Francis A. Drexel
LIBRARY

Books For College Libraries
Third Edition

Core Collection

SAINT JOSEPH'S UNIVERSITY

Regulating Safety:
An Economic and Political Analysis of
Occupational Safety and Health Policy

John Mendeloff

The MIT Press
Cambridge, Massachusetts, and London, England

Second printing, March 1980

This book was set in IBM Theme by To the Lighthouse Press and printed and bound by The Murray Printing Company in the United States of America.

Library of Congress Cataloging in Publication Data

Mendeloff, John.
    Regulating safety.

    Bibliography: p.
    Includes index.
    1. United States. Occupational Safety and Health Administration. 2. Industrial hygiene—United States. 3. Industrial safety—United States. I. Title.
HD7654.M46   614.8'52   78-10637
ISBN 0-262-13148-X

Contents

Figures   viii

Tables   ix

Preface   x

Acknowledgments   xii

1
OSHA: The Program and Its Problems   1

Operations   2

Criticism of OSHA   3

OSHA in the Context of Regulatory Policy   4

2
Political and Economic Perspectives on the Design of Occupational Safety and Health Policy   6

Rationales for a Government Role in Occupational Safety and Health   7

The Political Decision to Intervene: The OSH Act   15

Choosing the Method of Intervention   24

3
Consensus Standards and OSHA Enforcement   36

Adoption of the Initial Standards   36

Safety versus Health in Enforcement   41

Engineering Controls versus Personal Protection in the Enforcement of Health Standards   43

4
Social Values in Standard Setting: What Has Happened and Why?   47

Standard-Setting Procedures and Responsibilities   48

Two Cases: Vinyl Chloride and the Mechanical Power Press   52

Occupational Health Standards   58

The Role of Economics in Standard Setting   67

A Comparative Perspective on OSHA's Treatment of Economic Factors 71

Labor and Management Attitudes toward OSHA Standards 75

5
Should We Expect OSHA to Have an Effect on Injuries? 82

The Relevance of Standards: The Potential for Increased Safety through OSHA 85

Deterrence and Other Mechanisms to Achieve Increases in Safety 87

6
Tests of OSHA's Effectiveness 94

Identifying the Types of Accidents the OSHA Program Can Prevent 95

Developing a Model of Injury Rate Determination 98

A Test of OSHA Using Overall U.S. Manufacturing Injury Rates 102

Using State Data to Test OSHA's Impact 105

Evaluative Conclusions and Their Limitations 115

7
OSHA's Safety Program: A Policy Analysis 121

The Criteria 122

The Policy Alternatives 124

Accident Investigations 127

Targeting Inspections on High Injury Rate Establishments (THIRE) 133

Conclusion 142

8
Reforming Standard Setting 145

9
Analyzing OSHA: A Summing Up 151

Arguments for Federal Action 151

The Legislative Process: The Choice of Standards Enforcement as a Safety Strategy 154

The Implementation of the OSH Act 157

Evaluating OSHA's Impact   164

Designing Improvements in OSH Policy   167

Appendix: Econometric Issues in the Injury Rate Models   171

Glossary of Variables   177

Notes   178

Selected Bibliography   205

Index   213

Figures

2.1 Safety measures in terms of social benefits and costs 8

5.1 Rates for injuries reported under workers' compensation programs in California and Wisconsin, 1951–1975 84

6.1 Predicted and reported overall injury rates for California manufacturing,1948–1975 107

6.2 Injury rates in California manufacturing for four accident types, 1951–1975 109

6.3 Predicted and reported CIB injury rates in California manufacturing, 1951–1975 110

7.1 Relationships among safety regulation alternatives 125

Tables

4.1 OSHA responses to exposure limits recommended by NIOSH, 1972-1974   60

4.2 Estimates of instances of excess disease among 100 workers at the end of 40 years of exposure to asbestos   62

5.1 Serious violations cited in more than one fatality investigation, California, 1976   87

6.1 Work injuries categorized by accident type   96

6.2 Factors underlying the U.S. injury rate for manufacturing   104

6.3 Predicted and reported CIB injury rates, 1971–1975   111

6.4 Predicted and reported injury rates for three accident types, 1971–1975   114

7.1 Ranking safety performance   135

7.2 Evaluation matrix for safety alternatives   142

Preface

The design of good public policy usually requires many different perspectives, because "good" can mean many things: effective, constitutional, efficient, fair, politically feasible, administratively feasible, humane, and more. We generally subsume the criteria under two categories defined by the questions, Should a certain policy be adopted and implemented? and Can it be adopted and implemented? The simultaneous exploration of both the political underpinnings of a policy and its actual performance helps to focus analytic efforts on realistic solutions to substantive problems.

In scholarly practice the two questions have usually been addressed by different disciplines. For the vast number of policies involving issues of resource allocation, economists have given most of the answers to the first question, while political scientists have predominated in answering the second. This diversion of labor has evolved for good reasons, but it can hamper good policy analysis, since all the relevant criteria are unlikely to be considered by either discipline. The economist may ignore fairness and political feasibility; the political scientist, effectiveness and efficiency. If we care about all of these, then neither analysis will be satisfactory by itself.

Part of the problem might be met simply by ensuring that both perspectives are separately brought to bear on the policy issue. Yet this solution would fail to produce the additional insights that can be generated by bouncing back and forth among the perspectives, which requires either a multidisciplinary team or a multidisciplinary head. The advantage of this approach is that the bounces keep coming at new angles, forcing the analyst to approach the issues in new ways. For example, legal or political pressures may be forcing an agency to alter its behavior; knowledge of that agency's administrative practices and constraints can help an analyst develop feasible alternatives that will also be sensitive to the efficiency criterion. Or if an analyst finds that a policy's political support waxes instead of wanes despite a clear demonstration of its inefficacy, he is prodded into asking whether the objective he has been examining is really the one that matters most to the supporters. Since it has become axiomatic that most policies have objectives that are multiple, conflicting, and vague, these complexities should be anticipated.

One of the basic purposes of this study is to understand the way in which economic issues are considered in regulatory policymaking. Business and academic critics of regulation insist that the American people must be educated to understand exactly how much the regulation of social "bads" is actually costing them as consumers, workers, and stockholders. Supporters of regulation retort that, on the contrary, it is the benefits that are underestimated.

While popular views on this issue are certainly germane, so are the views of the policymakers themselves. Although examining only one policy area imposes obvious limitations—given the special characteristics of labor relations and health and safety issues—I nonetheless think it offers some general insights about how certain public actors approach economic questions. In order to understand their choices, we obviously have to understand the pressures brought to bear on them by other actors, but we also need to investigate their own understanding of the issues involved and their own sets of values, both of which are partly determined in turn by their bureaucratic and professional roles.

This study does three things: it examines why we have the occupational safety and health policy we have, assesses how well it is working, and proposes improvements. Methodologically, I think its main contribution lies in the way the first two are pursued in order to arrive at the third. I leave it up to the reader to judge the value of this approach. I should caution that this is not a comprehensive policy analysis; many important issues are left untouched, while others are only lightly fingered.

Acknowledgments

Among the many people at the Graduate School of Public Policy at the University of California at Berkeley who gave me guidance on this study, Lee Friedman, whose criticism was rigorous but supportive, deserves my biggest thanks. Bill Niskanen, who oversaw my early work on OSHA, did a wonderful job teaching me that policies have costs as well as benefits; Lee helped me recall that they have benefits as well as costs. Aaron Wildavsky spurred me on to consider the larger issues, especially the importance of understanding the concepts that guide policymakers' thinking about the relevance of costs.

Gene Bardach suggested ways to resolve problems at several critical points in the manuscript. Many pleasant conversations with David Good sharpened my thinking during the early phases of my writing. In addition, Lloyd Ulman, Bart McGuire, Tom Higgins, Claire Vickery, Steve Kelman of Harvard University, and Aldona DiPietro of the U.S. Department of Labor all read and commented perceptively on several chapters. Based upon their earlier evaluations of OSHA, Robert Smith of Cornell University and James Chelius of Purdue University provided several good suggestions about how to proceed. Cheng Hsaio and Cliff Orloff helped guide me through a few statistical thickets.

Jim Waldo of OSHA graciously helped me get settled while I was interviewing in Washington. I also want to thank all the people, named and unnamed—OSHA and other executive branch officials, Congressmen and their staff assistants, union and business lobbyists—who were willing to talk about OSHA with me.

Jean Powers, Karen Jones, Jim McKern, and the rest of the staff of the Work Injury Section of the Division of Labor Statistics and Research of the California Department of Industrial Relations were indispensable for my review of injury data. Cliff Erickson of the Cal-OSHA unit and Fred Ottoboni, special assistant to the secretary of agriculture and services, arranged my discussions with engineers from the Division of Industrial Safety—Elliot Berstowski, Harold Crabtree, and Fred Hull.

Peter Bouker of OSHA cheerfully helped to supply most of the enforcement and inspection data I needed. John Inzana of the Bureau of Labor Statistics provided me with the most complete available set of state injury rates. I have also benefited from conversations with James Kallenborn, John Seline, Dennis Donoghue, and other members of the OSHA evaluation staff and with Maurice Bresnahan of the BLS. Bert Concklin, Hamilton Fairburn, Adan Figueroa, and Mike Williams facilitated my examination of the files on OSHA inspections involving health hazards.

Several officials in other states provided me with data for the evaluation of

OSHA's effects: Lavinia Skipper in Florida; Frank Spanable in Ohio; Mark Gottlieb, Patrick Coleman, and Henry Gmeinder in Wisconsin; Rita Israel in New York; Bob Cashins and David Wegman in Massachusetts; John Patromanis in Iowa; Dave Cook in Nebraska; and Carl Jacobson in Oregon.

Dave Wegman and Les Boden of the Harvard School of Public Health bear the initial responsibility for getting me involved in the issue of occupational safety and health. The workers in the unions with whom we worked from 1970 to 1972 started the educational process. Talks with many consultants and company safety directors in 1975 gave me an additional perspective.

Aldona DiPietro and Ernst Stromsdorfer of the office of the assistant secretary for policy, evaluation, and research, U.S. Department of Labor, awarded a contract that supported the evaluation component of this study. The National Institute of Mental Health supported my research for several years. I also wish to thank the California Department of Industrial Relations for granting me time to work on my dissertation while I was employed there. The Graduate School of Public Policy provided not only a supportive environment and hot coffee but also a teaching assistantship in the introductory course on policy analysis, which provided both intellectual and financial sustenance. The dean of the Graduate Division came through with a grant to type the dissertation; Allen Pardini provided research assistance. My wife Fay provided a few good ideas and a lot more.

Regulating Safety

1
OSHA: The Program and Its Problems

Until 1971, state agencies bore the prime public responsibility for reducing the annual toll of several thousand work fatalities, approximately two million disabling injuries, and an unknown number of occupational diseases. The Occupational Safety and Health Act of 1970 (OSH Act) transformed the enforcement of safety and health standards from an overwhelmingly state function to a predominantly federal one. Under OSHA, fines for violations, which had been rare, became commonplace. Penalties were facilitated by the act's substitution of a simple civil procedure for the lengthy and costly criminal trials which states had relied upon. The procedural changes reflected a shift in enforcement philosophy; formerly, state agencies had seen their role as consultative—to educate employers, not to alter their incentives. Under the OSH Act, the goal of obtaining compliance became paramount, a goal pursued by levying fines to change the economic incentives that employers face.

Tougher enforcement made standards matter. As long as compliance had been largely voluntary, the content of the standards, no matter how protective they were, was not very consequential. The OSH Act also centralized the promulgation of new standards, reducing the influence of private standard-setting agencies. Especially in the health field, the act enlarged the public sector's ability to develop standards and also fostered a greatly expanded research program to identify new hazards. The act established the National Institute for Occupational Safety and Health (NIOSH) in the Department of Health, Education, and Welfare to oversee this research effort and to prepare reports on proposed health standards.

The changes in enforcement practices also altered the status of the employee in occupational safety and health affairs. Formerly excluded from the "consultations" between the enforcement agency and management, workers and their representatives were now accorded rights to participate in most steps of the process. Perhaps more importantly, workers now had certain guarantees that they would be kept informed of workplace hazards that affected them.

To establish an initial set of standards for the new Occupational Safety and Health Administration to enforce, the act required that safety and health standards under existing federal safety laws become standards under the OSH Act and that the so-called "consensus" standards, developed by private organizations, would also become effective within two years. Whether it was a case of adopting totally new standards or changing old ones, the act specified that while one consideration had to be "the attainment of the highest degree of health and safety protection for the employee," the "feasibility" of the standards also had to be taken into account.[1] In the health area, the act specified that standards would not only set limits on exposures but also prescribe medical exams, monitoring requirements, warning signs, and other matters.

OSHA's enforcement provisions require that citations listing the violations found during the inspection be prominently posted in the workplace. The citation gives dates by which each violation must be abated. Penalties of up to $1,000 may be imposed for "nonserious" violations and are mandatory for "serious" ones—those that involve a substantial probability of causing death or serious physical harm and that the employer either knew about or could reasonably have been expected to know about. Any employer who fails to abate a violation (whether nonserious or serious) within the period allowed may be fined up to $1,000 a day for each day past the abatement date. "Willful" or repeated violations can lead to fines of up to $10,000. The act set up an independent three-member Occupational Safety and Health Review Commission (OSHRC) to hear appeals from OSHA's penalties and citations. Unless appealed to OSHRC within fifteen days, these became "final orders" binding upon employers.

The act mandated that an employee representative had to be allowed to accompany the inspector, to observe any occupational hygiene tests, and to have access to the results. Employers must promptly notify employees whenever they are exposed to levels of toxic substances exceeding the legal limit. The act also provides procedures to reinstate and give back pay to any worker who is discriminated against for exercising his or her rights under the act (such as requesting an inspection).

A final major section allowed states to continue to provide safety and health enforcement if they could show that their programs were "at least as effective as" the federal program. For states choosing to operate under an approved OSHA plan, OSHA offered to pay 50 percent of the costs. Otherwise, state agencies had to turn over enforcement authority to OSHA.

Operations

By 1977, OSHA was operating with a budget of about $125 million, and NIOSH had another $35 million. OSHA employed about 1,250 safety and health inspectors; the twenty-three states operating under OSHA-approved plans added about 900 or more to the total.[2] The total number of OSHA-type inspections came to around 200,000, Only about 10 percent of them dealt with health. About 75 percent of the routine inspections discovered violations, usually several of them. The great majority of the violations have been cited as nonserious and carry an average penalty of only a few dollars. Penalties for the small number of serious violations average several hundred dollars. Although each year OSHA and its state counterparts inspect only a small percentage of the more than four million establishments covered by the OSH Act, in some sectors (like manufacturing) the inspections have covered workplaces that employed a majority of all employees.[3]

Within a month after the effective date of the act (the end of March 1971), OSHA had adopted all of the more than 4,000 federal and consensus standards. However, by the end of 1977, it had adopted only four new permanent health standards (for asbestos, vinyl chloride, coke oven emissions, and a group of fourteen carcinogenic chemicals) and only a slightly larger number of new safety standards.

Criticism of OSHA

The OSH Act arose out of the most bitter labor-management fight in many years and continues to generate controversy. Spokesmen for small business groups revile OSHA for its allegedly picayune but expensive inspections. Employers with good safety records complain that OSHA cites them for violations that are irrelevant to good safety performance. In the West a poster is in circulation depicting "The Cowboy After OSHA": he is wearing goggles and a helmet; a net surrounds his horse; and for good measure a box is located beneath the horse's rear to serve as an "antipollution device."

Large employers decry OSHA's failure to prune irrelevant requirements from the safety standards adopted en masse in April 1971. OSHA's alleged failure to weigh sufficiently the costs imposed by its standards has been a continuing complaint. On health standards, especially noise, employers denounce OSHA's requirement that exposures be reduced by engineering controls, rather than by giving workers earmuffs or respirators. Special ire is directed at the rule that even when exposures cannot be reduced to safe levels by engineering controls, controls must still be used; sole reliance on personal protective equipment is not allowed.

Labor unions have their bitter complaints as well. On some standards they charge that OSHA has sacrificed workers' health because of unwarranted concern for the costs of protection. OSHA's reliance on industry for its cost estimates draws fire as well. Unions often claim that penalties are skimpy, the inspectorate too small, and the percentage of violations cited as serious too low. They charge that the states that OSHA has allowed to administer their own programs provide a brand of enforcement that usually falls below the OSH Act's mandate. Finally, the unions have attacked OSHA's slowness in developing health standards and its alleged failure to give high priority to disease hazards.

Responding to criticisms from all these sources, the House and Senate Appropriations Conference Committee directed OSHA at the end of 1975 to upgrade the skills of inspectors, eliminate the "nuisance" standards and simplify the others, emphasize health enforcement, focus inspections on industries with poor safety records, and develop a consultation program to help employers achieve compliance.[4]

Echoing much of this criticism, an early draft of the 1976 report of the Council of Economic Advisers (CEA) went on to observe that OSHA had not perceptibly reduced injury rates in the industries in which inspections had been targeted but that "paradoxically, while ineffective, OSHA has been extremely costly to industry." The draft suggested that a tax on injuries would prove superior to the enforcement of safety standards, both because the standards applied only to a minority of all injury causes and because they did not ensure that injuries would be prevented in the least costly possible manner.

When the draft containing this criticism was leaked to the *New York Times,* union officials were outraged, and the Labor Department successfully negotiated the deletion of this section from the final report. A similar turmoil erupted in 1977, when a memo to the president from CEA Chairman Charles L. Schultze, Budget Director Bert Lance, and domestic adviser Stuart Eizenstat recommended a study of whether safety regulations should be replaced by some form of direct economic incentives to prevent injuries. Again this thrust was deflected by union leaders; the study was finally chartered to look at economic incentives as *supplements* to OSHA regulation.[5] Attempts to remold OSHA to fit economists' regulatory models have met with little success.

OSHA in the Context of Regulatory Policy

A crucial characteristic of almost all regulatory agencies, including OSHA, is that the bulk of the costs they impose (as well as the benefits) do not show up in the government budget but are incurred directly by the private sector and are therefore exempt from the usual congressional fiscal scrutiny. Although this study examines only OSHA, much of the discussion is relevant to other recent attempts to regulate private economic decisions. OSHA is one of the most prominent as well as the most controversial of the "new" regulatory agencies, the "newness" referring to both the economic and the political dimensions of their policies. The old regulatory agencies were established primarily to curb the misuse of market power or to stabilize the environment of a new industry.[6] Consequently, most of these agencies deal with a single industry—although some, like the Federal Trade Commission, range across the economy. Politically, the issues before the old agencies either show one firm pitted against another for some business advantage or, more often, show the industry making common cause to protect itself against alleged threats to its stability and prosperity. Although the beneficiaries of these policies are usually organized and clearly identified, the losers often are not.[7]

The new regulatory agencies deal almost exclusively with protecting the environment and the health and safety of citizens. In economic terms, their main concern is whether economic activities properly "internalize" all of the costs their processes and products impose on other people; or, more broadly, whether private markets (or those markets as modified by existing regulatory programs) generate the socially proper level of safety, air quality, and so on. Along with OSHA, the Consumer Product Safety Commission (CPSC), the National Highway Traffic Safety Administration (NHTSA), and the Environmental Protection Agency (EPA) are exemplars of the new regulation.

Another distinctive characteristic of the new regulation (related to its concern with externalities) is its focus on nonprice aspects of the product, which tend to involve highly charged topics like the value of human life or the value of preserving the environment. The emotional quality of such issues makes it easier to gain public attention for them, and it is difficult for legislators or bureaucrats to ignore popular attitudes. The recent growth of environmental and consumer lobbying and litigating groups has reflected the mass media's increased attentiveness and, along with the growth in political entrepreneurship among legislators who hope to profit from appeals to a broad public audience, catapulted these issues from obscurity to center stage.[8]

Yet although OSHA is part of the new wave of regulation, it is also a product of the ongoing conflict between labor and management groups. An understanding of the role played by each of these factors in the functioning of the agency requires a closer look at economic and political perspectives on OSH policy.

2
Political and Economic Perspectives on the Design of Occupational Safety and Health Policy

Any policymaker willing to adopt microeconomic analysis as his sole guide to policy choices would be ignoring the plurality of values that have a legitimate hold on the public and its officials. Yet any policymaker choosing to ignore that body of analysis would be forsaking the most useful guide we have to efficient resource allocation. Robert Smith has tried to summarize the guidance that economic analysis can offer to OSH policymakers. He offers three premises:

(1) There is nothing inherently immoral about discussing safety in terms of its costs and benefits. (2) Given a certain objective in terms of injury or disease reduction, society should choose the least costly method for achieving that reduction. . . . (3) There is no justification for seeking equal levels of risk in every occupation, factory, or industry, because the costs of reducing risks are likely to differ with techniques of production.[1]

From a broader perspective, however, these premises appear incomplete and potentially misleading. Consider the following modifications: (1) No method of valuing lifesaving can satisfactorily obviate the need for moral judgments by citizens and consumers about how much—if at all—they are willing to pay to protect the workers at risk. (2) Given a certain objective in terms of injury or disease reduction, society should assess the trade-offs among other objectives when considering each proposed method. No single criterion has a necessary presumption of dominance, and thus the least-cost solution will not necessarily be the most desirable. For example, procedural fairness and distributional equity must always be considered as well. (3) The third point derives from the second, since a least-cost solution requires that we reduce injuries where we can do it most cheaply. Taken together the two points are valid only if we are indifferent not only to the methods used but also to the distribution of costs and benefits.

Moral issues, trade-offs among objectives, distributional questions—all these terms invoke the political rather than the analytical process and suggest the limited relevance of a policy based only upon efficiency concerns. The rest of this chapter explores these three premises of economic analysis in greater detail, not only from the vantage point of the economist but also by examining the treatment accorded these economic arguments by the actors in the political process. Specifically, the three major issues addressed are: What is the rationale for new government intervention in the OSH field? If government intervenes, what strategies for preventing injuries or illnesses should it adopt? How are the costs and benefits of the OSH program distributed?

Rationales for a Government Role in Occupational Safety and Health

An economic formulation of the proper objective of public policy in the field of safety is that it should minimize the sum of accident costs and accident prevention costs.[2] This merely restates the premise that we should try to prevent accidents or illnesses up to the point at which it becomes more expensive to prevent them than to allow them to occur. In figure 2-1 this condition is met at the level of preventive measures indicated by "P." Up to that point additional preventive measures produce net social benefits. Beyond that point preventive measures impose net social costs. The implication is that some injuries and illnesses aren't worth preventing, that we can have too much safety and health as well as too little. (For the moment, I ignore the question of whether all the relevant criteria can be expressed in the money metric.)

A somewhat more realistic picture of the regulatory situation can be drawn by adding a set of lines to the usual diagram, depicting particular, discrete decisions that the regulators could adopt. In almost any regulatory context, some decisions will be socially beneficial and some will not. The marginal social cost and benefit curves describe the economic environment that determines whether regulation will produce small gains, large gains, huge losses, or whatever. (For example, if existing private or public policies already incorporate decisions 1 through 6, then added regulation is unlikely to produce net benefits. Or if the true marginal social cost curve shifted upward, the number of potentially beneficial decisions would drop.) But we need additional information for a realistic appraisal of the efficiency of a regulatory proposal.

The prognosis for regulation depends not only upon the locations and slopes of the curves but also upon the choices that public regulators make. These, in turn, depend on the quality of the information available to them—can they identify which decisions will have net benefits?—and on their incentives to use the information to achieve efficient outcomes. Just as assessments of whether we can rely on a private market to produce beneficial outcomes should consider the actual market (warts and all) rather than an imaginary, perfectly competitive one, so assessments of regulation should contemplate the behavior of real regulators, not omniscient servants of the "public interest."

The adequacy of the private market for safety depends primarily upon two assumptions: first, that firms know enough about safety technologies to choose the most cost-effective methods of prevention; second, that the firm bears all the costs of the injuries and illnesses resulting from its production. If

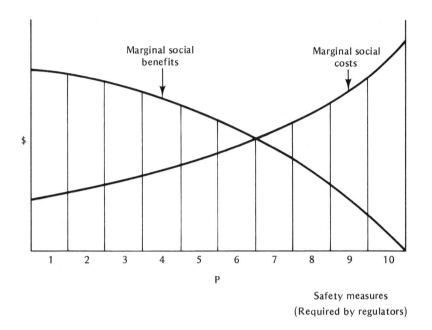

Figure 2.1 Safety measures in terms of social benefits and costs

some of these costs are thrown upon external parties who have no control over the level of safety, then the firm will have too many accidents. If the firm does not bear all these costs, the prices of its products will not reflect the true social costs of production; more of one good and less of another will be produced than if prices equaled the social (marginal) cost rather than the firm's (marginal) cost.

The importance of the first assumption can be simply explained. If employers either fail to perceive that prevention is possible, or if they overestimate its costs (or underestimate its benefits), then they will provide a level of safety that is too low (conversely, it could be too high). Here is a potential role for government: disseminating information about preventive measures and sponsoring research into new measures that no single firm or trade association would find it worthwhile to sponsor. As one witness observed during the hearings on the OSH Act,

It is almost impossible to believe, but true, that the first $100,000 granted the Public Health Service by Congress for coalworkers pneumoconiosis research was made available in 1963!
... Or byssinosis, lung disease, of some cotton workers. Again through the 1930's, 1940's and 1950's, no research, despite repeated reports from other countries that their cotton workers were ill.[3]

When will the second assumption, that the firm internalizes all of the social costs of injuries, be satisfied? Certainly many of these costs are automatically borne by the firm—the costs of broken equipment, downtime, accident investigation, the costs of hiring replacements, and some of the costs of training. Since the injured worker obviously bears a big portion of the costs, the assumption depends upon the existence of mechanisms by which workers are compensated.

Ever since Adam Smith discussed compensating advantages, many economists have argued that the labor market provides workers with risk premiums that barely compensate them for the risks undertaken for especially hazardous jobs. The compensation occurs before the fact rather than after. No one can ever be fully compensated for his or her death, but compensation can be paid for accepting a certain extra risk of death. Worker demands for risk premiums are expected to induce employers to undertake safety measures that would be successful enough in reducing hazards to pay for themselves in reduced wage premiums. For workers to play the role assigned by theory, they must have at least a modicum of accurate information about the risks they face. Some dramatic cases of employee ignorance have been documented, but we lack a general sense of how well informed workers are. In any event, from a theoretical perspective it is not clear how much information is "enough."[4]

The small body of empirical work on risk premiums, while far from conclusive, offers some weak evidence that, other things being equal, workers do tend to get paid something for accepting extra risks. Existing studies rely mainly on econometric analyses of samples of workers in different occupations or industries.[5] Occasionally they cite the "hazard pay" provisions found in over 5 percent of all union contracts, but they have overlooked a much more pervasive practice among unionized and nonunionized firms which builds risk premiums directly into the wage structure. That practice is "job evaluation," the determination of relative wages within a firm or industry by giving points based on a set of factors including experience, education, and working conditions. Probably most larger firms in the U.S., especially in manufacturing, use some form of job evaluation.

Two of the twelve factors used in many job evaluation plans are relevant here: "hazards" and "surroundings." Significantly, health hazards like dusts, fumes, and noise are not included in the "hazard" ratings but rather in the "surroundings" ratings, where they are considered only as disamenities. Thus this common job evaluation formula does not account for the risks of occupational disease. However, it is apparent that within firms or industries using job evaluation, some sort of risk premium is paid for danger.[6] Yet even here, it is difficult to believe that job evaluation ratings produce risk premiums that fully compensate the worker for two reasons. The first is that compensating differentials can run afoul of management's need to provide incentives for workers to climb the firm's job ladders. Strauss and Sayles give an excellent description of this problem:

According to worker logic, clean jobs are better than dirty ones. A new man should start at the bottom, at the hardest, dirtiest, least desirable job. Then, as he acquires seniority, he should move up to better, easier, higher-paying jobs. But this is contradictory to the logic of job evaluation, which says that more points should be given for hard work and dirty conditions. Yet people will resist being "promoted" into a higher-paying job that has lower status. In practice, this problem is solved by giving very low point values to the factors of physical effort and job conditions—or by socially separating the two kinds of jobs so that there will be little invidious comparison. At times management disregards the logic of job evaluation almost completely; dirty jobs are paid less than clean jobs. But the dirty job is a starting job through which all employees must move. As a man gets promoted, he moves by the ordinary process of seniority from a dirty, low-paid, low-status job to a cleaner, higher-paid, higher-status job.[7]

A second and related reason is that the risk premiums appear to be extremely "sticky." For example, a comparison of the 1963 and 1971 job classification manuals for the steel industry indicates that the hazard and surroundings ratings had not changed for even one of the more than 600 jobs described. It seems unlikely that no major changes occurred in any of those jobs during that time. A better explanation relies on the strong disinclination of management (and union officials) to disturb old and familiar relativities.[8]

In summary, although risk premiums apparently do exist—both within firms and industries through job evaluation and among occupations through more direct market forces—there are important reasons to doubt that they fully compensate the worker, much less that they reflect the concerns of all those who value his or her safety. Furthermore, as Robert Smith observes, "because so many injury-related losses are of a psychic nature ('pain and suffering'), we cannot begin to tell if the wage premiums are in fact fully compensating."[9]

Frequently, the analytical question that policymakers should address is not how well the unadorned market works but rather how well the market and the panoply of existing collective and public institutions work. Lack of faith in the existence of adequate risk premiums was one rationale for the establishment of workers' compensation (WC) programs over fifty years ago, although their major purpose was to provide income to disabled workers, not to alter employer incentives. The failure of most state WC programs to fulfill their main task very well—they replaced on average less than one-half of lost wages in 1970—may also weaken the safety incentives. However, the existing evidence, although not very thorough, does not indicate that higher benefits (and thus higher premiums) have caused injury rate decreases. That lack of impact is consistent with the theoretical view that higher WC benefits (ex post compensation) merely allow employers to pay lower risk premiums (ex ante compensation), without necessarily increasing their overall costs.

Yet even if one maintains the view that higher WC premiums can increase employer costs, several factors, in addition to low benefit levels, may have undercut the value of WC programs as a means for imposing the full social costs of injuries on employers. First, as an insurance program the first goal of WC is to spread the risks of injury losses so that employers will not bear all of the costs of the injuries their workers incur. Only the largest employers, especially those who are "self-insured," will pay for all of the compensable losses. (Even for a firm with 300 workers, for example, actuarial practices will only allow a 25 percent reduction in premiums for injury losses 50 percent below the industry average.)[10] Second, compensable losses constitute only one part of the employee's total losses; they don't include payments for "pain and suffering" or losses in nonwork activity. Third, in most states in 1970, WC coverage of occupational diseases was incomplete. For example, of the three states with over 50 percent of textile industry employment, neither Georgia nor North Carolina covered byssinosis, while South Carolina, which did, had never reported a single case despite informed estimates that over 17,000 textile workers suffered from the disease.[11]

Even with complete coverage, WC gives firms little economic incentive to prevent diseases with long latency periods. Private firms use discount rates of 10 percent and higher, and, at such rates, costs more than twenty years in the future shrink into insignificance. Whether that fact presents a problem may depend upon whether we believe that workers adhere implicitly to equally high discount rates. Even if they did, their opinions might be overridden either out of paternalism or from a belief that part of the costs of disease would be absorbed by taxpayers. In any event, prevention of these diseases must rely on programs other than WC.

Divergences between actual labor markets and the competitive model and shortcomings in the WC program may mean that employers are not forced to internalize all the costs of work injuries. That conclusion is supported by the knowledge that taxpayers also absorb some of the costs; for example, totally disabled workers receive benefits through the Social Security system. The most dramatic instance of taxpayers' picking up the tab is the federal "black lung" benefits program initiated by the 1969 Coal Mine Safety Act, under which total federal payments will be several billion dollars. (In his 1969 testimony on behalf of the administration's OSH bill, Secretary of Labor George Schultz specifically cited the threat of future epidemics like black lung and warned that occupational health programs in many states were inadequate; indeed eight states had no occupational health program at all.)

No social loss (other than administrative costs) occurs from making these transfer payments; funds are simply passed from taxpayers to victims. The social costs are incurred through the lost productivity of the worker, the medical resources used, the pain and suffering, and so on. Yet for public officials a "taxpayer benefit-cost" analysis (based on extra welfare payments and foregone tax revenues) may prove more compelling than the more basic analysis of social costs and social benefits. Consequently, once a mechanism has been established to shift some of the burden from victims to taxpayers, public officials are more likely to search for ways to avoid incurring new losses.

In cases like black lung, where a massive epidemic occurs many years after initial exposure and threatens to cripple a particular industry, the argument for public assumption of the benefit payments is strong.[12] The problem is that routine public assumption would give firms strong incentives to hide a disease or to pressure legislators to refuse to make it compensable in order eventually to force the state or federal governments to pay the bill. Nevertheless, once the situation exists, public assumption is sound.

Procedures need to be developed for relating the size of the externalized social costs to the extent of government intervention. For example, the existence of public funding for many medical care programs should not give the government carte blanche to regulate closely all activities that happen to cause injuries requiring medical care. Traditionally, economists have proposed to tax firms by an amount sufficient to close the gap between private and social costs. In practice, the measurement of the gap is often highly uncertain, depending upon solutions to the valuation problems discussed in chapter 4. In the absence of this approach, however, it becomes difficult to calibrate the proper degree of government intervention or even to understand what the impact of intervention on the externality really is. These problems raise the issue of the choice of methods for intervening.

Health versus Safety
One striking anomaly in OSH policy is that although labor and management leaders concurred in the view that occupational diseases presented the most serious case for government action, the actual deployment of OSHA's resources has heavily emphasized safety rather than health. Distinctions between the two usually stress the workers greater ability to recognize safety hazards, to make informed judgments about the risks he or she faces, and to press management for correction of the problem or compensation for enduring it.

Undeniably, workers can recognize common safety hazards—an unguarded machine, a catwalk without a railing, a slippery floor—more easily than they recognize the toxic effects of the chemicals they work with. Employers' incentives are conflicting when it comes to informing workers about hazards; certainly many examples of firms that did not inform employees about known health hazards can be cited. In a competitive industry, any firm that tried to take the lead in abating the hazard or compensating its workers would suffer severely. The industry as a whole would encounter similar obstacles when demand for the product is very sensitive to the price increases required by such extra efforts.

Yet resistance is not the only management response to claims that its employees are dying. The discovery in the late 1940s that the beryllium used in making light bulbs was causing acute and chronic diseases that were often fatal led the employers—General Electric and Sylvania—to replace it quickly with a less toxic substitute. Not only could these firms absorb the costs, but good substitutes were available. In the case of asbestos and vinyl chloride, where the toxic agent itself is the employers' product, substitution is more difficult. In the absence of the OSH Act, it seems unlikely that these industries would have moved so far or so quickly, even though they are dominated by large oligopolistic firms.

The rationale for an emphasis on health is often mistated, however. Workers may have no greater understanding of the safety risks they face than of the health risks, and potentially they can gain a much better estimate of the latter. Consider the probability that a given accident will occur and a particular injury result from it—a fall from a ladder, being struck on the head by falling boxes, back strain from lifting, getting a finger caught in a machine. The worker does not know the risks and, what is crucial, no expert does either. It follows that for regulatory purposes *the key distinction is not that workers know more about safety than they do about health risks; it is rather that experts know a great deal more about health than workers do but not much more about safety.* Properly informed by the experts, workers can learn what levels of exposure cause disease, and monitoring equipment can measure the actual exposures. The safety variables are even more complex and, more important, situationally specific.

Both health and safety hazards present problems in assessing very small risks of very large disasters. Peculiar to health, and particularly to diseases with long latency periods, is the problem of assessing events far in the future.[13] These situations may plausibly lead people to the "wrong" choice, wrong in the sense that if they thought it through they would come to a different solution. But since the normal prescription is not to set up a discussion group to explore the issues with the affected workers but rather to make decisions for them on the basis of how they should rationally respond, the paternalistic nature of government action is inescapable.

This paternalism may provide a needed input to offset the difficulties workers face. Again the problem is one of setting limits on disregarding the preferences workers reveal in their market behavior. To the extent that rank and filers agree with organized labor's support for these abridgements, the aura of paternalism is dispelled. One can favor a change in the rules even though it may deprive you of a choice that you would sometimes want to make. For people less directly affected, however, we are back to paternalism; we may support such a rule precisely because it deprives people of choices that we don't think they ought to make. During the hearings on the OSH Act, the issue was almost always posed in terms of money: "I don't think we should put workers in a position of having to bargain their health against two cents an hour." This concern carried more weight in the legislative process than arguments about efficiency, which were almost entirely absent from the hearings and debates. To understand why that particular balance was struck, we need to examine the political history of the act more carefully.

The Political Decision to Intervene: The OSH Act

For the policy analyst, the two-step procedure of investigating, first, the rationale for any government action and, second, the alternative forms it might take makes sense. The first step guards against rushing into needless interventions; the second helps to ensure that major options are not overlooked. For political actors, however, the distinction makes little sense. Private groups and public organizations inundate legislators with prepackaged proposals. Legislators choose the combinations of issues and groups that will best serve their political needs. They may do some repackaging, but it will be done more with an eye to marketing than to revamping the bills to suit their own policy preferences. As Bauer, Pool, and Dexter put it, "Instead of choosing among answers to fixed questions, [the congressman] is apt to be seeking issues that will meet fixed answers."[14] In consequence, a separation of the two steps— rationale and method of intervention—has an artificial quality in the discussion of the politics of OSH.

However, to the extent that legislators try to represent the interests of public or private organizations, it is critical to ask how the leaders of those groups perceive the policy issues. Even if legislators care little about the rationality of the policy, it may nonetheless have been carefully designed to meet the needs of the organizations with which they are allied.

The idea of enlarging the nation's OSH program, toughening its enforcement, and placing it under the federal aegis appealed to those top union leaders who had thought about the problem. For unions like the United Rubber Workers and the Oil, Chemical, and Atomic Workers, the problems of occupational disease appeared to be looming larger, and individual state efforts seemed inadequate to discover, monitor, and control the hazards. Enforcement of state regulations was generally tepid, partly due to fears that tougher enforcement would drive business away.

Part of the appeal of federal action to union leaders was that it offered a way to bypass their unions' weak position on these issues in collective bargaining. As one union leader explained,

The restraints on collective bargaining are very obvious; we don't have the power to get that stuff from management. Collective bargaining could be used more, but people tend to see themselves as impotent. OSHA helps to focus on the problem; how else could you get national attention to the problem of setting a level for some new material like vinyl chloride?[15]

During the hearings on the bills, Republican congressmen frequently taunted union witnesses by asking why, if these problems were so great, the union had done so little to win protections in the contract. One union safety director admitted that "in negotiating a contract, it appears that safety and health clauses come after the coffee break."[16] Many leaders feared that their own members would not be willing to trade off wages and other benefits for safety provisions. The passage of the OSH Act would achieve what collective bargaining could not.

Since the failings of collective bargaining derived mainly from members' disinclination to give up much in return for greater safety, one might wonder whether the OSH Act reflected the preferences of union members or only of their leaders. Actually, however, neither members nor leaders view benefit increases imposed by legislation as necessarily requiring a diminution of other privately set benefits. Worker fears of putting their own firm or industry at a competitive disadvantage are assuaged by the substitution of national legislation for collective bargaining.

Relying on the federal government to achieve ends the membership won't or can't reach through collective bargaining is nothing new for unions or other organizations. In the case of OSH, the turn to government resulted from a lack of technical capability as well as collective bargaining weakness. As Jack Sheehan of the United Steelworkers Union (USW) explained in an interview with the author,

None of us were real experts on safety and health. Now we have an industrial hygienist on our staff, but we still don't have the capability to have much input into a new standard. That's why we want a heavy government presence in this area.[17]

Since the labor view (shared by many outside of labor) is that "the Labor

Department is supposed to be our Department, whether it's a Democratic or Republican Administration," the expertise would be wielded by an arm of government that was not merely neutral but expected to serve the interests of labor.

Predispositions in favor of a new program, however, hardly guarantee action in its behalf. During the mid-1960s the OSH issue did not rank high on organized labor's political agenda. The initial impetus for new legislation came from the Labor Department officials who ran the existing, small-scale federal OSH programs. President Johnson decided to include such a bill in his 1968 legislative program, and on February 1, 1968, hearings began in the House before a subcommittee of the Education and Labor Committee. The provisions of the bill, introduced for the administration by Congressman James O'Hara, did little more than authorize federal inspectors to make inspections similar to those already being performed by the states and order HEW to conduct research on hazards and establish criteria for standards. Nevertheless, several business groups, most notably the U.S. Chamber of Commerce, opposed any direct federal role in enforcement. It was, they argued, a state function. George Meany came down to testify on its behalf, but after Johnson announced his withdrawal from the presidential race in March, the bill—along with much of the rest of his legislative package—made little headway.[18] Occupational safety and health was still not labor's issue, and its leaders would not fill the leadership vacuum.

Several quite similar versions of the 1968 bill were introduced by Democratic congressmen in 1969. The Nixon Administration countered with a bill introduced by Senator Jacob Javits and Congressman William Ayres (although Congressman William Steiger took the leading Republican role in the work on the bills), which differed primarily in its resistance to placing standard-setting, inspection, and enforcement functions in the Labor Department. Its supporters insisted that due process required placing these functions in different agencies.

During 1969 some labor leaders were beginning to mobilize around a different occupational safety and health issue and found themselves in strange company. The November 1968, Farmington, West Virginia, blast that killed seventy-eight miners precipitated a new wave of support of stricter enforcement of coal mine safety laws. Encompassing that disaster was the emergence of a grass roots movement to aid the victims of black lung. The organization generated by that movement, which led wildcat strikes and sent thousands of miners to the West Virginia statehouse to demand coverage of black lung in the state's workers' compensation program, also became a bulwark of the opposition building within the United Mine Workers (UMW) to the corrupt regime of Tony Boyle.

Ralph Nader participated in all of these developments, often through his aide Gary Sellers. Sellers had worked on the coal mine safety bills while employed by the Office of Management and Budget. He quit to work for Nader and quickly linked up with Congressman Phillip Burton to rework the bill which had been introduced in the House. Largely due to their efforts, the act that resulted was the first federal safety act to allow penalties for violations without the requirement that cumbersome hearings be held first. By establishing a federal benefit program for miners disabled by black lung (and for the widows and families of workers who had died from it), the act also heightened political consciousness of the costs imposed by employers' inadequate efforts to prevent occupational disease.[19]

By 1970 an OSH bill had become organized labor's top legislative priority, largely due to the support of the Steelworkers' president, I. W. Abel, who had recently succeeded Walter Reuther as head of the AFL-CIO's Industrial Union Division. Several explanations can be advanced for Abel's role: he was looking for issues on which to assert his new leadership; the traditionally close relationship between the Mine Workers and Steelworkers made the black lung movement and the Nader involvement in the Coal Mine Safety Act a potential threat if he did *not* push hard on the issue; the act might generate a helpful solution to the emerging cancer problem among USW members who worked in coke ovens. Along with these factors, Abel's close adviser Jack Sheehan, the union's chief lobbyist, was intensely interested in the issue. The importance of Abel's decision to lead a union campaign on OSH is attested to by Robert Nagle, who was counsel for the Senate Labor and Public Welfare Committee at the time of the OSH Act. In an interview with the author, Nagle said that "there is no doubt that without the Steelworkers' push, this legislation would not have come about."

Traditionally, the House Education and Labor Committee had been dominated by the AFL-CIO, which in conjunction with Speaker of the House John McCormack had handpicked the Democratic members chosen during the 1960s.[20] Now, although the AFL-CIO still exercised a veto over the committee's labor bills, it found itself in the unusual position of responding to initiatives from the committee's staff. Sellers, still working for both Burton and Nader (and thanks to Burton's aggressive use of congressional courtesy, sitting in as Burton's representative at subcommittee sessions), teamed with Daniel Krivit, the counsel for the Select Subcommittee on Labor, which handled the OSH bills. Drawing from the Coal Mine Safety Act, from suggestions from the Steelworkers, and from other people in the Nader network, they constructed a new bill which was far tougher than any of those on which the subcommittee had held hearings. The new bill (called the Daniels bill after Subcommittee Chairman Domenick Daniels) dramatically altered the proposed regulatory strategy. It included a citation system for the expeditious handling of violations; as with a traffic violation, the burden of appeal was placed on the alleged violator. It allowed "first instance" penalties, that is, employers could be cited merely for having a violation, not just for failing to correct violations cited earlier. Penalties for serious violations were made mandatory. The bill established procedures to keep workers informed about conditions in the workplace and made the health standards much more elaborate, transforming them from simple exposure limits to documents describing rules for the use of personal protective equipment, medical exams, monitoring, and other items.

The Daniels bill was introduced in March and approved by the House Education and Labor Committee in June 1970. In the Senate, the Labor and Public Welfare Committee headed by Senator Harrison Williams adopted most of the Daniels bill's innovations in the bill it approved in September. More importantly, the new administration bill championed by Congressman William Steiger went along as well.

The partisan battle was joined over political and procedural issues unrelated to the efficacy of the regulatory strategy. The main issue remained the location of authority. The administration wanted to establish one independent board to set standards and another to hear appeals, leaving the Labor Department only the job of conducting inspections. In the House, the administration won on this issue, the Steiger bill being substituted for the Daniels bill by a vote of 220 to 172. Meanwhile the Senate had adopted the Labor and Public Welfare Committee's bill after amending it with Senator Javits's proposal to set up an independent Occupational Safety and Health Review Commission to hear appeals; the other two functions were left in the Labor Department. The House-Senate Conference Committee resolved most of the major issues in favor of the Senate bill. In order to secure the standard-setting function safely in the Labor Department, organized labor was willing to concede on another of the most controversial issues, whether OSHA would have to procure a court order before acting in "imminent danger" situations.[21] In practice this provision has proved to be one of the least consequential in the entire act.

The conference committee's bill was approved by both Houses. Although a few business groups and congressmen asked the president to veto it, the Labor Department was willing to accept the bill, and the president, who already had vetoed one major labor bill that month—a proposal to create public employment to combat the recession—went along.

Arguments about Costs, Benefits, and Incentives for Safety

In interpreting this brief description of the OSH Act's history, several features merit special attention. The Republicans' focus on procedural issues was to some degree a screen for more substantive objections to the regulatory policy. Their objections to placing all authority in the Labor Department were phrased in terms of whether the same party should sit as judge and jury, but they also reflected concern about the department's partiality toward unions. As Senator Holland, a Democrat, observed on the Senate floor, "The judgment prevails not only on the part of employers, but also, I think, in the mind of the average citizen, that the Labor Department always—perhaps that is the right thing—is most sympathetic in its attitude toward the labor organizations."[22]

Certainly a concern with procedural issues per se was not absent. Ensuring that the government provides fair treatment to its citizens is an important norm, and the lawyers who dominate Congress have an abiding commitment to it. No one value has primacy, and policy that is perceived as effective but unfair is not less likely to meet opposition than one that is judged fair but ineffective.

The hearings on the OSH bills certainly were not devoid of testimony regarding the need for government action, but the most striking characteristic of the testimony and the congressional commentary was their idealism and their silence on the costs of regulation. In the whole legislative history, I found only two brief statements by Republican conservatives that point out that intervention can do more harm than good. In contrast, the idea that even one injury or fatality is too many is frequently repeated, along with assertions about the infinite value of human life. The language of the OSH Act only once even hinted at the notion that costs might have to be taken into account. In the section on standard-setting the act states,

The Secretary . . . shall set the standard which most adequately assures, to the extent *feasible,* on the basis of the best available evidence, that no employee shall suffer material impairment of health or functional capacity even if such employee has regular exposure to the hazard dealt with by the standard for the period of his working life. . . . In addition to the attainment of the highest degree of health and safety protection for the employee, other considerations shall be the latest available scientific data in the field, the *feasibility* of the standards, and experience under this and other health and safety laws.[23] (Emphasis supplied.)

The handful of references to "feasibility" in the debates did not attempt to make its meaning more precise.

Congressional aversion to hinting at the existence of costs and the possibility of trade-offs is, of course, not unique to the OSH Act. All proponents minimize the costs of action, just as opponents minimize the costs of inaction. Yet even other recent safety legislation has not been this oblique in its references to costs.[24] Although other reasons are involved, a sufficient explanation for the absence of any mention of costs was that organized labor did not want any. Certainly most of the legislators involved thought costs would be considered. The Senate's Nagle explained that, "in the Act the issue was not directly dealt with. That was intentional. We were afraid that if we said 'economic feasibility,' nothing but costs would be considered. We certainly imagined that costs would, in fact, be considered." On the House side, Subcommittee Counsel Krivit concurred that "the Act left it open and Congress did not face up to the issue of costs; although most of us believed costs would be a factor taken into account. We did have a few purists who thought that they should not be."[25]

Neither business groups nor Republican legislators had been willing to demand a more explicit requirement to consider costs. Our popular values don't countenance "putting a price tag on life," and thus politicians will not lightly adopt a position that opponents could easily turn into a political liability. However, another widely shared value is that reasonable people don't ignore costs. Although imbued with only practical, not moral, authority, this principle could have spearheaded a counterattack. But during the debate, politicians had little to gain from launching such maneuvers because business lobbyists were unwilling to adopt a more aggressive stance. The business spokesmen were trying hard to show that tough regulation was not really needed. A key element in that strategy was to portray business leaders as people who were as concerned about safety as anyone else. Taking a hard line on costs could have destroyed that image.

A few years later, when that particular strategic constraint no longer applied, some business groups did propose that the act be amended to require the consideration of costs. Senator Lawton Chiles of Florida introduced one bill (S 2823) to that effect, arguing that

while considerations of safety and health cannot be weighed in terms of cost, it should be the responsibility of the Labor Department to avoid regulations that are of minimal value in achieving worker safety. . . .
Accordingly, this bill directs the Secretary to recognize the cost-benefit ratio in promulgating a new standard and to publish information relative to the projected financial impact.[26]

Chiles still felt compelled to deny the possibility of making trade-offs at the very moment he was trying to get the Labor Department to do cost-benefit studies that do just that. (The bill was not, of course, reported out of the Senate Labor and Public Welfare Committee.) Yet even if a provision like Chiles's had been inserted into the OSH Act, it would have curtailed only slightly the discretion OSHA leaders have in weighing the importance of economic issues. To achieve greater control, Congress would have to pass a bill stipulating exactly how cost-benefit studies were to be performed and exactly how to weight them in the decision process. The first prerequisite would include rules for setting money values on human lives.[27]

Recognizing that Congress would never begin to take such steps, most business leaders have stopped trying to get amendments on cost issues. Instead, they are taking them up directly with OSHA standard setters, who can't pass the buck as easily as congressmen. But the congressional message on costs, which is conspicuous by its absence, is not lost on OSHA's administrators.

The debates over procedural and substantive issues often revealed underlying differences in perceptions of management behavior and the workings of the labor market. For example, the Republican position on the imminent danger provision not only reflected concern with due process but also a belief that any employer who was notified by an inspector that an imminent danger existed would immediately take steps to get rid of it. Thus the need for *any* extraordinary provisions to deal with these situations seemed unnecessary. The unions did not share this faith in employer responsiveness.

Administration spokesmen played down the need for penalties. As Secretary of Labor George Schultz observed,

Particularly in the kind of tight labor markets that we have, to become known as an employer with unsafe practices is to have the reputation of operating an undesirable place to work. And this in many ways is the most severe penalty that is involved.[28]

And the Labor Department's solicitor specifically explained that "it is our view that an employer who does not wilfully violate the act should not be subject to a fine."[29] Union spokesmen gave a very different picture of management's attitudes toward safety and the measures needed to improve them. The testimony of one local union safety committee chairman was typical:

Do you know when they do something at the Painted Post plant? After it falls down, literally comes off the beam, is when these people move. After one of our people is hurt is when they decide that something has to be done. That is why we are asking that the teeth that have to be put into this bill have to be very strong and have to be very sincere. We can't go on waiting forever.[30]

When Biemiller, the chief AFL-CIO lobbyist, reminded the House subcommittee that "it is the worker who suffers," Congressman Steiger retorted, "It is also fair to say, is it not, that the employer suffers from lost time, lost wages, inability to meet contract dates?" Biemiller responded, "Unfortunately, Mr. Steiger, over the years we have not found this great outstanding interest in health and safety on the part of employers that you seem to think exists."[31] Probably the most important point that business spokesmen made was that compliance with standards would have a relatively minor effect on injuries because most accidents were caused by some "human failure." Unfortunately, the issue devolved into a unenlightening debate about who was to blame for injuries, careless workers or negligent employers, rather than focusing on the relevance of standards.

Since they had taken the initiative, the unions and their allies had to overcome the inertia and control the centrifugal tendencies that plague any attempt to pass new legislation. Key legislators had to be stirred up to work for the bill, and once stirred they had to be kept from flying off to other issues. In such circumstances, activists have strong incentives to oversell their case, which in this instance meant belittling the adequacy of existing employer incentives to provide safety, implying that tough enforcement would force bad employers to make great strides in reducing injuries and illnesses. Employers, in turn, tended to avoid mentioning their irresponsibility in the occupational health area and tried to focus the debate on worker carelessness. Neither group is likely to provide reliable guidance for calibrating the proper degree of intervention nor for designing suitable methods to carry it out.

Choosing the Method of Intervention

In his study of the OSH Act, Robert Smith writes that "one can only guess why enforcement of a detailed set of safety standards was chosen by the authors of the act as the proper mode of government intervention.[32] The simplest answer is that the government had traditionally intervened in that manner, no one complained very much about it, and no one seriously suggested any alternative. However, even if the proposal favored by Smith and many economists, a tax on injuries, had been put forward during the debates on the legislation, neither business, labor, nor politicians would have rallied to it. The explanation for this lack of enthusiasm lies in the ideological and material interests that a standard-setting program serves, which a tax program would not.

For many years the federal government had run safety and health programs that operated through the enforcement of standards. The most prominent included federal contractors under the Walsh-Healy Act and coal miners and longshoremen under special industry legislation. The staff within the Labor Department's Bureau of Labor Standards, who had operated the Walsh-Healy program and who developed the initial legislative proposal for an OSH Act, naturally thought along these lines. The state programs, which were to be upgraded or replaced, also primarily enforced standards, although with a preference for persuasion rather than penalties. For state agencies and inspectors, any program that did not include state safety inspectorates would have been highly threatening.

Business safety spokesmen had become tightly enmeshed in the work of the private standard setting organizations—the American National Standards Institute (ANSI) and the National Fire Protection Association (NFPA). Developing standards by a consensus method, the committees of these organizations were overwhelmingly dominated by technical representatives from industry. During the hearings business lobbyists continually urged that these organizations be given a central role in the standard-setting procedures under the act. Labor union leaders and Naderites were critical of the standards approach, but only because of industry domination of the standard-setting organizations and weak enforcement of the standards by state and federal agencies.

The only discussion of any alternative occurred when a few congressmen speculated that it might be desirable to restore a system of tort liability, a system that could be very expensive for employers under present jury awards for damages. Union spokesmen had little patience with these speculations. The introduction of WC generally barred tort actions; the tort alternative could hardly be restored without abolishing or restricting the scope of workers' compensation, and the unions had developed a complex network of ties with the workers' compensation system. A labor bar had grown up to service compensation claimants; union leaders and union lawyers sought judgeships on the administrative courts that sit atop the claims system; and each local union had its own workers' compensation official, providing another concrete service to union members. For corporate leaders too, a return to the uncertainties of the tort system held few charms. Suggestions that WC benefits be increased to strengthen employer safety incentives were welcomed by labor leaders but were viewed as supplements to the OSH Act, not as substitutes.[33]

One strategy favored by economists did find support in the OSH Act—the provision of more information to workers. Better information can improve the workings of the market for safety, and the preferences of informed workers merit more respect than those of uninformed workers. As workers learn about new hazards, they are likely to demand either risk premiums or elimination of the hazards. In either case, employers' incentives to provide safe workplaces will grow. The inclusion of provisions to keep workers informed resulted, however, not from pressure from economists but primarily from the efforts of Nader's staff, whose skepticism toward both union and government bureaucrats led it to favor strengthening workers' capabilities to protect themselves.

The injury tax idea proposed by the Council of Economic Advisers in their quashed report was simply not on the table when the OSH Act was being created. Yet even when, as in the case of water pollution, economists' arguments for tax instruments have entered the legislative debate, they have gained little political following. Attempting to explain that failure, Charles Schultze and Allen Kneese have noted two factors.[34] One is the absence of analysts, especially economists, on the congressional staffs and the ensuing difficulties the committees have in considering a broad array of policy options. The other factor is the legal background of most congressmen, which inclines them to make the reallocation of legal rights and duties rather than economic incentives the usual tool for effecting changes in behavior. In the case of water pollution, although these factors are relevant, an explanation of congressional action probably doesn't need to look much further than the combined support of business, environmentalists, and municipalities for the present system (standards and treatment requirements) over an effluent charge system.[35] Although the roles played by legislators' own incentives and problem-solving procedures are important, an understanding of legislative behavior still requires the more traditional examination of the role of interest groups.

But before examining how the interests of affected groups shape attitudes on the issue of choosing between enforcing standards and an injury tax, it is necessary to understand why, judged by the efficiency criterion (and, to some degree, an effectiveness criterion as well), the standards approach seems inferior to the injury tax—at least in concept. There are three main reasons why OSHA enforcement of safety standards is not likely to reduce injuries at least cost. First, most injuries are not related to the violation of OSHA standards and would occur despite perfect compliance.[36] (Strains and overexertion, for example, cause one quarter to one-third of all lost-time injuries but are unaffected by standards.) While an employer can undoubtedly prevent some of these non–standards-related injuries more cheaply than those related to standards, OSHA, which provides no incentive for injury prevention per se, will deflect his efforts toward complying with standards.

Second, even for those injuries for which compliance with standards is relevant, totally different methods may be preferable to changes in the physical environment. The cheapest way to prevent a worker from losing a finger in a machine or ramming someone with a forklift truck may be to provide extra training or to give rewards to foremen whose departments have few injuries.

Third, even when physical changes are the best method, the particular standard required by OSHA may not be the least costly. It may be outdated or simply inappropriate in particular situations. In these cases greater use of "performance" as opposed to "specification" standards would be desirable. Instead of specifying that a ladder, for example, must have rungs one inch in diameter, the standard would state that the rungs must be capable of withstanding 400 pounds. Specification standards are also likely to impede technological advances.

Although safety standards are irrelevant to most injuries, health standards do cover almost all the known disease threats. Moreover, since diseases are contracted through exposure to toxic or physical agents, limiting exposures is the sensible method of prevention. Thus, the first two problems with safety standards do not apply to health standards.[37] What most bothers economists and businessmen about health standards is that OSHA has not adopted pure performance standards that would allow firms to use personal protective equipment instead of engineering controls. But this complaint pertains to the type of standard and not to the use of standards.

Unlike the standards approach, an injury tax would give employers an added incentive to prevent *all* types of injuries and would not constrain them from employing the least costly preventive methods. The tax, which ideally would be set to equal the externalized costs of the injury, would provide that incentive because it would raise the marginal benefits of injury prevention (the cost of the injury would now include the tax; thus that cost would be saved by the prevention of the injury). If, for example, the tax took the form of a 20-percent surcharge on an employer's total injury losses, he would spend no more than an extra 20 percent beyond what he would have spent in the absence of the tax.

Even if we disregard the objective of setting the tax to make the employer's cost equal the social cost, the tax remains a less costly instrument for achieving any given reduction in injuries. The crucial advantage of the tax derives from the likelihood that an employer will usually have better information about the least costly methods for preventing injuries at his workplace than the government does. In cases where a government agency does know more, the enforcement of standards may in fact be cheaper. More realistically, a standard may be desirable when, although it is inappropriate at some workplaces, the resulting losses are outweighed by the gains achieved by preventing other firms from erroneously concluding, perhaps owing to high information costs, that the measure would not be worthwhile.

The theoretical case for taxes is subject to a number of qualifications.[38] For example, it assumes that firms are cost minimizers, an assumption that some critics of the tax approach dispute. While some standards are surely worthwhile, firms are probably sufficiently well informed and engage in enough cost-minimizing behavior to make an injury tax a cheaper way to reduce injuries than the present safety enforcement program. How much cheaper it would be is open to speculation, as are the distributive consequences that a change would bring. We also don't know what the effect of a given tax on the injury rate would be, although one possible virtue of the tax would be that the rates could be readjusted to home in on the desired target.[39] The administration of a tax system is also far more burdensome than is usually recognized. Yet even given all these problems, the critical weakness of the tax proposal is political.

The Politics of the Injury Tax and Safety Standards

Why don't business groups rally around the injury tax proposal? The tax would almost certainly impose smaller net costs on firms than the standards approach, if one ignores the tax payments themselves. That is the rub, for while the social calculus does not treat the tax as an additional (resource) cost, the firm must.

Firms may differ in their opinions on an injury tax. Those for whom injury reduction is cheap compared with compliance with standards may prefer a tax; firms for whom the reverse is true will not. At the extremes, there is some tax rate low enough for all firms to prefer a tax, and some rate high enough for all to oppose it. Since about two million disabling injuries a year occur in the private sector, even a tax that averaged $250 per injury would impose annual tax payments approaching $500 million (on the plausible assumption that the great bulk of injuries would still occur at this tax level).[40] Quite possibly, this amount exceeds what firms spend annually to comply with OSHA safety standards. (See chapter 7 for "guesstimates" of the amount of this spending.) It seems reasonable to conclude that the tax rate would not have to be very high to bring most firms into opposition.

If it were guaranteed that the tax receipts would be returned to industry, perhaps through a reduction in the average corporate profits tax rate, the position of industry groups might change, but the political feasibility of such a bargain is very low.[41] Another reason for opposition to an injury tax might be corporate fears that, once established, such a tax would be easy to change. While this flexibility is an advantage for many proponents, for employers it carries the threat of turning the tax into a hungrily-eyed source of revenue rather than a method to internalize social costs. Union leaders have reason to value cost-effectiveness—the chief virtue of the injury tax—only to the extent that they feel that workers will end up bearing the costs of prevention. As explained below, they often think that such an outcome is unlikely, at least in any visible, short-run sense. In addition, unionists do have ideological reasons for disliking the injury tax. Just as the effluent tax fell victim to the environmentalist claim that it was a "license to pollute," so an injury tax could become a "license to maim." It carries the implication that if the tax does not supply enough of an economic incentive to prevent an injury, then the injury should be allowed to occur. One can hardly expect unions to accept such a policy. Even though a standards approach may prevent fewer injuries—although no one ever knows that for sure—it retains an explicit commitment that workers shall be provided a safe place to work.

By allowing employers to choose the methods for reducing injuries, the injury tax could lead to difficult problems for unions: replacing or firing workers with bad accident records; stricter discipline for violation of safety rules; requiring workers to wear safety shoes or safety glasses. While some of these measures, like the last two, may also be required by OSHA, the union is placed in a less difficult position vis-à-vis its members precisely because "this is what the government requires"; union leaders are not as likely to be held responsible. Moreover the union could use its influence in Washington to try to ensure that such practices are not required.

The substitution of a tax for standards of enforcement would also eliminate union powers that the OSH Act has augmented. Prior to OSHA, a union threat to call in a safety inspector provoked only mild concern on the part of employers. Even if the inspector discovered violations, no penalty would result, and even if the violation went uncorrected no extra penalty would usually be levied. By increasing the size and certainty of fines—and by adopting procedures that help keep unions informed of inspection results—OSHA gave local unions a useful weapon. If management expects that an inspection will cost it anywhere from several hundred to several thousand dollars, then it may often be willing to grant various union demands in exchange for not requesting inspections. In this manner local unions can use OSHA as a lever to increase their bargaining power.[42]

At the national level, the thrust of the entire injury tax program would depend upon one basic decision: the size of the tax. Attention would be diverted from the particular injuries suffered by particular groups of workers. As a result, union leaders might well fear that OSHA policymakers would give less of an edge to safety than they would in the average standard-setting procedure. Under an injury tax policy, union leaders would also lose the opportunity to use their influence with Labor Department officials to try to sway decisions on standards of particular interest to their union.

As for politicians, probably their legal backgrounds do disincline them to use economic incentives, as Kneese and Schultze observe; yet a Congress composed of men and women trained in economics would be subject to the same political pressures and might not behave very differently. Their point about staff analysts is also relevant: if economists had served on the subcommittee staffs, more potentially efficient policies might have been considered. But then the question becomes why economists don't serve on these staffs and why even when they are involved in the OSH field their influence is so meager.

In his description of the House Education and Labor Committee, Fenno noted how little demand there was for staff expertise. As one congressman explained,

Expertise? Hell, everyone thinks he's an expert on the questions before our Committee. On education, the problem is that everyone went to school. They all think that makes them experts on that. And labor matters are so polarized that everyone is committed. You take sides first and then you acquire expertise. No one accepts anyone as impartial. [43]

Although the Education and Labor Committee presents an extreme case, a more fundamental reason for the lack of analysis is that congressmen have little incentive to investigate new policy options unless some powerful groups are already proposing them. For congressmen, the cost of a failure to analyze options is very low. As Mayhew explains,

The important point here is that on measures lacking particularized benefits the congressmen's intrinsic interest in the impact of legislation vanishes. Hence, it is a misallocation of resources to devote time and energy to prescription or scrutiny of impact unless, again, credit is available for legislative maneuvering. On matters where credit-claiming possibilities wear thin, therefore, we should not be surprised to find that members display only a modest interest in what goes into bills or what their passage accomplishes. [44]

The opposition of business, labor, health activists, and safety professionals would almost certainly ensure that politicians too would oppose an injury tax. But there are other reasons as well. Ideologically, the standards approach appears as a form of equal opportunity legislation which surrounds it with an aura of legitimacy. It takes the middle road between a radical egalitarianism that would try to equalize all risks—to make being a lumberjack as safe as being a stockbroker—and the injury tax approach, which would elicit safety improvements only where they could be achieved cheaply enough. The standards approach guarantees that all workplaces meet certain (sometimes irrelevant) minimum standards, but doesn't guarantee equal results. What could be fairer?

Moreover, the likelihood that an injury tax would be tagged a "license to maim" would trouble politicians as much as if not more than it troubled labor leaders. According to Mayhew, members of Congress "are much inclined to incorporate popular conceptions of instrumental rationality into the statute books. Attentive publics judge positions on means as well as on ends. Hence the congressional penchant for the blunt simple action."[45] The "license to maim" label conjures up an image of passive legislators, derelict in their duty to protect the American workers. Thus for politicians, even more than for union leaders the injury tax would be too automatic. The standards approach offers greater opportunities for intervention. Some of these emerge in the standard-setting process, but most grow out of the enforcement process. Employers who claim that OSHA is persecuting them and unions who claim that employers are being coddled supply a steady stream of casework in congressional offices.

The congressmen who gain the most from the opportunities for intervention are the chairmen of the subcommittees that wrote the act (and also Congressman Steiger, who cosponsored it). Because the committees' jurisdictions are continuing, they will normally have to approve any changes in their own legislative creations (unless the full House or Senate is willing to override them). Vested with oversight authority, the committees are in a good position to ensure that administrators do not subvert the intent of the legislation. While this appears to protect an important democratic principle, the exclusive committee jursidiction also tends to exclude any groups that lack influence in the committee from having any say in the policy area being considered. Unsurprisingly, in light of the alliance between the unions and the Democratic majorities, business lobbyists complain that the oversight hearings are held only to stiffen OSHA's spine and make it tougher in its enforcement.

Distributive Features

The methods of intervening to improve occupational safety and health conditions are of concern because the distribution of benefits and costs can vary depending on the method used. A preeminent concern with finding the least-cost methods of injury prevention implies indifference about the identity of beneficiaries. We all expect the leaders of the Textile Workers Union to show more concern about the health of textile workers than of farmers in Kansas or school bus drivers in California. Consequently, the union would be unswayed if someone could demonstrate that it cost more to prevent the deaths of textile workers. Perhaps on no single issue are economists' and lay views as far apart as they are on the issue of social cost. Few people think about using up society's resources; rather, they ask who will pay.

Standard economic theory would suggest that since workers are compensated for the risks they take, a reduction in risk will lead to a reduction in wages as well. Workers would take more of their income in safety and less in money. Yet, although the theory indicates that workers will pay for at least some of the safety improvements, it does not require that they pay for all of them.[46]

Unions seldom appear to act as if they believed that wholesale passbacks were likely. In part, this skepticism developed as a shield against the litany of management threats about the financial consequences of acceding to union demands. Protected by three-year union contracts, by aversion to tinkering with relative wages, and by the firm's need to remain competitive in those jobs for which an external labor market exists, workers and unions will usually have only minor, long-run adjustments to make.

In some cases workers will suffer because of OSHA. Unemployment is one reason. Although reduced demands for goods whose relative prices have been raised by OSHA will be offset by higher demand for those whose relative prices have been lowered, the movement of workers from one industry to another is hardly frictionless, and unemployment will result. No one knows the number of workers laid off as a result of OSHA, but some undoubtedly have been. Higher costs in the American textile industry, for example, have probably caused some marginal firms to succumb to foreign competition. The difficulty of attributing plant shutdowns to any single factor can generate claims of either massive impact or no impact. Since the employers who close down are unlikely to have much political clout (while in some cases, strong firms may look on approvingly at the shakeout), the only strong complainant may be the union of the affected workers. Even if the unemployed workers are unorganized, pressures on other firms may jar the union into action. Although unions' political support of OSHA may restrain them from complaining about such losses, the recent reversal in the United Auto Workers' longstanding support for strict auto pollution controls reveals the potential sensitivity of union leaders. Perhaps significantly, however, the UAW did not call for any weakening in OSHA enforcement, which auto manufacturers had also blamed for cost increases; auto union members benefit more visibly from OSHA than from reductions in auto pollution.

Other losers are workers who prefer facing job hazards to the OSHA alternatives. OSHA required employers to offer medical exams to workers who have certain levels of exposure to toxic materials. When those exams indicate that continued exposure would be harmful, the employer is required to remove the worker, OSHA does not require that the worker receive employment elsewhere, much less guarantee a job at equal pay. Unless the union can enforce such a claim or the firm decides to grant it, the worker may find himself unemployed or working at a worse job. Workers who have to surrender risk premiums are also potential losers under OSHA; however, because of the rigidities in the wage system, it seems unlikely that very many immediate losers have been created in this way. Workers who are now forced to wear personal protective equipment also may be losers. If they had previously been fully informed about the hazards but still refused to wear equipment because of the discomfort, then they will be made worse off by having to wear it.

In the context of a competitive labor market, workers can be faced with some especially hard choices. Suppose a worker, previously unaware that noise was damaging his hearing, did not wear the earmuffs offered by his employer. Since OSHA, he has become aware of the damage and has also been compelled to wear the muffs. He might feel satisfied doing this if he got an extra 25¢ an hour more (plus whatever he eventually receives from workers' compensation), but the firm might find someone who doesn't mind the discomfort and fire the veteran. More generally, whenever workers discover that a job is riskier than they had thought and do demand some sort of premium, management has a strong incentive to try to replace them with less risk-averse workers. Mandatory standards and especially mandatory engineering controls serve to protect workers who want to take fewer risks. They also protect unions against those members who might want to take greater risks.

In some respects the OSH Act relies on unions to activate it, through worker complaints and surveillance of management, both of which are more likely to occur at unionized workplaces, where unions can use the act to gain leverage in bargaining. Yet if OSHA were totally dependent upon worker invocations, it would largely fail to correct hazards at nonunion plants, handing them a potential competitive advantage. The desire to exploit the strengths that unionism confers must be tempered by the danger of undercutting the unionized sector.

Ideally, unions might prefer a system that provided strict and inflexible enforcement at nonunion workplaces but that would respond flexibly to union preferences at the local or national level. (Conflicts between local and national leaders about how flexible enforcement should be complicate the picture.) If union members at a workplace are willing to tolerate conditions that violate OSHA standards, perhaps in return for a little extra money, then why should OSHA enforce its standards there?[47] If such bargaining is mutually profitable to both parties, then why should OSHA prevent it? In the absence of externalities, this question occurs naturally to economists. Politically, however, it is apparent that the public support for the OSH Act rests partly upon a desire to discourage risk-taking in the workplace; it does not sanction the use of OSHA to help workers get more money for taking the risks they take.

OSHA does not encourage such bargaining; once inspectors are called in, they appear to behave similarly at union and nonunion workplaces. (However, one difference is described in chapter 3.) Yet there are no public means to prevent unions from winning concessions from management in exchange for not pressing for OSHA enforcement. From an economic perspective, the bargaining may partially restore the efficiency gains that a flexible enforcement policy would have provided.

Beneficiaries and Equity

Several sources indicate that risky jobs tend to be relatively low-paying jobs in spite of any risk premiums that may exist. For example, figures for New York State around 1950 indicate that the correlations between an occupation's compensable injury rate and fatality rate, on the one hand, and its median income, on the other, were -0.38 and -0.16, respectively. Using 1967 data for a national sample, Thaler and Rosen also found that the simple correlation between life expectancy in an occupation and its average earnings was negative. Surprisingly, however, within the steel industry, jobs that are more hazardous tend to be better-paying. For over 600 nonsupervisory job classifications, the simple correlation between job class, which largely determines relative wages, and hazard ratings was $+0.20$.[48]

If the benefits from OSHA's program were directly proportional to the level of risk encountered on the job, then OSHA's benefit structure would almost certainly be progressive. However, there is no reason to assume that any such neat relationship exists. The discussion of OSHA's impact on safety in chapter 6 indicates that employees in manufacturing and construction have reaped the reward of the greatest reduction in injuries, mainly because the hazards in those industries are most closely related to OSHA standards. The OSH Act's expansion of health hazard research promises its greatest benefits to workers in petrochemical and related industries, workplaces in which the introduction of new, potentially dangerous substances is occurring at the fastest pace. Although exceptions exist, these industries are not among the lower-paying ones in the economy.

The simplest accurate statement about the beneficiaries of OSHA's programs is that they are overwhelmingly blue-collar workers, mostly unionized, and mostly men. Support for OSHA based on a concern with income distribution and improving the lot of the least fortunate does not seem well grounded. Even if it were, more direct transfer programs would serve those goals more efficiently. One might support the OSH Act in the hope that it would reduce status inequalities by improving the working conditions of blue-collar workers, but the OSHA program's role in any such improvement is likely to be meager, so support on those grounds would be largely symbolic.[49]

Such a search for reasons to support the OSH Act may seem unnecessarily far-fetched, since quite solid reasons are right at hand. The expanded research program is long overdue; efforts to estimate the future benefits of current research are notoriously uncertain, but there is good reason to believe that the private provision of research has been inadequate, and the prospect of staunching future losses from presently unknown health hazards is bright. OSHA's health standards provide a conceptually sound way to approach health hazards. The OSH Act's procedural requirements increase the flow of information to workers about the hazards they face, facilitating the proper working of market processes. The value of OSHA's safety program is more doubtful, although some of the measures are probably worthwhile. The two most serious questions about the OSH Act are whether the enforcement of safety standards constitutes a desirable form of regulation and whether OSHA properly weighs the costs and benefits of protection in its safety standards and especially in its health standards.

3
Consensus Standards and OSHA Enforcement

Within a month of its legal birth, OSHA adopted thousands of preexisting federal and consensus safety and health standards, but it adopted only a handful of additional standards during the following six years. Thus the standards OSHA enforced were far from new. For example, before OSHA, compliance with the federal standards had been required from all employers with federal contracts larger than $2,500. The consensus standards, established as guidelines by private groups through a consensual process, had been incorporated into the labor codes of many states. Yet because both state and federal enforcement agencies had almost entirely eschewed penalties before 1970, firms had usually remained free to disregard standards with which they did not wish to comply. Thus OSHA's impact during these first six years has been due primarily to its tougher enforcement of preexisting standards.

OSHA's enforcement has been subjected to criticism on three major grounds. Perhaps the most common criticism it has faced is that the standards are often irrelevant, petty, or simply not effective enough to justify their costs. A second and related criticism is that despite the legislative preoccupation with occupational disease, the great bulk of the enforcement has been devoted to safety hazards, not health. A third criticism is directed at OSHA'S requirement that engineering controls—and not personal protective equipment—be used to prevent harmful exposure to health hazards. Each of these three criticisms touches upon basic issues in OSHA's enforcement program, and an evaluation of their validity requires a knowledge of the political, economic, and organizational factors underlying the choice of these policies.

Adoption of the Initial Standards

The thousands of standards OSHA adopted in early 1971 included the consensus standards developed by groups like the American National Standards Institute (ANSI) as well as the federal standards already enforced by the Labor Department under the terms of the Walsh-Healey Contracts Act and other laws.[1] The "consensus" method essentially meant that committees composed primarily of corporate safety engineers, with a light sprinkling of labor and government representatives, overwhelmingly agreed that a certain technique or protective device had desirable safety features. In many states these consensus standards, as well as exposure limits for toxic materials, had been incorporated into state safety codes in the 1950s and 1960s. Although many standards were out of date, they generally represented a model for industry to strive toward.

Every OSH bill had explicitly mandated the adoption of consensus standards. The 1969 Nixon Administration bill also gave ANSI a central role in the ongoing process of establishing new standards, since the Labor department would have had to rely on ANSI to approve new standards. Business spokesmen generally favored this proposal because they wanted to curb the department's discretion. Some had criticized Labor Secretary Wirtz's adoption of standards under the Walsh-Healey Act; he had picked them from "out of the blue" according to one business lobbyist I interviewed. The bills considered in 1970 no longer gave ANSI a special role in new standards, but they still required OSHA to adopt the consensus standards.

During the hearings on these bills, Democrats described the consensus standards as watered down and out of date. The senate Labor Committee's report expressed its support for the adoption of the consensus standards in the following terms:

The purpose of this procedure is to establish as rapidly as possible national occupational safety and health standards with which industry is familiar. These standards may not be as effective or up to date as is desirable, but they will be useful for immediately providing a nationwide minimum level of health and safety.[2]

The committee's counsel, Robert Nagle, later recalled, "It was true that people were not fully aware of what the adoption of consensus standards meant. In fact there was a general feeling that most of them were a little weak because they had emerged from a watered-down process. But we did know that they were *not* generally followed by industry." The OSH Act's cosponsor, Congressman William Steiger, took a somewhat different view: "We were misinformed by industry, which kept telling us that these standards were widely used and generally accepted. That simply turned out not to be true."[3]

Some business spokesmen had presented a different picture. In 1972 an official of the U.S. Chamber of Commerce lamented,

Perhaps the greatest problem in this entire standards area results from the impression that the consensus standards had the blessing of the business community as the last word on safety.

On October 16, 1969, we testified before this subcommittee in an attempt to correct this assumption. We stated:

"National consensus standards are expressly intended to be guides—not ironclad limitations. Their real value lies in their flexible application to a number of diverse employment situations. It would, therefore, be both a basic and grave mistake to adopt such standards as inflexible and wooden rules and we urge that they not be so treated."

Unfortunately, this advice was not heeded and failure to do so has in large measure resulted in the hearings being held today.[4]

Yet business leaders had had several reasons for not empahsizing these warnings about consensus standards. First, they wanted to convince legislators that industry voluntarily adopted good safety practices and that no need existed for punitive public enforcement. To oppose adherence to the mild and innocuous-sounding "consensus" standards, which had essentially been developed by industry, would have spoiled the image they were trying to project. Second, at least until the summer of 1970, their lobbyists did not think that enforcement under the act would differ much from the mild practices followed in states like California and New York. As long as enforcers either lacked teeth or refused to bite, the content of the standards didn't really matter very much. Thus although many states had previously made the consensus standards into formal requirements, their enforcement agencies' decisions to eschew penalties and stick to education kept the real role of the standards purely advisory.

By the time the Steiger bill appeared, containing the same basic enforcement procedures that the Daniels bill had, it was too late for business to oppose all legislation. Moreover, the lobbyists still thought the provisions of the act would allow the head of OSHA broad discretion about which consensus standards to adopt. Since they had a close relationship with Labor Secretary James Hodgson, they had good reason to believe that the decisions about the adoption of these standards would be made by a sympathetic official. Indeed, Leo Teplow and Frank Barnako, both from the steel industry, later claimed responsibility for having George Guenther appointed the first assistant secretary for OSH.[5]

However, in this respect at least, Guenther confounded their hopes, Section 6(a) of the act required that within two years of the act's effective date (April 29, 1971), the secretary of labor shall promulgate any existing consensus standards and federal standards "unless he determines that the promulgation of such a standard would not result in improved safety or health for specifically designated employees." In addition, Section 4(b)(2) dealt with the federal standards and mandated that "standards issued under the laws listed in this paragraph and in effect on or after the effective date of this Act shall be deemed to be occupational safety and health standards issued under this Act. . . ."

On May 29, 1971, OSHA promulgated *all* of the consensus and federal standards. The agency still had twenty-three months to go before its deadline expired. The standards occupied three hundred densely packed pages of the *Federal Register*, which still omitted many that were incorporated by reference. The effective dates of most of the standards were delayed for three months; for some, the delay was nine months. During the three months, OSHA inspectors could only cite violations of the act's "general duty" clause, a much clumsier enforcement tool.

As many observers, including the Occupational Safety and Health Review Commission, have noted, this hasty and wholesale adoption generated many errors. A few standards were actually not relevant to safety or health. Some were so vague as to be unenforceable. In some cases, OSHA had printed the consensus standards improperly, with significantly different wording and requirements.[6] Most importantly, the standards had been adopted in a "wooden and inflexible" manner. No care was given to limiting their application only to particular situations. No attention was paid to how effective they would be, nor to how much compliance with them would cost. As Frank Barnako explained later, no one thought that OSHA would adopt all of the consensus standards. He wondered whether the business community bore some of the responsibility; perhaps it should have established a crash program to review the standards and recommend which should be weeded out.

Why did OSHA promulgate these standards so quickly and indiscriminately? If it had waited eighteen months, it would have had time to do some of the weeding itself. The rush to promulgate standards may have been part of a strategy aimed at achieving a delay in the date when they became effective. The language of the act appeared to provide little support for such delays, but OSHA leaders were eager to give employers time to become acquainted with the standards. Early promulgation may have been a way to appease union critics and to forestall lawsuits against the delayed effective dates. The Nader study of OSHA suggests that this action did hold off legal attacks.[7]

Yet even if it had used the full two years, OSHA would have lacked both the time and the resources for an intelligent assessment of more than a small minority of the consensus standards. As OSHA's standard setters quickly learned, the information needed to make such assessments is highly precise and rarely available. The act had given the consensus standards a presumption of effectiveness; the burden of proof was placed on OSHA to show that they were not effective. This presumption ensured that any widespread pruning of the standards would encounter a wave of lawsuits that OSHA would find very difficult to win.

In *Bitter Wages*, Page and O'Brien do hint at a strategy that probably would have left all the parties better off.[8] If OSHA had quickly adopted a subset of the more important standards and then waited a year or two until adopting more, it would have been able to avoid making so many errors and have had the time to try to convince the unions that not all of the standards should be adopted. By then the outcry against even these more firmly grounded standards might have persuaded the union leaders that OSHA should tread more lightly. Yet this strategy would have demanded a willingness on OSHA's part to risk enlarging the rift between the agency and organized labor. The unions and their allies would almost certainly have been reluctant to trust Guenther's discretion about which standards to omit or postpone.

Ironically, the speedy adoption of all the consensus standards has redounded to the disadvantage of both OSHA and the unions. Some union officials have speculated whether the move, which stirred vast annoyance and gave OSHA's enemies good ammunition, had been intended by the department's top Republicans as a way to discredit OSHA. Many of OSHA's strongest backers have been highly critical of what they view as its nitpicking enforcement. Former Counsel Nagle's assessment, for example, is that "the problem is not with the penalties. The problem is that enforcement had been misdirected to emphasizing compliance with standards that have relatively little effect on safety and health." Asked whether he though this misdirection had been intentional, he laughed and said, "I've seen enough stupid things at the Labor Department to know that it wouldn't need to be intentional. Whatever the feelings are at the top, the pressures on the inspectors in the field can explain the outcomes."

One congressional staffer felt that it would be all right not to level penalties when the employer immediately abated a violation, although he quickly added that he was not against first-instance penalties. He felt there had been too much "Mickey Mouse business" on minor violations and too much downgrading of serious hazards. He didn't think that employers should be penalized if their railings were 26 inches and the standard required 28. What was really needed, he concluded, was good judgement. Another legislative staff member felt that inspectors should know what the special hazards in each industry are and look especially for them, not bothering about all the little things. She admitted that inspectors must cite every violation they see, but added that "they don't have to look for everything."[9]

Although they are unhappy with the strict enforcement of many relatively unimportant violations, legislative and union leaders have been unwilling to give up the policies that are responsible. The underlying issue is the exercise of discretion by inspectors. Unions fear that inspectors will use discretion to weaken enforcement against serious as well as minor hazards. Neither the unions nor OSHA leaders have been willing to trust the good judgement or professionalism of the inspectors. Consequently, OSHA had employed the usual method of limiting discretion in the field, which is to require strict enforcement of all regulations; for OSHA inspectors, this entails citing all the violations detected, even if they are trivial.

Two avenues of escape from this dilemma appear open. The first is to upgrade the quality of the inspectorate to create a level of professionalism that will instill greater trust in their judgments. The second is to declare that many safety violations are simply not worth bothering about,[14] which would prompt inspectors to exercise discretion in order to avoid getting bogged down in trivial problems. The two avenues clearly converge, for it is best to vest the exercise of discretion in professionals. OSHA's recent leaders, Morton Corn and Eula Bingham, have moved in this direction by giving priority to health enforcement and to improved training for inspectors. In 1976, Congress facilitated these changes by temporarily prohibiting penalties for nonserious first-instance violations. If violations are not considered serious enough to warrant a penalty as a deterrent, then it becomes harder to justify citing them at all.

Safety versus Health in Enforcement

During the hearings on the OSH Act, both labor and management leaders agreed that health hazards, not safety hazards, presented the strongest case for government action. Yet since the act took effect, the overwhelming bulk of inspections and violations have dealt with safety, not health. For example, for the calendar years 1973, 1974, and the first six months of 1975, OSHA conducted approximately 190,000 inspections; fewer than 20,000 of them included tests for air contaminants, excess noise, or any other health threat—slightly over 10 percent of the total number of inspections.[11]

Why did health concerns recede into the background in enforcement? One important reason is that a large segment of the occupational health problem does not readily lend itself to solution by enforcement. To discover that diseases are occurring and then unravel the causes requires research, not enforcement. In addition, violations of safety standards were simply more prevalent than violations of health standards, a situation that had been guaranteed by the mass adoption of the consensus standards. Excessive noise is a common problem in industry, but it is hardly as pervasive as wet floors, cluttered aisles, and substandard electrical plugs.

Unions could still fault OSHA for not aggressively seeking out the users of hazardous materials like asbestos. However, OSHA faced a serious constraint in developing its health enforcement program—the lack of trained industrial hygienists. As late as June 1973, OSHA employed only 68 hygienists. and was still struggling to post one in each of its forty-nine area offices. Why did OSHA have so few hygienists? According to some estimates, fewer than 2,000 industrial hygienists worked in the United States in 1970 (and only about 600 of them had been certified by their professional association), and 75 new hygienists were being trained each year.[12] The OSH Act spurred the demand for hygienists by all sectors, not just by OSHA. With this competition, OSHA did well to increase its hygiene force to 168 by mid-1975. If OSHA's managers or the Congress had insisted on making health inspections performed by hygienists the bulk of the enforcement program, they would have had to be content with a much smaller agency. Naturally, OSHA's leaders, along with its union and congressional allies, wanted OSHA to become large. With four million workplaces to cover, a couple of hundred inspectors would never do.

But does the number of health inspections have to be limited by the number of hygienists, or can less highly trained personnel provide a partial substitute? Legal and political factors figure importantly in the answer to that question. The formal demands on OSHA as a law enforcement agency restrict the extent to which substitution can take place. OSHA must be able to present credible evidence for the violations it cites. There is some danger that quickly trained inspectors may not be proficient enough with the instruments needed to measure toxic exposures. Professional skills have been especially needed since the OSHRC placed on OSHA the burden of proving that engineering controls were technically feasible.

OSHA could certainly have used safety inspectors to ferret out health violations to a much greater extent than it did. The evidence indicates, for example, that safety inspectors rarely conducted any tests for noise or toxic exposures, even when they visited workplaces where exposures were likely. If they had made such tests, they could have screened for violations, allowing for a more efficient use of hygienists' time. The most likely result of such a policy, however, would have been a sharp rise in the number of health violations detected. Given the evidential standards, more hygienists would have been needed to prepare the cases for these additional violations. Moreover, an outreach effort of this nature could have sharply raised employer compliance costs, because noise and toxic hazards tend to be very costly to abate. It seems unlikely that such an aggressive policy would have appealed to the policymakers,[13] not only because the administration was sensitive to business concerns, but also because the result could have been an intensification of attacks upon OSHA.

Engineering Controls versus Personal Protection in the Enforcement of Health Standards

When OSHA sets new health standards, it must decide whether exposures must be limited by the use of engineering controls or whether firms can rely on personal protective equipment such as earmuffs or respirators. In the few new health standards that OSHA has adopted, engineering controls have been required "except to the extent that such controls are not feasible."[14] For the over 400 health hazards for which OSHA has not yet established new standards, the language of the Walsh-Healey standard is controlling: before personal protective equipment can be used as an acceptable means of compliance, "feasible administrative or engineering controls must first be determined and implemented in all cases."[15]

How do OSHA enforcers decide whether engineering controls are feasible at particular workplaces? These decisions have major consequences. For example, even if the standard requires engineering controls, an enforcement policy that freely granted employer claims of infeasibility would allow widespread reliance on personal protection instead of engineering. In attempting to estimate the costs of reducing employee exposures to a certain toxic material, it makes an immense difference whether or not personal protective equipment will be allowed as a means of compliance.

OSHA stated its policy on "feasibility" in its *Compliance Operations Manual (COM)*. Feasiblity was construed so broadly that if the policy were followed in the field reliance on personal protection would rarely be allowed. The *Manual* stated,

A determination regarding the feasibility of engineering controls should involve an evaluation of engineering ability to accomplish this control. In most instances there is sufficient engineering and scientific knowledge to perfect engineering controls satisfactorily abating a hazard. The question of economic feasibility of implementing such controls will not normally be a factor. But, if a major reconstruction of a plant or a capital expenditure, which would seriously jeopardize the financial condition of the company, is the only method that would achieve effective engineering controls, and if there were feasible alternative administrative controls or protective devices available, engineering controls would not be considered feasible. However, spending that has less serious consequences, for example, replacement or installation of large units of machinery or equipment, even though amounting to thousands of dollars but not otherwise jeopardizing the financial condition of a company would be considered feasible.[16]

This policy can be criticized on several grounds. It runs counter to an efficient solution in many and probably most situations. Evidence that personal protective equipment could be used successfully or that workers would be willing to wear it is dismissed as irrelevant. According to the associate solicitor for OSH, the general rationale for this approach was the feeling, "Why should we allow somebody to provide less protection just because it would cost them a lot of money?" The OSHRC upheld this view in several cases. For example, it required B. F. Goodrich to undertake expensive noise controls at one plant, noting that the sum was small in comparison with the corporation's total assets.[17]

If the basic policy had been based upon efficiency criteria, then it would make little economic sense to exempt firms from it on the grounds that their existence would be "jeopardized." Firms that can't stay in business when they are forced to bear the full social costs of production should not be helped to stay in operation. That conclusion follows if the firm also captures all of the social benefits it generates. The converse is often asserted in arguments that a firm's importance to a community justifies subsidies. If a firm does shut down, at least some workers will experience more than just frictional unemployment, creating some social costs that the firm is unlikely to bear. Usually these costs will not be significant enough to justify easier enforcement, but in some cases they may be.[18] Yet even in the cases where easier enforcement for marginal firms seems efficient, it will remain inequitable in its effects among firms.

OSHA's reasons for adopting the tough definition of feasibility had little to do with efficiency and not much more to do with equity. By treating economic factors as normally irrelevant, the *COM*'s writers not only avoided having to specify how to make the trade-offs but also saved OSHA's field staff from the enormous problems of trying to apply the criteria in thousands of cases. Attesting to the success of this effort, in 1975 OSHA's chief compliance officer could not recall a single case in which an employer had been allowed to use personal protective equipment as the permanent abatement method because of financial infeasibility.

OSHA's exceptions for firms "in jeopardy" indicates the Labor Department's sensitivity to the problem of putting firms out of business and, more importantly, of putting workers out of jobs. OSHA can show critics this *COM* policy and assure them that no one need be put out of work.

The image of rigid enforcement of the engineering requirement fades, however, when one looks at the lengths of time OSHA allowed for abatement. One indication of this looseness was that the solicitor's office was very hard put to find a case in which a firm had been fined for failure to abate a health violation, although one case was finally found.[19]

In order to examine how OSHA's abatement policy on engineering controls had worked in practice, I reviewed the case records for a random sample of fourty-three health inspections that had been conducted out of the San Francisco Area office during 1972 and 1973. That review confirmed that none of the employers cited for violations of health standards (most of them for noise) had been exempted from engineering controls because of economic considerations. In fact, none of them had been exempted from the requirement for technological infeasibility either. However, OSHA had set initial abatement periods averaging two years, and extensions of another one or two years were common. In consequence, by May 1976 there were only three closed cases out of the twenty-three cases in which noise violations had been cited. In four or five of those cases the abatement date had passed, but OSHA had not yet made the follow-up inspection required before the case could be closed.

One other feature of these noise cases merits attention. OSHA set shorter initial abatement periods at unionized workplaces than at nonunion workplaces. For both 1972 and 1973, the periods were 7 months longer at the latter (27 months compared to 20 months). Although the number of cases is small, the difference for the two-year period is statistically significant.[20] This pattern persists if one excludes the inspections triggered by complaints (of which there were none at nonunion plants) and looks only at cases referred to the industrial hygienist by a safety inspector. One possible explanation for this difference is that OSHA acts tougher because the union is there to counterbalance any tendency to show consideration to the employer. Since postponement of engineering controls extends the period during which the workers have to wear earmuffs or plugs, the union is likely to look unfavorably on extended abatements unless it feels that financial jeopardy is involved. That concern ties in with the second possible explanation: the unionized workplaces tend to be larger and are often branch plants of large national firms with relatively great financial resources. Thus OSHA, as well as the workers, may take these resources into account in setting abatement dates.

Whatever the explanation for the difference between union and nonunion firms, the fundamental point is that OSHA has used lengthy abatement periods as a means to avoid dealing with the complexities of determining either technical or economic feasibility. Initially OSHA placed the burden of proving infeasibility on the employers but without explaining to them what criteria it would use in judging their arguments. Employers responded by also sidestepping the issue of feasibility and instead simply asked for the extensions that OSHA was very willing to confer.[21] OSHA's leaders chose not to try to resolve the issue of feasibility.

Eventually the OSH Review Commission did step in. First, it ruled that the burden of proof for showing that compliance was technically feasible fell on OSHA. The industrial hygienist must be able to refer to similar hazards that have been abated at other plants or to references in the literature that describe engineering controls. More recently, in September 1976, the OSHRC took the major step of ruling that the determination of economic feasibility included considerations beyond the financial jeopardy of the firm. It had to include some "weighing of benefits and costs"; exactly how OSHA should carry out this weighing was left open. The Labor Department, supported by the unions, is appealing this ruling.[22]

Associate Solicitor Mintz's description of the situation in 1975 remains accurate in 1978: "We just don't have any settled law on the definition of the feasibility of enforcing engineering controls. We're in the same shape as we are in determining the feasibility of a standard."[23] However, although they have been totally successful in avoiding the controversial weighing of costs and benefits when it comes to enforcing standards, OSHA's administrators have not been able to avoid the scales when it comes to setting new standards. That they nevertheless have often claimed not to be using scales presents a paradox that is worth exploring.

Social Values in Standard Setting: What Has Happened and Why?

Assistant Secretary Stender has said that we will never trade lives for dollars, and my staff supports that completely. I don't believe anyone can argue with that philosophy.

Now let's not be naive and think that OSHA's role is just to promulgate NIOSH's recommendations without considering other factors, such as "feasibility," that are specified in the law. . . . I believe it would be unconscionable for us in the federal government to set standards without consideration of the questions of economics and feasibility.
Daniel Boyd, Chief, OSHA Office of Standards Development

We have often said that it is impossible to put a price tag on the lives or health of workers. This is most certainly correct. But general principles don't settle concrete cases, and upon completion of the rule-making proceedings the Department of Labor will have to decide on the basis of the record what the proper [noise] level should be.
Benjamin Mintz, Associate Solicitor for OSH

We never have suggested that there should be a trade-off between dollars on the one hand and the protection of health or the environment on the other, nor do we do so now. But the economic problem is there, and is relevant to any reasonable administration and implementation of this legislative proposal. . . .
Dr. C. Boyd Schaffer, Director of Technology, American Cyanamid, Inc.

We don't object so much to the consideration of economic feasibility, but OSHA is not competent in this field. Nor is it possible to equitably balance economic considerations with the paramount consideration of life. Thus far, OSHA's cost of compliance studies have amounted to little more than opinion polls of industry management.
Sheldon Samuels, Director of Health and Safety for the Industrial Union Department, AFL-CIO

Each of these statements[1] denies the legitimacy of balancing or trading off human lives and resources expended on safety measures, yet each statement also asserts that economic considerations can or should be considered. What does it mean to "consider" economic costs if they are not to be balanced against the health effects?

Political expediency could explain these contradictory sentiments. Each speaker is just protecting his flanks. If he omitted either the denial of trade-offs or the need to consider costs, he would leave himself vulnerable to criticism. Yet discussions with OSH policymakers suggest that the paradox cannot simply be explained away as political hypocrisy. Many of them, for personal reasons, do not like to think about the trade-offs they are explicitly or implicitly making all the time.

Attempts to deny the contradictions in these statements don't hold up. After examining his statement Daniel Boyd explained that the paradox could be resolved (at least in the case of health) by using personal protective equipment to provide a cheap method of controlling exposures.[2] Boyd's suggestion could constitute an excellent resolution except that OSHA has never allowed personal protection as a substitute for engineering protection in its standards. As chapter 3 showed, OSHA ultimately does enforce the engineering requirement; therefore, the Office of Standards Development (OSD) is not proposing engineering "where feasible" and assuming that weak enforcement will really allow personal protection in most cases. Each of these men is aware that OSHA standards could be made stricter and save more lives—at a price. Their statements allow them to show that they are "reasonable," they "consider costs," while at the same time they refrain from the sin of putting a price on life.[3]

In chapter 2 I showed that private market failures present a necessary but not a sufficient condition for public intervention, and that the success of regulation depends largely on the quality of the regulatory response. Unless public regulators have the information to make better decisions than employers can and the incentives to weigh the social costs and benefits properly, the results of public regulation could end up inferior to the status quo ante. The statements I have cited suggest that OSHA leaders have a difficult time deciding how to weigh economic considerations in setting standards.

Standard-Setting Procedures and Responsibilities

The OSH Act's Section 6 sketches out the procedures for the development of permanent standards. According to Section 6(b)(1) the secretary of labor can propose, revoke, or modify a standard whenever he "determines that a rule should be promulgated in order to serve the objectives of this Act. . . ." The sole formal check on the secretary's authority is the right of people adversely affected by a standard to appeal its validity in a U.S. court of appeals. Even here, however, the act states that "the determinations of the Secretary shall be conclusive if supported by substantial evidence in the record considered as a whole."[4] A series of circuit court decisions have set forth exactly what the secretary must do to pass judicial muster, most clearly in a case upholding a standard dealing with a carcinogenic chemical against a challenge by the producing firms:

It seems, then, that judicial review of a Section 6 standard properly includes at least the following:

(1) determining whether the Secretary's notice of proposed rulemaking adequately informed interested persons of the action taken;

(2) determining whether the Secretary's promulgation adequately set forth reasons for his action;

(3) determining whether the statement of reasons reflects consideration of factors relevant under the statute;

(4) determining whether presently available alternatives were at least considered; and

(5) if the Secretary's determination is based in whole or in part on factual matters subject to evidentiary development, whether substantial evidence in the record as a whole supports the determination.[5]

Clearly, the judicial constraints have been primarily procedural rather than substantive.[6] Once the Labor Department learned the rules of the game, it had little problem winning its cases, but the court decisions have fostered greater thoroughness in documenting the issues involved.

Probably the most important case, and the one that came closest to addressing substantive issues, grew out of a union challenge (*IUD* v. *Hodgson*) that OSHA had improperly given weight to economic factors in promulgating the permanent asbestos standard in 1972.[7] I have already shown (chap. 2) how drafters of the OSH Act took care to avoid any explicit mention of economic considerations in the discussion of criteria for setting standards. Section 6 referred only to the need to consider the "feasibility" of the proposal. Only one meager piece of legislative history is cited by the court to illuminate the meaning of "feasibility," and that citation sheds little light. In it Senator Javits explained that "as a result of the amendment, the Secretary, in setting standards, is expressly required to consider feasibility of proposed standards. This is an improvement over the Daniels bill, which might be interpreted to require absolute health and safety, regardless of feasibility. . . ."[8]

With this meager guidance, the court opined:

There can be no question that OSHA represents a decision to require safeguards for the health of employees even if such measures substantially increase production costs. This is not, however, the same thing as saying that Congress intended to require immediate implementation of all protective measures technologically achievable without regard for their economic impact. To the contrary, it would comport with common usage to say that a standard that is prohibitively expensive is not "feasible." . . . The thrust of [Senator Javits's remarks] would seem to be that practical considerations can temper protective requirements. Congress does not appear to have intended to protect employees by putting their employers out of business—either by requiring protective devices unavailable under existing technology or by making financial viability generally impossible.

This qualification is not intended to provide a route by which recalcitrant employers or industries may avoid the reforms contemplated by the Act. Standards may be economically feasible even though, from the standpoint of employers, they are financially burdensome and affect profit margins adversely. Nor does the concept of economic feasibility necessarily guarantee the continued existence of individual employers. It would appear to be consistent with the purposes of the Act to envisage the economic demise of an employer who has lagged behind the rest of the industry in protecting the health and safety of employees and is consequently unable to comply with new standards as quickly as other employers. As the effect becomes more widespread within an industry, the problem of economic feasibility becomes more pressing.[9]

The court concluded by noting that factors like the impact on the competitive structure of the industry or its ability to compete with imports might be considered in determining feasibiliy.

The court's decision makes explicit the requirement to consider the economic impact of standards. Moreover, the language does seem to set some limit on the allowable impact—putting most or all of an industry out of business. The imprecision of this limit, if that is what it is, makes it a weak constraint on policy. OSHA must not be oblivious to costs, but the decision still leaves OSHA broad discretion in deciding how to weigh them in the standard-setting calculus. And despite the court opinion that legitimate standard-setting apparently must incorporate economic considerations, the act's lack of explicitness still allows precisely the opposite argument to be made: in 1975 the chief counsel for the Senate Labor and Public Welfare Committee argued that "if OSHA considers costs at all, it may be considering them too much. The Act talks about feasibility; it doesn't talk about economic feasibility."[10]

Although employer-backed amendments to the OSH Act have concentrated on enforcement, several of the bills introduced in 1973 did include provisions for the explicit consideration of costs by OSHA. More than twenty senators cosponsored either the Curtis bill or the Domenick bill, both of which would have required OSHA to develop estimates of the costs and economic impact of all proposed standards and to consider them in its decisions. To some degree the court's decision in *IUD* v. *Hodgson* achieved what the Curtis and Domenick bills were seeking: a requirement that costs be considered.

Compared with its attention to OSHA's enforcement procedures, Congress has paid relatively little attention to standard setting, although several key legislators and their staffs do show an active if limited concern for this issue.

However, even the handful of congressmen with special OSHA concerns do not testify at public hearings on the standards. As Krivit reports,

We do let OSHA know what we feel about the substance of a standard, but we don't testify at hearings. We're not technical people and we don't like to give the impression that people should listen to us because of our position in Congress. Mainly, we see our job as mediating. We should stay more in the role of seeing that the law is enforced, making sure their treatment of a standard isn't arbitrary or capricious. But we do try to get people together to work out some of their differences.[11]

This mediating role is not one of neutrality; rather, it includes advising and sometimes coordinating the efforts of those groups with whom you are allied. For Krivit and his counterparts in the Senate, these allies are labor unions and health-oriented groups. For Congressman Steiger, the allies are employer groups. Prodded by these allies, congressmen occasionally publicly express their positions on the substance of a standard.

Congressman Steiger had a unique role as the Republican coauthor of the act. His support of the program was often crucial in forestalling attacks upon it by members of his party. The Republican administration—in particular the first head of OSHA, George Guenther—consulted closely with Steiger. The second Chief, John Stender, complained that "Steiger tried to interpose himself far too much. He was trying to run the OSHA program and he was encouraged by Schubert [Richard Schubert, the undersecretary of labor]. I felt they were in league."[12]

A memo to Steiger from one of his top staff reveals that he relied heavily on Schubert to keep a rein on Stender but that especially in the area of standards the aide felt the reliance had been misplaced because the undersecretary had failed to prevent Stender from making several major mistakes.[13] Even a congressman as involved as Steiger had to recognize that the responsibility for standard setting rested primarily with the administrators.

Within the Labor Department, decision-making authority on standards is officially delegated to the head of OSHA.[14] Although leaders who lack technical training—like the first two OSHA chiefs—are dependent upon their staff for technical justifications for the standards OSHA proposes, they have not been bound by staff decisions. In several instances, for example, Stender altered the recommendations of his OSD, perhaps most importantly in the case of noise. According to former OSD chief Daniel Boyd, his office had wanted to retain the existing 90-decibel (db) noise standard (carried over from the Walsh-Healey standards). The Environmental Protection Agency urged OSHA to adopt an 80-db standard. A compromise was reached on 85 db, but Stender refused to accept the compromise. OSHA's October 1975 noise proposal favored the retention of the 90-db level. Mindful of the immense costs involved, Stender had been unwilling to require heavy spending to abate a nonfatal hazard. Stender denies that he received any instructions from higher officials in the Labor Department about the noise standard.[15]

Two Cases: Vinyl Chloride and the Mechanical Power Press

The two most recent assistant secretaries for OSH have both had academic backgrounds in occupational health. While their technical expertise allowed them to become more involved in the earlier stages of the standard-setting process, the basic problems they faced were no different from those faced by their predecessors. Two brief studies of standard-setting—for vinyl chloride and mechanical power presses—will illustrate just what those problems are and how OSHA's leaders have addressed them. While both the vinyl chloride and the power press standards required decisions to be made in the face of a high degree of uncertainty regarding costs and benefits, OSHA's actions in the two cases diverged dramatically.

The Vinyl Chloride Standard
After a third worker at its Louisville, Kentucky, vinyl chloride plant died from a rare form of liver cancer, B. F. Goodrich informed NIOSH of the fatalities. Less than three months later, on April 5, 1974, OSHA issued a temporary emergency standard that reduced the permissible exposure level from 500 parts per million (ppm) to 50 ppm. Even before these deaths, several studies had indicated that exposure to vinyl chloride levels below 500 ppm could generate tumors in laboratory animals. Based on its own studies, in the 1960s Dow Chemical began efforts to reduce exposures in its plants to below 50 ppm, but other firms chose to ignore the published Dow results and rely on other studies.[16]

Shortly after OSHA issued the emergency standard, a new study revealed that cancers developed in mice exposed to the proposed 50 ppm level. NIOSH had refrained from recommending any specific exposure level before the emergency standard. As it had done with the standard on fourteen carcinogens the previous year, it chose to rely instead only on specifying the permissible work practices. Spurred by this new evidence, however, NIOSH recommended that "no detectable level" of exposure be permitted. Given NIOSH's skepticism about the possibility of accurate measurements, this really constituted a 1.5 ppm ceiling on exposures. OSHA accepted the NIOSH arguments and proposed a permanent standard calling for "no detectable level."[17]

At the public hearing, the Society for the Plastics Industry, a trade association, claimed that the "no detectable level" proposal was totally infeasible. It released a study prepared by Arthur D. Little, Inc., which claimed that adoption of the OSHA proposal would destroy 1.6 million jobs and cause a $65 billion loss in production.[18] OSHA turned to another contractor, and in late August, after less then eight weeks of study, that firm announced its preliminary conclusion that OSHA's proposal was indeed impossible to meet in the plants where vinyl chloride monomer (VCM) or polyvinyl chloride (PVC) were produced, plants that employed about 6,000 workers. (Over 350,000 other people are exposed to lesser risks in plants that fabricate products using vinyl chloride.)

The report stated that the costs of controlling VCM rose sharply below a 2-to-5-ppm time-weighted average (TWA). Firestone—the only firm that attempted to estimate the costs of a "no detectable level" standard—estimated that for its plants, "no detectable level" would cost 16 to 60 times more in capital costs and 15 to 40 times more in annual operating costs than a 2-to-5-ppm standard.[19]

In its standard document, OSHA acknowledged that both the industry and the study it had commissioned believed that a 1-ppm ceiling was infeasible, although it noted that union spokesmen disagreed:

Since there is no actual evidence that any of the VC or PVC manufacturers have already attained a 1 ppm level or in fact instituted all available engineering and work practice controls, any estimate as to the lowest feasible level attainable must necessarily involve subjective judgment. . . .
We agree that the PVC and VC establishments will not be able to attain a 1 ppm TWA level for all job classifications in the near future. We do believe, however, that they will, in time, be able to attain levels of 1 ppm TWA for most job classifications most of the time. It is apparent that reaching such levels may require some new technology and work practices.[20]

Addressing the prospective benefits of a standard, OSHA admitted that no evidence had been presented that cancers had occurred with exposures less than 50 ppm. Although stating that some sort of dose-response relationship probably existed, OSHA cited the views of many cancer experts that "safe exposure levels for carcinogenic substances can not be scientifically determined." In other words, there is no threshold level beyond which we can be sure that no cancers will be instigated. Following this reasoning, OSHA continued,

It would be imprudent to assume man to be less sensitive to VC exposure than experimental animals in the absence of conclusive evidence. It would also be unfounded to assume that animals will not develop tumors when exposed at concentrations of VC of less than 50 ppm. Should a sufficiently large number of experimental animals be exposed to VC at concentrations of less than 50 ppm, Schneiderman said that it would be expected that some would develop VC induced tumors.

In conclusion, OSHA noted that no one disputed the carcinogenic properties of vinyl chloride, but everything else was disputed,

... the precise level of exposure which poses a hazard and the question of whether a "safe" exposure level exists cannot be definitively answered on the record. Nor is it clear to what extent exposures can be feasibily reduced. We cannot wait until indisputable answers to these question are available, because lives of employees are at stake. Therefore, we have had to exercise our best judgment on the basis of the best available evidence. These judgments have required a balancing process, in which the overriding consideration has been the protection of employees. . . .

The standard that OSHA promulgated on October 4, 1974, set an exposure limit of 1 ppm TWA, with a ceiling exposure of 5 ppm, not to be exceeded for more than fifteen minutes. Since NIOSH had believed (incorrectly, it later turned out) that exposures could only be measured with an accuracy of 1 ppm ± 50 percent, the final standard deviated very little from the proposed standard. Industry and labor groups reacted accordingly. The Society of the Plastics Industry filed suit to overturn the standard. The president of Firestone's plastics division stated that the standard "puts the vinyl plastic industry on a collision course with economic disaster."[21] One union leader expressed concern about OSHA's apparent wavering on the question of requiring the use of engineering controls, the alternative being to allow firms simply to supply respirators to their workers. Looking back at the issue, George Taylor, head of the AFL-CIO's Standing Committee on OSH, describes the VC standard as the best OSHA has promulgated. "It has come closest to what a standard should be, mainly because it essentially includes the criterion of 'no detectable limit' "[22]

Grover Wrenn, head of health standards development, recounts how he, OSD Director Dan Boyd, and an associate decided that the evidence for dose-response curves in man for cancer was very limited and thus that no safe level of exposure to vinyl chloride existed. They felt that this position was consistent with that taken by other federal government agencies, including the Environmental Protection Agency (EPA) and the surgeon general.[23] The fabrication industry had testified that it could comply with any standard that was set; it was concerned that its supply of VC not be cut off. The problem was the fifty-four plants producing VC. Wrenn, who had an industrial hygiene degree and special knowledge of chemical control technologies, felt that technical measures were available to deal with VC exposures. Moreover, he strongly suspected that the costs would turn out to be lower than anticipated.

The cost arguments didn't matter very much, however, because, according to Wrenn, "We discounted the cost arguments entirely. We were ready to let some plants shut down." Wrenn believes that the industry had no inkling that OSHA would actually stick with its initial proposal in the final standard. If the companies had known, he suspects that they would have descended on Stender with such pressure that he would have backed off from the 1-ppm standard. OSD kept Stender briefed as the standard developed, but Wrenn reports that he did not follow OSD's work closely. Wrenn had originally opposed Stender's decision to make the wearing of respirators optional during the first year the standard was in effect (when exposures did not exceed 25 ppm) but conceded that it had allayed opposition.

Within OSHA and among outsiders, the VC standard is generally regarded as a great success. OSHA responded quickly, and many believe correctly, by promulgating a permanent standard nine months after the news of the first 3 deaths came to NIOSH. Through October 1975, over 40 additional deaths have been reported worldwide from VC-caused liver cancer, including 13 in the United States and 9 in Canada.[24] Although it is clear that the first deaths were only the beginning of a wave, the long lag between exposure and disease will make it difficult to know whether the present standard has been effective until many years have passed.

However, it is known that the judgment that a 1-ppm TWA standard was not feasible was wrong. In December 1975, OSHA Assistant Secretary Morton Corn warned that industry couldn't afford another credibility loss like the one on VC:

That's the word I'm getting out. You told everybody the industry is going to shut down. And lo and behold, we've got the best compliance with VC than with anything we've done [*sic*] . . . and look how quickly. Industry didn't shut down and, as far as I know, nobody went out of business.[25]

A 1976 study did indicate that the standard had caused two plants to close and PVC prices to rise 6 percent, but these effects hardly confirmed the industry's predictions.[26]

The Mechanical Press Standard

The standard on mechanical power presses was adopted by OSHA through the consensus route, along with the great mass of other safety standards. In the year OSHA became law, the power press committee of the American National Standards Institute (ANSI) had adopted a provision that methods be used to prohibit the need for press operators' hands to enter the area between the dies, at the press's point of operation. Labor unions had representation on this ANSI committee, but they were absent during deliberation on the standard. Although the firms that manufactured the presses were more enthusiastic about the "no hands in dies" provision than the firms that used them, the standard had little trouble gaining the consensus needed for ANSI approval. Before OSHA, of course, the ANSI standards were merely advisory; although some state laws did incorporate ANSI standards, the enforcement method treated compliance as essentially voluntary.

OSHA's adoption of the "no hands in dies" provision—or rather its failure to exclude it from the wholesale adoption of consensus standards—provoked trade associations to petition for its revocaton. As adopted, the standard did not require employers to observe the provision until August 31, 1974. Agreeing to consider the question, OSHA asked for comments in January 1973 and received over three-hundred replies during the next three months. Metal stampers and other firms using presses supplied the bulk of the comments, which were almost unanimously in favor of revocation.

OSHA requested that the ANSI committee reconsider the "no hands in dies" provision, but a reconstituted committee, with a smaller percentage of press builders and a larger percentage of press users, was unable to reach a consensus. The majority report retained the provision as a "goal" but allowed employers to provide redundant safeguarding (that is, two or more safeguards) when "no hands in dies" proved impractical. Faced with this indecision from ANSI, OSHA's first response was to consider postponing the effective date of the provision three years, until 1977, allowing time for further study of power press injuries. But by early 1974, OSHA policy had changed, and a proposal to revoke the provision was published. The OSHA proposal did not include the revised ANSI provision for redundant guarding.

Anticipating controversy, OSHA scheduled a public hearing for mid-May.

Of the 31 witnesses who testified, 6 were from unions, and only 2 of those were familiar with the issues and the data bearing on the effectiveness of "no hands in dies" in preventing injuries. Two of the other union witnesses were rank-and-file workers who operated presses and listed the injuries that had occurred in their shops. Power press manufacturers stayed away from the hearings, giving enormous technical superiority to business supporters of the proposal.

Witness Richard Berman of the U.S. Chamber of Commerce testified that OSHA was "swimming in statistics to support revocation" and that far more data existed about the effects of this standard than for almost any other standard OSHA had considered.[27] Yet in reviewing the evidence, OSHA concluded that "the statistics often do not indicate whether employee injuries were at the point of operation; what guards or devices were in use, if any; whether the employer was engaged in 'hands in dies' operation; or what the cause of the accident was."[28]

While information to estimate benefits was missing, OSHA received an overabundance of figures purporting to represent the costs of complying with the standard. Business estimates of the cost of the basic press modifications ranged from $1,500 to $35,000; the AFL-CIO's George Taylor had written OSHA claiming that "an operating press can be modified to meet the standard by an outlay of about $50 per press."[29] When United Auto Workers Vice-President Douglas Fraser was questioned by the representative from the solicitor's office, he conceded that he was unfamiliar with the sort of modification but said that "if there is a price to pay—and I suspect there is—then we should be willing to pay it unless it's so completely exorbitant that this becomes unreasonable and I don't believe it's that." Fraser went on to say that firms that had introduced these procedures had not suffered losses.[30]

In late November of 1974, Stender announced that OSHA's permanent standard would include the revocation of "no hands in dies" and that it would not follow the ANSI B-11 committee in its alternative of redundant safeguarding but would aim at improving the single safeguarding that was required. OSHA reached these decisions by placing the burden of proof on the proponents of "no hands in dies" and redundancy. Its stance toward the evidence was noncommittal:

The accident statistics are not helpful in determining the effectiveness of "no hands in dies" when compared with appropriate safety devices or guards. . . . In view of the absence of evidence on the precise reliability of any of the safety devices, additional safety in using two such devices is even more speculative.[31]

Consequently, these points were weighed in favor of revocation. The rationale for the permanent standard continued by noting that many employers had shown that other safeguarding methods appeared to work well; moreover, "no hands in dies" might actually create hazardous pinch points in the feeding apparatus.

The last three arguments were that the provision would not be technically feasible for all operations in the near future; that the associated costs would be "prohibitive"; and that its adoption would make many short production runs economically infeasible. The use of the word "prohibitive" echoes the Court of Appeals' earlier language in *IUD* v. *Hodgson,* decided earlier that year, when it set forth examples of "infeasible" standards. The idea that costs would be prohibitive was challenged by a letter sent to OSHA after the hearings by the National Machine Tool Builders Association. It assured OSHA that "fortunately the success of hands out of the die and improved safety at the point of operation on mechanical power presses is not limited to a condition of true automation. Many methods of far less expensive 'semiautomation' will provide improved operator safety and increased productivity at low cost."[32]

As with almost all major OSHA standard actions, review was quickly sought in the courts. On December 31, 1975, the Third Circuit remanded the standard to OSHA for a more complete statement of reasons why various alternatives were not chosen.[33] OSHA should have little difficulty presenting enough data to meet the court's weak "substantial evidence" test.

A 1973 survey revealed that a substantial minority of mechanical power presses lacked *any* point of operation guards.[34] Thus enforcement of even the single guarding provisions adopted by OSHA, or of the general machine guarding standards that also apply, might help to reduce the approximately 10,000 lost-workday injuries that mechanical power presses cause each year.

Occupational Health Standards

Even though OSHA had promulgated only four new health standards by the end of 1977, the health area offers a better prospect than safety for viewing the standard-setting process and the considerations that shape its results.[35] As intended by the OSH Act's developers, OSHA's initial step in the health field was to adopt en masse the "threshold limit values" (TLVs) that had been established for about four-hundred toxic substances by the private American Conference of Governmental Industrial Hygienists (ACGIH). The asbestos standard was promulgated in 1972, the standards for the fourteen carcinogens and for VC in 1974, and the coke oven emissions standard in 1976.[36] By the end of 1974, NIOSH had submitted about twenty additional criteria documents to OSHA. OSHA had proposed standards for nine of them by the end of 1976; for two others, heat stress and ultraviolet radiation, it had definitely decided not to propose any standard in the near future. Thus, in addition to four permanent standards, there is a set of eleven standards on which OSHA has taken some action regarding NIOSH recommendations.

Although the first few health standards emerged through the emergency route, the usual mechanism for determining which health standards OSHA will consider is the transmittal of a criteria document from NIOSH. Many OSD staff are dissatisfied with NIOSH's authority to set the agenda for OSHA in this fashion, and difficulties have ensued. NIOSH sets its own priorities for developing criteria documents (CDs) by looking at five factors: numbers of people exposed, toxicity, incidence of disease, quantity produced or used, and the trend in the use of the material.[37] The NIOSH criteria documents can be roughly described as the health "baseline" from which to examine deviations related to economic considerations. Although NIOSH eschews recommendations that it knows are technically impossible, the criteria documents make no reference to economic constraints, and the agency's spokesmen affirm their duty to ignore them.

My discussions of health standards deal almost exclusively with the issue of exposure levels, although other provisions (those dealing with medical exams and warnings to workers, for example) have stirred up important controversies.[38] The strict compliance through engineering controls required by OSHA inspectors means that the setting of exposure levels is critical. Its importance is even more apparent in the new health standards, which require engineering controls even when they won't reduce exposures below the permissible limits.[39]

Table 4.1 lists all of the health standards for which OSHA proposed a standard or received a criteria document from NIOSH through 1974.[40] For each standard, the table provides the year the criteria document was received by OSHA, and the exposure levels that were advocated at various steps—the NIOSH proposal, the OSHA proposal, and the final OSHA promulgation. Before reviewing any of these standards in detail, I will note general points illustrated by the table which should be kept in mind. First, the only four permanent standards all deal with carcinogenic substances. Second, NIOSH's recommendations during 1972 were out of phase with OSHA policy, but they appear to have drawn closer together since then. Of the five 1972 CDs trans-

Table 4.1 OSHA responses to exposure limits recommended by NIOSH, 1972–1974

Standard	Year of NIOSH CD	NIOSH	OSHA Proposal	OSHA Promulgation
		Exposure limits		
Asbestos[a]	1972	5[a]; 2 in 2 yrs.	5; 2 in 4 yrs. C = 5 (rev. 1975) .5	5; 2 in 4 yrs. C = 5
14 carcinogens	1973	WP	WP	WP
Vinyl chloride	1974	WP	NDL	1 ppm; C = 5
Beryllium[b]	1972	.001 C = .005	.001 C = .005	
Carbon monoxide	1972	35 ppm; C = 200		
Heat stress	1972		Not proposed	
Noise	1972	85 db	90 db	
Ultraviolet radiation	1972		Not proposed	
Inorganic lead[b]	1973 (rev. 8/75)	.15 (rev. < .15)	.1 (10/75)	
Coke oven emissions[c]	1973	.2 (CTPV)	.3 (Respirable particles)	.15 (BSFTPM)
Chromic acid[b]	1973	.05 C = .1		
Mercury[b]	1973	.05		
Toluene	1973	100 ppm C = 200	100 ppm C = 200	
TDI	1973	C = .02 ppm TWA = .005		
Trichlor-ethylene	1973	100 ppm C = 150	100 C = 150	
Inorganic arsenic[b]	1974 (rev. 5/75)	.05 (rev. .002)	.004 (1/75)	
Sulfur dioxide	1974	2 ppm	2 ppm; C = 10	
Ammonia	1974	C = 50 ppm	C = 50 ppm	
Cotton dust[b]	1974	WP	.5; .2 in 7 yrs.	

Note: C = ceiling, the exposure that is not to be exceeded at any time, unless a peak excursion is allowed or a number of minutes is specified; P = peak exposure; all other exposure figures are 8-hour time-weighted averages. NDL = no detectable level. WP = work practices.
[a] Measured in fibers per cubic centimeter.
[b] Measured in parts per cubic meter.
[c] Each group involved in the coke oven emissions standard picked a different substance as the measure of harmful exposure: CTPV (coal tar pitch volatiles), B (a) P (benz (a) pyrene), respirable particles, and BSFTPM (benzene-soluble fraction of total particulate matter); all measured in milligrams per cubic meter.

mitted by NIOSH, only two have been proposed, while two have definitely been set aside by OSHA. Moreover, in the case of noise, the standard proposed was quite different than the NIOSH proposal. Of the seven CDs transmitted in 1973, four have been proposed; none have been rejected by OSHA and only the coke oven standard has aroused major interagency conflict. The greater congruence appears to have continued with the eight CDs transmitted in 1974; four had been proposed by the end of 1976.

A third and related point is that while OSHA proposals are sometimes less strict than what NIOSH suggested, they are usually not; and when they are less strict, the differences are usually not great. On asbestos, OSHA moved back the 2-fiber requirement by two years; on the carcinogens, it dropped the permit system recommended by NIOSH; on vinyl chloride, it moved almost imperceptibly from "no detectable level" to 1 ppm. The major exceptions concern noise, heat stress, and ultraviolet radiation (sunlight). In all these cases, the number of affected workers is very large (NIOSH estimated from over one million for heat to over seven million for noise), but the incidence of fatal or seriously disabling diseases is low. Carbon monoxide may provide another example of this category.

A final point illustrated by table 4.1 is the great uncertainty that pervades decision making in this area. In these cases, the uncertainties pertain to benefits and are reflected in NIOSH's major revisions of standards to reflect new scientific knowledge. NIOSH revised its recommended exposure limits for arsenic and lead after OSHA had made its initial proposals. With asbestos OSHA has already proposed to cut the exposure levels it set in 1972 by 75 percent, down to 0.5 fibers per cubic centimeter. The coke oven emissions standard is the most tangled web of all, for no one is quite certain exactly what causes the cancers associated with this exposure. Consequently, NIOSH, the advisory committee, and OSHA have differed not simply on exposure levels but also on what substance should be the measuring rod for exposures.

Uncertain Benefits and Costs: Asbestos and Noise

The difficulties OSHA faces in getting information about the projected consequences of new standards appeared with the very first health standard that OSHA promulgated. After NIOSH proposed that the 5-fiber asbestos standard adopted on an emergency basis in 1971 be continued for two years and then dropped to 2 fibers, OSHA commissioned Arthur D. Little, Inc., to assess the wisdom of this proposal. After surveying employers (including U.S. government shipyards) to develop estimates of costs and surveying doctors to get their opinions about dose-response relationships, the study concluded that

reduction of the exposure of workers to asbestos dust from present levels to 5 fibers/cc will significantly reduce asbestos related diseases and achieve more than 99% of the benefits attainable from the control of dust levels.[41]

Since Arthur D. Little estimated that compliance with a 2-fiber standard would cost twice as much as a 5-fiber standard, it recommended that "a 5-fiber standard appears to be cost-effective at this time."[42]

The consultants derived their estimates of the health effects of different TLVs by polling medical experts on asbestos. They were asked how many workers out of a hundred exposed for forty years would be expected to experience each type of asbestos-caused disease—asbestosis, lung cancer, and mesothelioma (a rare cancer of the lung lining). The responses of the ten experts consulted appear in table 4.2. Union spokesmen noted that almost all of these experts had been financially supported by asbestos manufacturers. The unions pointed instead to the views of Dr. Irving Selikoff, a leading expert on asbestos who had worked closely with unions and who had refused to participate in the Arthur D. Little poll.[43] The table presents Selikoff's estimates alongside those of the other experts.

OSHA did not accept the Arthur D. Little argument in favor of a perma-

Table 4.2 Estimates of instances of excess disease among 100 workers at the end of 40 years of exposure to asbestos

Average exposure[a]	Asbestosis		Bronchogenic cancer		Mesothelioma	
	Panel	Selikoff	Panel	Selikoff	Panel	Selikoff
2	0 (20-0)	55	0 (1-0)	12	0 (0.1-0)	4
5	1 (55-0)	85	0.3 (5-0)	20	0 (0.2-0)	7
12	9 (70-6)		1.5 (10-0.05)		0.1 (1-0)	
30	19 (75-9)	95	3.4 (15-1)	20	0.1 (2-0)	5

Source: Arthur D. Little, Inc., "Impact of Proposed OSHA Standard for Asbestos: First Report to the U.S. Department of Labor" (Cambridge, Mass., April 1972), table 2, p. 18; Paul Brodeur, Expendable Americans (New York: Viking, 1974), p. 146. Brodeur did not provide Selikoff's estimates for the 12-fiber standard.
Note: The first figure in the panel estimates is the median; the figures below in parentheses show the range of the estimates.
[a] No. of fibers (> 5 ml) per cc (8-hr time = weighted average).

nent 5-fiber standard, although it did accede to a further two-year delay before requiring that the 2-fiber TWA be achieved. Union leaders attacked this delay bitterly, accusing OSHA of caving in to the asbestos industry. While the delay did represent a concession, prompted by the issues raised in the study, the critical fact is that OSHA had adhered to the 2-fiber level recommended by NIOSH, despite the impressive (but incorrect) medical support for the safety of the 5-fiber standard. OSD chief Boyd, who was not with OSHA at that time, feels that the decision was made on scientific grounds and with an extra margin of safety. "Except for Selikoff's views, the five fiber standard represented the main scientific views. Now those views and data support a 0.5 fiber standard."[44] The bulk of the new evidence regarding cancers has been developed by Selikoff and his associates and demonstrates that his estimates were more accurate than the panel's "consensus." OSD now feels that, although the 2-fiber level may be stringent enough to prevent asbestosis, numerous cancers may be generated at lower and less frequent exposures.

The 1972 asbestos standard engendered the most thorough attempt at a benefit-cost study of a standard yet attempted, a study performed independently of OSHA by Russell Settle for a Ph.D. dissertation at the University of Wisconsin.[45] In spite of the fact that it is thoughtfully and carefully executed, the Settle study reveals several of the difficulties of using benefit-cost analysis for decision making. The problem for decision making arises from Settle's approach to the myriad assumptions that any such study must make. While it is important to demonstrate how sensitive the results are to the choices among assumptions, Settle leaves the decision maker with a bewildering array of estimates to choose from. He presents seventy-two different estimates of the net benefits of the 2-fiber standard. The benefit-cost ratios range from 0.07 to 27.70, an almost 400-fold difference.[46] This enormous range probably represents "truth in benefit-cost calculations"; narrower ranges could be attained only by making stronger assumptions. Clearly benefit-cost analysis gives a decision maker wide latitude to choose the assumptions that will produce the outcome he wants. Settle did conclude that on balance "the benefit-cost analysis seems to favor the [asbestos standard]; especially if 'low' discount rates are considered appropriate for evaluating public programs." Alternatively, the middle and high estimates of deaths prevented receive a predominantly favorable judgement as long as the broader concept of benefits is employed.[47]

When Settle presented his findings at a conference convoked for the purpose of evaluating OSHA's effects, the audience—especially the members most sympathetic to labor—breathed a sigh of relief that his study seemed to suggest that the regulation of asbestos met the benefit-cost criterion. Yet Settle's study was based upon the assumption that the 2-fiber standard would be totally effective in preventing all disease.[48] Yet the labor unions had been correctly arguing all along that a 2-fiber standard would not have that effect and that only a zero-fiber standard would prevent all of the cancers. Settle's various estimates of the number of deaths prevented by the 1972 asbestos standard thus have an upward bias; they would not all be prevented by a 2-fiber standard. The importance of this bias depends largely upon the costs of attaining the new 0.5-fiber standard and upon how effective it will be. Another factor adding to Settle's upward bias in his estimate of the benefits of regulation is that his calculations of asbestos-caused deaths are based on epidemiological studies that trace the mortality record of groups of workers whose exposure began twenty or thirty years ago, when exposure levels were often higher than they have been in recent years.[49] Consequently, he has over-estimated the potential disease reduction attributable to the reduced exposures required by OSHA. The 1972 asbestos standard appears to be a case where the judgment of whether benefits exceed or fall below costs could go either way.

Agnosticism has not characterized the views that other analysts have expressed about more recent OSHA proposals. Robert Smith has argued that even the proposal to retain the existing 90-decibel (db) noise standard will impose costs that far exceed the value that the affected workers would place upon the reduced annoyance and loss of hearing. He estimates that current expenditures of approximately $15,000 would be required to prevent each case of what on the average would amount to only a slight hearing loss ten to forty years in the future. Smith expressed doubt that many workers would opt for the protection if they had to pay this bill.[50] For both his cost and effect data, Smith relied heavily on an OSHA-commissioned study estimating that full compliance with the 90 db standard would cost over $13 billion, while with an 85 db standard the cost would be $31 billion. The next year, the firm, a leader in the acoustical engineering field, revised its estimates downward to about $10 billion and $18 billion, respectively. Concurrently, its estimates of the numbers of cases of hearing loss that would be prevented declined roughly in proportion, so that the cost-effectiveness figures used by Smith did not change markedly.[51] If these figures are more or less correct, Smith's argument is fairly persuasive and does show how a benefit-cost approach can be valuable. That is a big "if," however, and it would loom even larger if Smith had not chosen one of the only standards involving no clear risk of death.

Economic critiques of OSHA standards have come from within the federal government as well as from outside. Congressional efforts led by conservative Republicans and southern Democrats to require OSHA to estimate costs and benefits have died in committee, leaving the initiative in this area to the executive branch. In 1975 a new agency began to intervene in OSHA's standard setting, the Council on Wage-Price Stability (CWPS). Established the previous August as a watchdog agency whose only powers were to publicize government actions deemed inflationary, the council assumed a more structured role following President Ford's November executive order requiring that "inflationary impact statements" (IIS's) accompany new agency regulations and legislative proposals.[52] Stender responded by requesting that OSHA be exempted from filing statements. As he explained later, "We had a mandate from the act to enforce safety; these things would usually be a waste of time, since when an economic impact would be big, we would have to consider it anyway." In addition, he felt that the IIS documents would not be very helpful. "You can make your study; I can make my study. Nobody really knows. That Bolt study on noise [the study OSHA had commissioned in 1974] was just a big guessing game."[53]

Within OSHA, the reaction to the IIS program was even more hostile. One memo circulated among top OSHA officials argued that the act did not allow OSHA to consider costs, even though the court's ruling in *IUD* v. *Hodgson* had appeared eight months before. The memo expressed worry that OSHA might be forced into proving the employers' case that a standard was too costly. Perhaps most importantly, it said, "If we file these, then presumably we are agreeing that whoever reviews these can enter into a dialogue with OSHA policy officials."[54]

The Office of Management and Budget (OMB) denied OSHA's request for exemption. In conferences with OMB and CWPS, top Labor Department officials worked out the criteria for IIS's. Whenever the impact of a regulation would exceed $100 million in one year (or $150 million in two years) for the whole economy, IIS's would be required; smaller costs would trigger IIS's if they impinged on particular industries. Criteria for energy and employment effects also were written up.[55]

Several people within OSD expressed the view that the IIS requirement represented a political move to retard the development of standards. To Don Elisburg, chief counsel of the Senate Labor Committee, "Most of this stuff is hokum. OSD is putting one-third of its 1977 budget into the development of IIS's. That's too much."[56] Within ASPER, the view is different, as one official's remarks indicate:

These IIS's are a pain in the neck. Their costs probably exceed their benefits. But at least they do have benefits, which is more than you can say about a lot of the activity in OSHA. The IIS's have forced those people to look at standards in terms of economic impact.[57]

Neither of the first two OSHA IIS statements (coke oven emissions and arsenic; the revised BBN study really constitutes a third) differs much from some of OSHA's more thorough earlier studies—vinyl chloride, for example—although along with the cost analysis, the IIS studies do try to make a more thorough assessment of effects on the larger economy—prices, employment, and output in other sectors.

The economists at CWPS espouse benefit-cost analysis and chide OSHA for failing to quantify the effects and ask how much the beneficiaries would be willing to pay for them. The CWPS economist responsible for OSHA explained that "to us, benefit-cost analysis means rational thinking." As examples of the potential use of benefit-cost analyses by OSHA, he referred to Settle's and Smith's studies as ones that could have helped decision makers choose more rationally.[58]

At hearings on standards, CWPS has strongly criticized OSHA for its rigid requirement that engineering controls be used for abatement. Only CWPS has taken the step of joining cost and effectiveness data, a move that has led it on several occasions to observe that the apparent cost of preventing a fatality under a proposed standard could amount to several million dollars. Although CWPS spokesmen at hearings emphasize the importance of quantitative assessments of willingness to pay, they note their agreement that factors should not be left out of the analysis just because they cannot be quantified.

If "benefit-cost analysis means rational thinking," CWPS can lead OSHA through an IIS, but it can't make it think. Realizing the political dangers of moving beyond a purely critical stance, CWPS has not ventured to advise OSHA about how it should value the saving of a life or the prevention of cancer. Because the council's authority is restricted to reviewing agency proposals and publicizing errors, its success depends upon finding a receptive

audience in Congress, the White House, the Labor Department's upper eche-
lons, or within OSHA itself.[59]

The Role of Economics in Standard Setting

The statements introducing this chapter revealed the paradox that pervades
OSHA decision making: the belief that while a consideration of costs is necessary, sacrificing lives for economic reasons is unacceptable. If we take the
statements literally, the paradox applies only to decisions about potentially
lifesaving standards, but the important point is that a refusal to weigh the
costs against the benefits makes the "consideration" of costs an empty ges-
ture. The view that costs are irrelevant certainly jars anyone accustomed to
economic reasoning. More to the point, that view does not appear consistent
with the choices individuals themselves make about reducing risks. People
recognize that safety can be costly, that other goods must be sacrificed to
increase safety, and that they are not always willing to pay the price.

Many economists believe, in Robert Smith's words,

> The criterion for any standard must be, "would the beneficiaries be willing to
> pay the costs of this standard if they were fully informed as to the hazards
> involved?" This criterion underlies the use of benefit-cost analysis and must
> be used to prevent the diminution of social welfare from "too little" (as in
> the case of asbestos hazards) or "too much" (as in the case of the seatbelt
> interlock system) protection against risk.[60]

At another point, Smith emphasizes that "the estimate of benefits must
attempt to discover (or guess) what the beneficiaries themselves are actually
willing to pay for the benefits—not what someone thinks they would be willing to pay."[61] This concept of the benefits of lifesaving, although hard to put
into practice, is certainly far more attractive than measures based upon the
discounted present value of foregone production or consumption. Yet a central problem arises in defining the beneficiaries. Certainly, they include not
only the workers at risk but also their families and friends, to the extent that
the workers' own valuations do not incorporate theirs. In addition, the beneficiaries also include everyone else who places a value on reducing the risks
the workers face. Although motives like envy and caring have only recently
been admitted into economic analysis, on theoretical grounds it is impossible
to deny that the valuations of this last group should be included.[62] The
interesting question is whether the magnitude of its valuation can be large
enough to add significantly to the demand for safety by the workers themselves.

The magnitude of charitable contributions and of "public-regarding" voting patterns suggests that caring on the part of seeming "outsiders" may be significant.[63] Such caring undoubtedly carries more weight in the political arena than in the marketplace, mainly because people often fail to "put their money where their mouth is." The quandary arises precisely over what to make of this lack of alignment. If, as some economists claim, only market behavior reliably reveals preferences, then their statements can be dismissed as hypocritical. However, since private markets can't do a very good job of reflecting my willingness to pay something to make coal mining safer, for example, such a dismissal would be premature, and the political process may be needed to take account of preferences like mine. Moreover, if I felt that passage of the OSH Act requires all citizens (whether as taxpayers or consumers) to chip in to make blue-collar jobs a little safer, I might support it even if I would not pay an equivalent amount out of my own pocket toward that objective. The reason is not only that my $10 alone is too small to have any perceptible effect but also because I would feel, "Why should I give if others don't?" Government action makes everyone give, and that seems fairer.

The implications of a broad class of beneficiaries for risk reduction has some interesting analogues on the cost side. Paternalism has a bad image, and consequently OSHA's leaders have strong reasons for accepting unions' contentions that the affected workers will usually not bear most of the compliance costs. If workers did bear the full costs, then OSHA would have to ask, "How much should we make the workers pay to protect themselves?" However, if costs are diffused among stockholders, workers, potential workers, and consumers, then the question begins to turn into "What are we, as a society, willing to pay to protect workers?" Because the actual incidence of costs is so messy and uncertain, the legitimacy of any given group to complain about costs is undermined, and it becomes easier for OSHA officials to refer to their own feelings in deciding how much "society" is willing to pay.

No matter how we modify the willingness-to-pay approach, it remains alien to the OSHA experience, which is characterized by the refusal to explicitly trade off lives and dollars. That refusal does not mean that OSHA always requires the safest possible standard. In the case of mechanical presses, for example, we saw that it did not. Yet, in many other cases, OSHA has espoused the most protective standard without any attempt to weigh whether the added protection was worth the cost.

Making Life and Death Decisions
Why do OSHA decision makers refuse to acknowledge a responsibility to

trade off the loss of some lives for greater economic goods? Some of the explanations are embedded in general cultural attitudes towards lifesaving. However, since other federal agencies do use explicit valuations of lifesaving, a more discriminating discussion is required. The first point to establish is that OSHA officials feel they lack any clear decision-making criteria for setting standards. As David Bell, chief of OSD's economic analysis unit, explained, "We don't have any algorithms, no rules of thumb. OSHA has never really come up with any mechanism or decision rules for producing standards." In Grover Wrenn's words, "Our system of setting standards is still ad hoc; we have no formal model for doing it. . . I don't think we will *ever* have any formal rule for trading off costs for lives or injuries. Currently, we have great latitude in making those decisions, although as case law develops, that discretion may narrow."[64]

Responding to criticisms that OSHA has failed to conduct enough benefit-cost studies, Bell emphasized the absence of any consensus about how to measure the value of lifesaving and—even more of an obstacle—the gaps in the information needed to conduct the studies.

Here at OSHA, we have no recognized way to put a value upon the life of a man. How do you treat a man retiring at age 65? From some economic viewpoints, it would be preferable to kill him rather than injure him, because then you have only burial expenses.
Moreover, our data base doesn't really tell us what the real social costs of injury and disease are. What are the costs for medical care or for welfare payments of black lung disease? I can't stand still for these attempts to put a money value on the benefits as long as we can't weigh the elements fully and equitably.

When asked what he thought about studies that assigned money values to lifesaving, Bell responded, "Good for them, but I think it's a matter of morality as well as of professional judgement." The depth of his feeling indicated that the differences transcended judgments about the quality of data. During the interview, Bell referred to a statement Congressman David Obey had made recently and noted that Obey had become one of his heroes. Obey had stated, "Quite frankly, I believe that when you're dealing in questions related to human life, economic costs are irrelevant."[65] Regardless of whether Bell actually agrees with this statement, the point is that he and many others in OSD and OSHA generally find this assertion of a preeminent commitment to lifesaving tremendously appealing.

Obey's views are obviously inconsistent with maximizing output, but whether they are rational is an altogether different question. Rationality consists in undertaking actions so that more rather than less of the things one values are attained. If a person derives satisfaction from thinking of himself as someone who will not "reduce" human life to economic terms, it may be rational for him to dismiss the costs of lifesaving as irrelevant. If such views are widely shared among citizens, then rational action may require that collective decisions eschew the guidelines that economic analysis provides. In other words, people may be willing to give up some material benefits in exchange for the psychic benefits of satisfying criteria they value more.[66]

Discomfort with the processes and criteria of economic analysis is evident in the following example drawn from the environmental area:

It somehow goes against the grain to learn that cost-benefit analyses can be done neatly on lakes, meadows, nesting gannets, even whole oceans. It is hard enough to confront the environmental options ahead, and the hard choices, but even harder when the price tags are so visible. . . . Economists need cool heads and cold hearts for this sort of work and they must write in icy, often skiddy, prose.[67]

The economist would retort that making the price tags visible makes it easier, not harder, to confront the options in a rational way. But if the issue involves values that are considered absolute, the economist would not be right, as the following example suggests:

Economist Walter Mead, addressing an offshore oil conference, is discussing the "social cost" of the 1969 Santa Barbara oil spill. He quickly arrives at a knotty question: What is the cost, in dollars and cents, of one dead sea gull?

Taking a lunge at it, he puts the figure between $1 and $10. "I don't think anyone would say they have a value of more than $10 a bird," he reasons. But he hasn't asked environmentalists.

While the oilmen in the audience remain silent, the environmentalists stare at each other in pained disbelief. A murmuring fills the room and one environmentalist voices agreement with the notion that economists "know the price of everything and the value of nothing." The next day Jacques Cousteau, the oceanographer, assails the Mead analysis as "shocking" because each species is "precious in itself."[68]

While many people might balk at the preciousness of sea gulls, deeper cultural roots nourish the belief that human life must be treated as sacred or of infinite value. Many people find it painful to believe that they, their profession, or their society lack a wholehearted commitment to this principle. At a conference on evaluating OSHA's effects, the director of HEW's Division of Health Evaluation, commenting on Settle's benefit-cost study of the asbestos standard, insisted that the link between asbestos and cancer was so clear that exposures *had* to be controlled. Economic studies had a role, he felt, only when the standard dealt with dermatitis or some other nonfatal disease.

Claims that needs are absolute, benefits are priceless, or costs are irrelevant all take decisions out of the realm of economic analysis. One characteristic of priceless goods is that they can't be bought and sold. If, in fact, they are being marketed, then it follows that the market has overstepped its legitimate bounds.[69] Whenever moral or religious beliefs are involved, the sway of economic thinking will be restricted.

A Comparative Perspective on OSHA's Treatment of Economic Factors

Just as individuals may choose for various reasons to forego the balancing of benefits and costs that economic analysis prescribes, so collective institutions with the task of representing and carrying out popular preferences may by extension make similar choices. But the tension between the rejection on moral grounds of putting a money value on lifesaving and the economic insistence on rationality is resolved differently in different contexts. Most pertinently, unlike OSHA, several federal government agencies do employ specific figures for the value of lifesaving. Examining the differences between these agencies and OSHA can help to explain why OSHA's standards themselves vary in the attention they give to costs, for, although the general drift of OSHA standards has been to adhere to the safest possible level, some standards appear to be more protective than others.

The number of agencies with major responsibilities for safety and health is large; at least two of them—the Federal Aviation Administration (FAA) and the National Highway Traffic Safety Administration (NHTSA)—conduct benefit-cost studies. In studies done at different times, the FAA has placed various values on lifesaving, but the more recent ones have been around $200,000. NHTSA, established in 1966 and made part of the Department of Transportation (DOT) in 1967, used a $240,000 figure in its recent studies of the air bag and other passive restraint systems.[70]

A significant impetus for the growth in both benefit-cost and cost-effectiveness analyses came from the influx of economists that accompanied the attempt to install the program-planning budgeting system (PPBS) in domestic agencies in 1965. The more sophisticated of these studies require a moderate degree of economic training. The absence of any Ph.D. economists within OSHA restricts its capability to perform such studies on its own and, more importantly, tends to limit the enthusiasm within the agency for valuations based on "willingness to pay." The obvious question is, Why are there no Ph.D. economists in OSHA? Or why aren't the economists in ASPER assigned to OSHA make sure it carries out such studies? The reasons are essentially the same ones invoked to explain the relative lack of success in implementing PPBS in federal agencies.[71] The use of analysis depends not only upon having staff who are competent to supply it but also on agency or departmental heads who have the desire or incentive to demand it, and OSHA differs from the FAA and NHTSA in several critical respects.

Identifying the Victims
It has been frequently observed that a social willingness exists to pay great sums to rescue trapped miners, identifiable individuals facing imminent death. Several economic explanations for this response are available. Under the most plausible assumptions about risk averseness, people will pay more for a given reduction in risk when the threat of death is very large than when it is small; that is, we will pay more to go from certain death to a 90 percent chance of death than from a 20 percent chance of death to a 10 percent chance. In this perspective, major rescue efforts can be justified because they reflect the individual's own high valuation. In another sense, the social rescue effort is like an insurance policy. We are willing to pay great sums to rescue people because we would want to be rescued ourselves if we faced death.

In vivid contrast to the rescue of known individuals facing imminent death, NHTSA sets standards each one of which is usually aimed at protecting everyone who rides in a car. Similarly, most FAA safety regulations apply across the board to the tens of millions of people who fly in airplanes. The circumstances OSHA deals with don't exactly match that of the trapped miners, but they are often closer to it than to dangers that affect millions of people who have no more identity than a statistic. Some OSHA standards involve only the fifty workers at the plant that manufactures an exotic carcinogen; more commonly, they involve several thousand workers at a dozen plants. Other OSHA standards—noise, carbon monoxide, electrical standards—do apply to millions, much in the style of the FAA regulations.

The moral responsibility attached to making life-and-death decisions regarding other people becomes far more wrenching when the people affected are identifiable individuals. Their spokesmen can testify at hearings, bringing along those already afflicted owing to lax standards or enforcement in the past. They can ask, "What will you do to protect us?" In this situation, the culture's strictures against putting a money value on life are heavily reinforced. OSHA officials do appear to show less concern for costs when the potential beneficiaries are more easily identifiable.

That response probably reflects popular attitudes, at least about the relative amounts of protection to give. If the identifiable groups of workers are also the groups who face especially large probabilities of death, then these predilections will jibe with the economists' conclusions as well. However, an additional consideration is that jobs with great dangers may have been selectively filled by workers who are less risk-averse than most people. If so, their willingness to pay for reductions in risk would be smaller than the average person's. Before deciding how protective to be, we would want to know whether the workers knew about the risks before taking the job or at least before their seniority partially immobilized them. Here again, it can be seen that many variables are relevant to a proper determination of the value of life-saving; no single figure can serve for all cases.

Paternalism and Sharing the Risks

A second distinction between the transportation agencies and OSHA is that while standard setters do drive cars and ride airplanes, they do not operate punch presses or work in arsenic smelters. Chauncey Starr has suggested that "we are loath to let others do unto us what we happily do to ourselves."[72] A complimentary observation appears to be that we are loath to do to others what we might happily do to ourselves. The belief that our society morally censures decisions to sacrifice human lives for economic reasons puts the people to whom decision making has been delegated in a bind. But if decision makers face the same risks as everyone else, they can at least decide knowing that they will have to bear the consequences. That knowledge may make it easier for them to rely on their own personal appraisal of the risks because they feel they will be representative. When the risks are not shared in this way, the decision makers are placed in a more paternalistic position and are likely to adopt a more protective standard. With responsibility for decisions about the health of their "patients," standard setters seem to copy physicians in the preeminence they give to the patient's well-being.[73]

The Politics of Regulation

Although the factors I have just discussed influence the way in which OSHA treats economic analysis, the most important features distinguishing OSHA from the FAA or NHTSA are political. The organized labor movement is the Department of Labor's (and OSHA's) chief client, and the department is expected to show at least some partiality to the interests of organized labor. OSHA, established at labor's behest, is overseen by congressional committees dominated by the AFL-CIO and depends primarily upon labor backing to ward off attacks upon its authority.

Neither OSHA nor the Labor Department feels that the higher prices to which workplace safety measures can lead is primarily its concern. While this lack of responsibility is partly attributable to a legislative mandate that glosses over the issue of costs, the more fundamental cause is that the agencies reflect the views of their constituencies. Labor leaders usually want to give scanty weight to cost concerns, and their views help mold OSHA's. In contrast, the FAA faces a constituency comprised of interest groups (the airlines, airport authorities, the pilots' association, and air-traffic controllers, to name some of the major ones) that press for several competing values—safety, convenience, cost savings—and push the FAA to work out a reasonable balance among them.

The congressional committees to which a disgruntled group might appeal an FAA safety decision are also organized to act more as the overseer of the transportation sector than as the protector of the passengers. Because of this committee orientation, and because no highly ideological positions are involved, it is unlikely that any group could successfully make a major issue out of the way the FAA values lifesaving. And when the threat of public attacks diminishes, the importance of popular values in policymaking also declines—except to the extent that the decision makers themselves share them.

Like OSHA, NHTSA is charged only with a safety mission, and unlike the FAA it has been embroiled in controversy. Ralph Nader has been attacking NHTSA ever since his efforts helped get it established. However, despite Nader's efforts, the consumer movement still lacks the power over regulatory agencies that organized labor has over OSHA, and consumer issues (including consumer safety issues) do not evoke the ideological fervor that marks labor-mangement issues. Although corporations have refrained from even asking OSHA to set money values on the benefits of measures to protect their workers, the automakers have confronted NHTSA with their own benefit-cost studies of its regulations protecting consumers. This kind of external pressure on the agency to be explicit about its economic assumptions has reinforced internal bureaucratic pressures. NHTSA was placed in the Department of Transportation along with the FAA and other agencies, and for the department safety is again only one of several competing interests. In addition, the presence of more than one safety agency creates a departmental interest in devising a yardstick for comparing them. Rationalists will urge the department's leaders to force the agencies to become explicit about their valuations. When disparities exist, the department will feel pressure either to compress them or figure out ways to rationalize them. Given the political problems with the latter course, the former will usually be chosen.[74]

Labor and Management Attitudes toward OSHA Standards

Since OSHA's approach to the treatment of economic factors is so heavily influenced by organized labor, union leaders' views deserve a closer examination. They would have severe qualms about highly protective standards if they believed, first, that sharp and sudden unemployment of union members would result or, second, that all the costs of compliance would be subtracted from a fixed pool of funds used to pay for improvements in wages and benefits.

Neither of these threats is likely to materialize, although an occasional plant will be an obvious candidate for a shutdown in the event of stricter standards. Some of the factors buffering unions from the second threat are long-term contracts and firms' needs to maintain internal wage differentials and to stay competitive in the external labor market. The first threat, unemployment, arises because of the strong likelihood that at least some and perhaps all of the added costs will be passed on to consumers. The effect on the existing work force is likely to be small, however, because of the combination of several factors. The most important is that the increase in costs attributable to standards typically represents only a small percentage of the price of the final product. The elasticity of demand is almost invariably less than unity, so that whatever price increases result will not, in percentage terms, have as large an impact on sales or employment.

Second, although the opposite effect may be more likely, the effect of standards can sometimes actually be an increase in employment, at least in the short run. This may occur either because standards increase the relative price of capital inputs (for example, by requiring ventilation systems and guards for machinery), leading to some substitution of labor for capital, or because a standard mandates work practices that require additional workers.[75] For example, most estimates are that the coke oven standard will force the steel industry to hire thousands of extra workers, hiring that can offset the impact on employment of higher prices and reduced sales.

In the long run, of course, since standards are established to protect workers from harmful exposures, they create incentives to design new technologies to get the workers out of harm's way and perhaps out of the way altogether. Therefore, over a period of several years, reductions in employment below the level that would have prevailed in the absence of the standard are very possible. While stunted growth can reduce opportunities for current employees, these foregone chances are not likely to be well perceived; even if they were, they would not count as heavily as a reduction in current status.[76] Union leaders may worry that reduced growth in employment will decrease both union dues and the political power that larger treasuries and memberships make possible, but this concern is likely to pale before the immediate benefits of political credit claiming and the personal gratification the leader receives from providing greater protection.

In chapter 3 I described how OSHA's policy for determining the "feasibility" of engineering compliance mirrored the union approach for determining when to grant wage concessions to weak firms. Typically, unions make concessions only when the padlock is about to be placed on the plant gate. Union reasons for discounting management claims apply just as forcefully to standard setting as to standard enforcement. First, the situation is very uncertain, and to give in easily could encourage firms to bluff. Expressing widely shared union views, Jack Sheehan of the Steelworkers made this comment on the coke oven standard:

What difference does it make what the cost estimates are? You don't know what it really costs them. You don't know the tax advantages they will take or whether they would have put in new facilities anyway. You don't know if the new way will turn out to give higher productivity.[77]

Second is the view that workers should not be asked to sacrifice their "right" to a healthful working environment simply because their particular employer has failed to make much profit. At least in regard to wages in the auto industry, unions felt that "so long as a company was not at a crisis level, those who were employed should not, as a matter of equity, be asked to forego 'justified'—i.e. pattern—increases in order to assist those who were or might be unemployed, even if the unemployment effects were reasonably predictable."[78] Such an emphasis on rights would clearly conflict with the suggestion that standards differ among industries, varying with the costs of compliance in each one.

Another factor ties together the enforcement process and standard setting. Unions can gain bargaining leverage from the enforcement of a standard only if it is set at a stringent enough level to demand extra efforts to reach it. A union representing members of a firm that already complies with the terms of a proposed standard will gain nothing. Often the firms that will find compliance most difficult will be small, frequently nonunion firms. Given a sufficiently strong enforcement effort, those firms may be driven out, or at least any competitive advantage they may have over unionized firms will diminish.

Union leaders realize that their members are sometimes willing to accept greater risks in exchange for higher pay, and the union may advocate this position in collective bargaining. The most explicit form of risk premiums—provisions for "hazard pay"—have been included in a small proportion of union contracts. But many union leaders feel uncomfortable about accepting hazard pay provisions. They feel, sometimes correctly, that the workers don't understand the hazards; in any event, they dislike the aura of selling away their members' health. As the industrial hygienist employed by the United Rubber Workers (URW) expressed it, "I don't think we should ever get 'hazard pay' for any kind of environmental health condition. Our basic philosophy is that the company should use any extra money to make improvements that would make the environment safer." He recounted his discussion with URW members at a Pottstown, Pennsylvania plant manufacturing vinyl chloride:

Most people accepted the situation, but there were some in the local union—mostly the younger people—who expressed the same kind of feeling as the newspapers have reported about the Painesville plant: "Let's get maybe 10¢ or 25¢ or 30¢ an hour because we're working with VC." Now, 10¢ more an hour comes out to be about $200 more a year. If I were to offer you $1,000,000 for your life, would you take it? You know you wouldn't. Life's pretty damn precious to everyone. So, after we spent a fair amount of time talking to our people at Pottstown, they understood this concept of hazard pay, and they didn't press the issue further.[79]

In dealing with occupational safety and health, as in dealing with racial discrimination or union corruption, tough federal standards can be invoked by union leaders to curtail behavior that they disapprove of but that they had previously felt powerless to change.

Another influence that reinforces union leaders' tough position on standards, at least in the health area, may be the company they keep. As many political scientists have observed, agencies and clientele groups can become symbiotic.[80] A similar type of relationship can develop between union leaders and the experts (both within and outside of government) on whom the unions have come to rely for technical assistance. The outside scientists who offer their services to the unions tend to be very strongly dedicated to the goal of protecting workers, even going beyond the health profession's usual attitudes. Having come to rely on these rather uncompromising experts, some of the union leaders may feel pressure from them to uphold protective standards.[81]

While unions' aversions to setting explicit values on lifesaving are easily understandable, the failure of employers to assert the need to make these judgments is more puzzling. In their everyday activity businessmen do make implicit or explicit decisions about the value of lifesaving. In the auto industry, the issue arises in designing safety features; in all businesses, it arises in setting the size of the budget for worker safety. It is important to make it clear that business executives share the social taboo about valuing lives; it is precisely because they do make such valuations in their daily behavior that the taboo has its strength. I asked the safety director of one of the nation's ten largest manufacturers if he agreed with Obey's statement that "when we are dealing with lives, the costs are irrelevant." He replied, "Well, I wouldn't say what he did in that flatout way; you've got to be realistic. No employer would ever deliberately let someone be exposed to a deadly hazard, but you do try to choose the least costly method of abatement." In the course of the interview, he told two anecdotes about events in his firm. The first was about a crane that had been allowed to operate in a very unsafe manner due to an unusual operation. Finally, the crane collapsed from the extra strain, killing one worker. He also recounted how he had convinced a top executive to approve some protective measures by pointing out to him that the maximum workers' compensation death benefits in that state had just been raised sharply.

The safety director gave no indication that he recognized any contradiction between his statement that employers would not deliberately expose workers to deadly hazards and the corporate behavior revealed in the two anecdotes. Yet just as workers deliberately accept some risks, so employers deliberately assign workers to risky jobs, sometimes paying some sort of risk premium in compensation. In this context, it is quite reassuring for management officials to believe, along with the vice-president of the American Petroleum Institute, that

no one can put a price tag on human life or human suffering and we would never attempt to do so. We value the life and health of every one of our employees, and we want to do everything we can to make sure that the working environment is free from any condition that could cause accident or injury.[82]

Even if management officials were willing to be totally frank with themselves, they would still have good reasons to keep their frankness from going any farther. Imagine an executive testifying before Congress that "we will not try to prevent injuries or illnesses unless the expected benefits exceed the expected costs." Even if he added that the measure of benefits was how much the *workers* valued the safer environment, he would encounter withering skepticism about his firm's ability and incentive to measure those benefits correctly.

I have shown that neither labor nor business interests are willing to indicate to OSHA what precise rules or even (in operational terms) what general rules it should follow in considering economic factors in standard setting. Both regularly appeal OSHA's promulgations to the courts, but the judiciary has shown that it will not step beyond the limited role of determining whether OSHA presented "substantial evidence" to support its decisions. Congress, which was not even willing to use the word *economic* to clarify what was meant by *feasibility* in Section 6 of the OSH Act, is not going to do more than suggest the broad political limits of standard setting. Even the watchdog CWPS, despite its exhortations about the general approach OSHA should adopt, refrains from guiding it through the actual steps it should take. The wish to avoid confronting the morally controversial and politically dangerous issue of valuing workers' lives encourages this restraint, but the other major factor that allows OSHA to escape the stripping away of discretion that characterizes most agencies dealing with labor-management relations is the great uncertainty about costs and effects.

Dealing with Uncertainty

The common agreement to eschew valuation is undergirded by the pervasive uncertainty about the costs and effects of OSH standards. If the range of costs could be pinned down and if experts would agree on the range of mortality and morbidity effects, then the pressures to monetize the benefits would mount. One party or another would be tempted to seize the opportunity to demonstrate that even an outlandish (or paltry) figure for the value of a life would still rule out (or justify) a proposed standard.

But even if better studies of costs and effects were available, the atmosphere of labor-management conflict reduces their usefulness in resolving issues of fact. In OSHA, one ASPER economist reports, "studies are viewed merely as weapons." On the congressional side, one staff member discounted the economic studies that OSHA had contracted for with the tart comment that "you've got a cadre of sycophantic consultants around here who say they can do anything."[83]

While economists often see their role as inventing ingenious methods to find out how much the beneficiaries value the risk reduction, OSHA still sees the economist's job as contributing information on costs and economic impact. In the view of many of the top OSHA standards people, the economists' performance has been miserable. According to Anson Keller, a lawyer and former special assistant at OSHA,

The problem with economists is that they just don't know anything. Economics in this area is dealing with unknowns. If they would be honest—say that it may cost $31 billion or it may cost $10 million—that would be OK. But they try to act as if they know something. It upsets me to see the economics creep in under the OMB pressures and with IIS's. Those requirements slow down the process of promulgating standards.
    We do lack economic and engineering expertise. The most crucial part is the engineering knowledge. If I had my way, we would go out and hire engineers. The economists all get their data from industry; they don't gather raw data. The economists said the vinyl chloride standard wasn't feasible; they said the same thing on asbestos. Back at EPA, they said it about pesticides regulation. They said we would have a boll weevil invasion that would dwarf any Egyptian plague. It bothers me. They've cried wolf so often that they may eventually have a good point and no one will listen. I know that when I walk out of one of those meetings, I think to myself that I just don't believe their conclusions; they all depend on so many assumptions that could go awry.[84]

In the face of the vast uncertainty described by Keller, techniques for rational calculation tend to break down. Some writers have stated that a rule of "minimax regret"—"to adopt strategies that avoid the worst logically possible outcomes, thereby minimizing the maximum possible loss"—has some resemblance to observed political behavior.[85]

More generally, the advice tendered to decision makers is to delay in the hope that more information will become available. OSHA has come to act as if it thought this was good advice. With several early exceptions, OSHA's setting of health standards has proceeded at a pace that has drawn the wrath of union leaders. This slowness is striking testimony to the importance of uncertainty, since it must counteract the opposing tendency to do something to show that your commitment to the people and problems is real.[86]

Partly because of the small number of standards examined, it is difficult to "hold other things constant" and isolate the effect of each variable. Nevertheless, the vinyl chloride and power press cases suggest other distinctions that seem to figure in the minds of standard setters. Substances causing cancer receive especially protective treatment. Certainly, a dread of cancer is pervasive and can plausibly justify special efforts to prevent it.[87]

Although not unique in this regard, the carcinogens typically present the problems of uncertainty in their sharpest form. The lack of clear dose-response relationships in humans makes it very difficult to define the extent of the hazard. The unguarded machine can be counted upon not to cause 1,000 cases of gastric cancer twenty-five years from now, but that certainty is often missing when the issue is controlling toxic exposures. OSHA's embrace of the "no detectable level" guideline, of going as low as you can go, still doesn't provide certainty, but it does provide reassurance that "we in OSHA have done all that we can." Top OSHA decision makers also appear to make a distinction between health and safety standards. Within OSD there remains a (partially valid) image of the worker subjected to a health hazard as a passive victim; safety standards, in contrast, are often designed to keep workers from getting themselves into trouble.

This chapter and the previous one have examined how OSHA has been implemented and why. Insights into how OSHA performs have been garnered from this investigation of policies, but before attempting to design recommendations for improvements in the OSH program, it would be desirable to go beyond the policies and procedures to see whether the program is actually having any effect on injuries. The added insights that such an evaluation generates turn out to be helpful.

5
Should We Expect OSHA to Have an Effect on Injuries?

The legislative history of the Occupational Safety and Health Act is replete with references to the objective of reducing occupational injuries and illnesses. Attempts to estimate how well the act would achieve that objective were rare, however. Testifying before Congress in 1968 about an earlier version of the OSH Act, Secretary of Labor Willard Wirtz asserted that it would annually save thousands of lives and prevent hundreds of thousands of disabling injuries.[1]

Appearing before the same House subcommittee in 1972, two years after the act's passage, one state safety official told its members that "the Williams-Steiger Act needs a goal. Now that the law has seasoned a bit, it would be appropriate to require the Department of Labor to establish a plan for a 10 percent reduction in injuries by 1980." Congressman Steiger, cosponsor of the act, responded with dismay: "It would be difficult to obtain a 10 percent reduction in eight years? I would hope it would be more like 50 percent or something like that. I have no basis for doing that other than hope."[2]

Later on the fourth anniversary of the act's passage, Steiger wrote,

The most appropriate measure of OSHA's success is the valid comparison of illnesses, injuries, and deaths prior to OSHA and for the first three years of OSHA's activity. Unfortunately, record-keeping before 1970 was woefully incomplete. Also, the current method of compiling data differs enough from earlier methods to make any comparisons invalid. The only accurate assessment will be the decline in deaths and injuries as industry adopts the safety standards. If a decline does not occur, we will know that there is something seriously wrong with the program. I am confident that just the opposite will be true.[3]

Empirical evaluations of OSHA's impact are certainly desirable. Even if a consensus existed about which views were correct, the theoretical issues raised in chapter 2 regarding the state of the labor market and the extent of externalities provide very little help in understanding the actual magnitude of OSHA effects. This chapter tries to provide a better understanding of OSHA's mechanisms, their potential and their limitations. The paucity of new standards promulgated under OSHA means that its impact, if any, will mainly derive from tougher enforcement of the preexisting federal or consensus standards.

Sometimes evaluators of public programs are confronted with a large jump or drop in the measure of program effects. Their job is to investigate whether the change could have resulted from something other than the program itself. The evaluator of OSHA faces an altogether different situation. National trends are hard to depict because of the change in reporting practices and the lack of data for 1971, but the pre-1971 patterns persisted: rates that were going up continued to go up, while rates that had leveled off remained unchanged. Rates based upon state WC reports—which are not subject to definitional changes or data gaps—show the same general pattern (see fig. 5.1). In fact, for both the states and the United States as a whole, the 1972-74 jumps in the manufacturing rates are probably the largest percentage increases for any two-year period since World War II. (I say "probably" because the U.S. rate is based upon a sample and thus subject to sampling error.) Do the data show that OSHA has failed to curtail injury and illness rates? Simply glancing at the overall rates can't answer that question, although it should induce skepticism about OSHA's impact.

It should be noted that this discussion of the basic conceptual issues underlying the evaluation of OSHA's effects deals almost exclusively with injuries and ignores illnesses, for two main reasons. First, many diseases have long latency periods and the effects of enforcement could not show up for many years. Second, even for acute illnesses pre-OSHA reporting was highly unreliable, and current reporting remains much less reliable than for injuries. [4]

The first step in approaching an evaluation of OSHA is to clarify why OSHA might be expected to have any effect at all on injury and illness rates. If, for the moment, it is assumed that firms try to maximize their profits, then it follows that in health and safety decisions, as in other areas, they will adopt all safety measures for which the perceived private benefits exceed the costs to the firm. The benefits of safety measures can include such items as lower workers' compensation or other insurance premiums, less downtime due to accidents, savings in training costs, and perhaps the ability to get workers to accept lower wages because of the improved safety and reduced risk. With the information available to it, the firm decides how much "safety" (including safety training and management emphasis on safety as well as physical hazard reduction) to provide.

The government can directly alter the results of the firm's calculus by instituting an enforcement program that raises the expected costs of noncompliance with certain safety and health standards. Before OSHA, state safety agencies relied almost entirely upon persuasion; employers were fined only on rare occasions. This avoidance of fines fit the prevailing philosophy of the state agencies, but it was abetted by practices that insulated enforcement from the employees—keeping it a matter between management and the inspector—and by legal requirements that fines could be levied only after cumbersome judicial proceedings. In California in 1970, for example, five

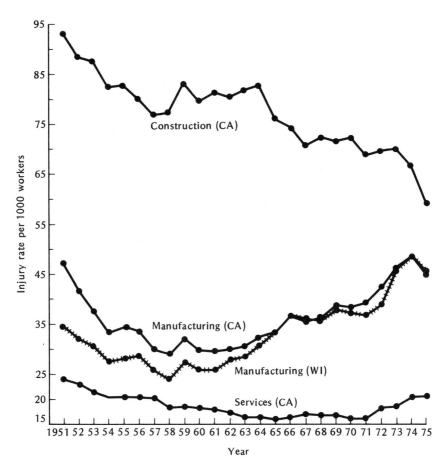

Figure 5.1 Rates for injuries reported under workers' compensation programs in California and Wisconsin, 1951–1975. Source: Through 1971, rates are taken from State Dept. of Indus. Relations annual reports on "California Work Injuries," which were also used for number of injuries in 1972–77. The 1972–77 rates were constructed using average annual employment figures from the unemployment insurance program, published in "California Employment and Payrolls." For the overall manufacturing sector the two series differ by much less than 1 percent. Annual figures on number of injuries reported in Wisconsin manufacturing (likely compensable injuries) were provided by Patrick Coleman and Mark Gottlieb, Wisconsin Department of Industry, Labor and Human Relations. The rate was computed using employment figures in the Bureau of Labor Statistics *Handbook*. Note: For California, injuries involve one or more lost workdays; for Wisconsin injuries involve four or more lost workdays.

firms were prosecuted and fined, although 20,000 inspections that year had turned up 200,000 violations. Employers who failed to correct violations were usually simply told again to correct them. A few states prosecuted somewhat more frequently than California; many others never fined employers. Altogether, it seems unlikely that in the whole country more than a few hundred employers a year were fined; the total penalties probably did not exceed $50,000.[5]

The deterrence effects of law enforcement programs on "risk-neutral" people are assumed to be a function of the probability of being caught times the penalty or fine for the violation. Although except in rare circumstances OSH Act penalties are civil, not criminal, offenses, the deterrence concept may provide a fruitful starting point for analyzing the safety behavior of firms, once a more fundamental question has been examined: How great can OSHA's impact on injuries be even if we assume that the deterrent force of standards enforcement is overwhelming?

The Relevance of Standards: The Potential for Increased Safety through OSHA

In order for the deterrent effect of the OSHA program to reduce injuries and illnesses, a crucial condition must be met: compliance with standards must actually have some safety value. Moreover, even if every standard's enforcement did indeed prevent injuries, it would still be possible that the vast majority of injuries could not be prevented through compliance with the existing standards.

(It is important to realize that the issue involved here is not the one that received so much attention at the OSH Act hearings: whether workers or unsafe working conditions are to blame for most injuries. The relevant question is whether OSHA can secure compliance that will prevent injuries. Thus noncompliance sometimes involves worker misbehavior (such as failing to wear safety devices), while many accidents involve no violations even thougn workers bear absolutely no responsibility for them. The point that most injuries result from both factors—people making errors in a hazardous environment—can perhaps be driven home by asking whether lumberjacking has an injury rate twenty times higher than insurance because lumberjacks are twenty times more careless than insurance clerks.)

The set of injuries that could be prevented by compliance with standards must itself be subdivided. Many violations occur briefly and intermittently and are unlikely to be perceived by inspectors on their very occasional visits.

Since OSHA policy does not usually penalize employers retroactively for violations that did in fact cause injuries, the full set is larger than the proportion of injuries OSHA could prevent by having inspectors go out and detect violations. (I will refer to the full set of injuries caused by violations as ICV injuries and to the subset of injuries caused by detectable violations as ICDVs. Obviously at some point the two converge, probably where there is one government inspector for every worker.)

How large are the ICV and ICDV categories? Some estimates have been based upon the scanty information contained in employers' reports of injuries filed under the WC programs. In one study, a team of California safety engineers reviewed over nine hundred such reports, whose content can be conveyed by a few examples: "lumbar muscle sprain (bent over)"; "pain and numbness in back and leg (slipped on street while delivering)"; "leg badly bruised (door hinge came loose, fell on leg)." Only the last of them was judged preventable by outside inspection. Overall the team judged that 18.4 percent were preventable in this way (corresponding roughly to the ICDV category), while another 8 percent could have been prevented by "in-house" inspectors. The combined figure of 26.4 percent is not far from an earlier New York State study that gave an ICV estimate of 22 percent.[6] These figures should not be taken too literally. Aside from the ambiguity of key words like *cause* and *control*, these studies are based upon the scanty information provided by the injury reports. The director of the California study reports that she and the engineers often had to guess at the supporting details in order to classify an injury. The proportion of ICDV injuries is probably upwardly biased in these studies because engineers may tend to exaggerate their own effectiveness.

Different sets of data from Wisconsin and California provide more reliable estimates of the ICV category. They are based upon actual accident investigations (AIs) in which the finding that a violation contributed to the accident usually imposed significant costs ($500 to $1,000 fines) on the employer. Data from both states indicate that violations contributed to 10 to 15 percent of the deaths covered by the state WC programs.[7] However, these figures overstate the proportion of fatalities that inspectors could realistically hope to prevent, because many of the related violations were momentary or occurred during unusual procedures and thus were unlikely to be detected. Table 5.1 displays the standards that were cited as serious violations in two or more California investigations of fatalities. The descriptions of these standards make it plain that they rarely pertain to obvious defects in permanent

Table 5.1 Serious violations cited in more than one fatality investigation, California, 1976

Standard violated	Number of times cited as serious in an AI report of a fatality	Number of times cited, excluding AI reports	
		Serious	General
Minimum distance from overhead power lines	5	7	7
Use of safety belts and lifelines	3	31	53
Prohibition of sources of ignition when gases may exceed 20% of lower explosive limit	3	0	9
Precautions to prevent contact with overhead lines	2	4	1
Locking out machine power during repairs	2	13	112
Blocking movement of parts during repairs	2	0	5
Prohibition of work under forks on forklifts, unless blocked	2	0	0
Provision and use of protective equipment	2	0	47
Precautions for work in confined spaces	2	0	1
Machine design appropriate to its use	2	1	41

Note: See note 7 for a description of the data upon which this table is based. The first column of figures includes only those serious violations that were cited as contributing to the fatality. The other columns include violations cited under all other circumstances.

fixtures. Six of the ten standards were cited fewer than fifteen times outside of AIs. In part, this paucity of citations corroborates the difficulty of detecting violations of these standards on routine inspections.[8] My own examination of all 512 California AI reports in which violations were cited in 1976—for both fatal and nonfatal accidents—suggests that inspectors probably could have detected the violations in less than half of the cases. My own best guess of the proportion of injuries caused by detectable violations is in the range of 5 to 10 percent with the low end more likely. For all injuries caused by violations, the range is 10 to 30 percent, again with the low end more likely.

Deterrence and Other Mechanisms to Achieve Increases in Safety

Will OSHA achieve any of this potential reduction? The first reason to expect that OSHA might have some impact is that the OSHA penalties increase the costs of safety violations. Employers will find it more worthwhile to spend money on the particular safety measures covered by standards.

Many observers, however, have expressed skepticism about OSHA's deterrent force. OSHA's average penalty per violation has been about $24. Only a small percentage of all firms is inspected each year; in 1974, inspections by OSHA or by states operating under OSHA procedures numbered about 170,000, while over five million establishments are covered by OSHA. Even if firms are inspected, many violations will not be detected, since inspectors aren't familiar with all the thousands of standards and aren't as thorough as they could be. After establishing all these points, Robert Smith concluded,

The small probabilities of inspection, the likelihood that many violations may never be detected even if an inspection is made, and the low fines combine to provide extraordinarily weak incentives for compliance with OSHA standards in advance of inspection. Incentives to comply after inspection are much stronger, given that fines for willful and repeated violations average $1,104. However, only 23 percent of the plants with violations are subject to a follow up inspection, so that even failure to abate is not certain to be detected. . . .
To expect that businessmen can be induced to invest thousands of dollars to comply in advance of inspection by a less-than-10 percent chance of being fined $170 [the average penalty per inspection] assumes that they would profit from compliance even if there were no chance of inspection. This assumption, in turn, presumes that businessmen are woefully ignorant of how profitable safety really is and presumes that OSHA standards can be shown to have a marked effect on the injury rate.[9]

Even a 10 percent chance of being detected and fined $25 would create an expected cost of only $2.50. Only if the costs of compliance with this particular violation exceeded the expected benefits (reduced injuries, and so on) by less than $2.50 would OSHA's deterrent force be sufficient to gain compliance. While this might occur in some cases, especially if it became known that a certain violation was always cited as "serious" and thus carried a fine of at least $500, the numbers are likely to be very small. Calculations of this sort would induce minimal compliance with OSHA. Only as firms came to be inspected and reinspected would any deterrent force be felt. Until then, they would view OSHA with benign neglect.

Yet businesses—especially the small ones least likely to be inspected by OSHA—have responded with noisy concern, not neglect. Many of the businessmen who come to complain at congressional hearings have spent money for compliance without any prior inspection. At the other end of the size spectrum, a Conference Board survey of large firms elicited reports that most had undertaken some compliance activity.[10] My own guess is that private-sector expenditures that would not have occurred in the absence of OSHA have amounted to between $500 million and $1 billion annually, although the figures might be as low as $200 million or as high as $1.5 billion.[11] But if these spending estimates are anywhere near correct, then why would firms spend so much, given the small probabilities of inspection and the small penalties? I will suggest as an explanation two institutional factors that the current discussion has ignored, after reexamining the arguments about infrequent inspections and small penalties.[12]

Three considerations help to explain how, within the narrow deterrence framework I have described, OSHA could achieve a major part of its potential for preventing injuries caused by violations inspectors can detect. First, the arguments that OSHA's deterrent must be weak because only 1 or 2 percent of all covered establishments are inspected each year either miss or underemphasize the importance of OSHA's focus on larger establishments. Within manufacturing, for example, since 1973 the number of inspections at establishments with over 500 workers (which employ 42 percent of all manufacturing employees) has approximately equaled the number of such establishments. Even if no more than one-fourth of these inspections toured the entire facility, the resulting coverage of workers would still be substantial.[13] OSHA does have a direct measure of employee coverage, since each inspector must state the number of workers affected by an inspection (that is, specifically taking into account the partial nature of many inspections). Since 1974, for example, the coverage for federal OSHA in all industries has reached about fifteen million workers a year.[14] Adding in the state-operated programs almost certainly brings the total above twenty million. Since about sixty-five million private-sector workers are protected by the OSH Act, the proportion who see an inspector is not trivial.

Second, the argument that OSHA's inspection effort is trivial ignores the sectoral relevance of OSHA enforcement. Millions of telephone operators, stockbrokers, and department-store salespeople may never see an OSHA inspector, but workers in those occupations and industries suffer relatively few injuries that compliance with standards could prevent. The standards have the greatest relevance in manufacturing and construction; in 1974 almost 80 percent of OSHA's inspections were in those two sectors (which have only 35 percent of private-sector employment).[15] It seems plausible that at least since 1974 the workplaces of most manufacturing workers have been inspected each year.

These first two points suggest that the strength of OSHA's preinspection deterrent is not necessarily a critical factor. Inspectors will visit the workplaces of a large proportion of employees, and since postinspection compliance will usually be economically rational (except for some major engineering changes), OSHA is likely to provide some protection. Nevertheless, if OSHA can pick out the violations that are most likely to cause injuries and give higher penalties to them, then the injury impact of the preinspection deterrent may be greater than a casual look at the expected costs of noncompliance would suggest. Chapter 6 shows that accidents involving getting caught in machinery and falling from heights are the types that enforcement of standards is most likely to prevent, and a disproportionate number of the "serious" (and thus highly penalized) violations are cited for these standards.[16] We don't know how well employers perceive differences in the expected penalties, but if a firm has a one-in-three chance of being inspected and fined $650 for a particular violation, it is quite possible that the expected cost of $217 will fill the gap between the private benefits and costs of compliance.

Because of these three considerations, it seems plausible that despite its small inspectorate and low average penalty, OSHA's deterrent may be large enough to induce substantial compliance. It is conceivable that even with greatly expanded resources and larger penalties, OSHA would very quickly run up against a more fundamental constraint—the limited proportion of injuries caused by detectable violations.

It is important to realize that one need not rely on a simple model of deterrence to explain how OSHA could possibly have any effect on injuries. If institutional factors are admitted into the discussion, several other possibilities present themselves. One important factor may keep a profit-maximizing employer from ignoring OSHA—his workers and their unions. OSHA's effects here may operate in two ways. First, OSHA has several provisions likely to increase workers' awareness of hazards. The most important of these include the right of a worker to accompany the inspector on his tour; the requirement that all citations for violations be posted at or near the site of the violation and that they include a date by which the violation must be corrected; and the requirement that all workers exposed to significant levels of air contaminants or noise be kept informed of their personal exposures.

If workers do become more aware of the hazards, they may exert pressure on management to correct them. The pressure may take the form of grievances, strikes, or demands for higher wages. By far the most common change in contract safety provisions since the OSH Act became law has been the growth in employer and employee pledges to obey all federal and state safety provisions.[17] Now that workers are more likely to know when violations exist, they can use the grievance route, going to arbitration if necessary.

Second, OSHA's stronger penalty system strengthens the bargaining position of workers, especially if they are organized. If the union is aware of a violation, it can request an OSHA inspection—a request that is almost always granted. Thus, the filing of this form makes the probability of inspection and detection equal to one. (Even if no violation is cited, the firm will incur costs of $50 to $500 simply from taking time to escort the inspector. Moreover, he can find and cite violations other than those noted in the request for inspection; few workplaces are totally free of violations.) If a violation is cited, the union can monitor compliance, again raising the probability that noncompliance would be detected to a virtual certainty. Note that under pre-OSHA practices, which rarely utilized penalties, the union would not have been able to impose costs upon the firm so easily. Most OSHA officials with whom I have spoken agree that the vast majority of requests for inspections are filed from unionized workplaces. In 1973, these complaint inspections numbered over 7,000—about 13 percent of all non–follow-up inspections.[18] Once the role of workers and unions as enforcers of OSHA standards—supported by OSHA procedures and penalties—is recognized, OSHA's impact no longer seems to apply only to those firms that have already been inspected and cited.

Finally, if the strict assumption of profit-maximizing behavior is relaxed, several other factors may lead OSHA's enforcement program to alter firms' safety practices. For example, several plant safety directors have explained to me that they are free to make decisions on safety expenditures below stipulated amounts. Several of them had never been asked to calculate explicitly the expected benefits of safety measures, even for the larger expenditure decisions which the plant manager had to make. Many local union leaders have told me that when OSHA took effect in 1971, their safety directors took checklists of OSHA standards around the plant, noted violations, and sent in orders to the maintenance staff to begin abatement.

The safety director of one branch plant of a manufacturing corporation with over 100,000 employees reported that the corporation's president had made a videotape for local plant officials announcing the firm's policy of compliance with OSHA standards. The safety director felt that "in a direct way OSHA hasn't done anything to improve our safety record—we already had a first-rate program—but it has helped me." He explained that he can make safety expenditure decisions up to a $1,000 limit; the plant manager must authorize anything above that amount. "But if the expenditure is necessary to comply with OSHA, I don't need to show what the benefits will be. If it's just something that I think we ought to have, then I have to review past accidents and show how it will prevent reoccurrences."

Since about 80 percent of firms inspected by OSHA are cited for violations, it can be assumed that full pre-OSHA compliance was uncommon. Larger firms which employ professional safety engineers would have been the most likely to have attained a high level of compliance. General agreement seems to exist among safety professionals that smaller firms are relatively more likely to ignore the standards or to insist that cost considerations preclude compliance. Only among firms with over 250 employees do we begin to find that more than one-half have "resident" safety directors, according to Gordon's survey of California employers.[19] (None of the firms with under 100 employees had one.) Although plant safety directors are responsive to managerial concerns about costs, they also identify with professional goals, one of which is compliance with safety and health standards. At the higher levels of the corporate hierarchy, proclamations of intent to comply with the law signal the growing desire of corporate leaders to make their organizations appear socially responsible. Profitability can become more of a constraint than a maximand, especially when business is booming.

(Other factors may make at least limited compliance a sensible policy, even in the absence of a strong deterrent force. In some markets, firms will generally be able to pass the added costs on to consumers reducing the incentive to avoid possible inefficiencies. The assumption of risk neutrality may fit managerial attitudes less adequately in the field of safety than in other areas. At any rate, it can become very difficult to distinguish risk-averse behavior from behavior based on law-abidingness.)

The possibility that OSHA could produce at least a temporary *increase* in injury rates should not be totally ruled out. Some safety directors have claimed that the clamor to meet OSHA standards misdirected safety efforts away from the usual emphasis on training. If the effectiveness of the compliance efforts fell below that of the foregone training, then injury rates could rise. Once they had recognized this, however, firms could be expected to reallocate resources; depending upon their value, either compliance efforts would be dropped or staff would be added to carry out both functions.

Finally, if workplace environments were made safer as a result of OSHA, the effect on the injury rate might be less than expected because workers might become less vigilant. If I feel that the new automatic safety devices on my machine are sure to protect me, I may become less cautious than I had been on my old, less trustworthy machine. If the engineer considered the machine alone he might overestimate the ensuing injury reduction. [20]

One final point is that a number of important OSHA standards really require compliance only from the producers of equipment, not the users. If all tractor and construction equipment manufacturers automatically install roll-over protective devices (ROPS) because of standards requiring such equipment on all purchases after a certain date, then compliance becomes relatively easy to monitor.

In summary, the OSHA enforcement system, despite the small size of its usual deterrent, may nevertheless generate substantial compliance activity. This conclusion rests partly upon the importance of union and employee pressures and partly upon the discretion exercised by safety directors and by image-conscious corporate leaders. A deterrence theory alone does not seem adequate to explain the response to OSHA, but it should certainly not be disregarded. Because the deterrence effect is sometimes miniscule, the actual effect that OSHA has had on plant safety must fall below the estimates of its potential. Yet given the substantial compliance that might still be expected to occur, careful tests may be able to discern some of the effects OSHA has had on the injury rate.

6

Tests of OSHA's Effectiveness

Only a minority, and probably a small minority, of all injuries can potentially be prevented by compliance with OSHA's safety standards. Yet despite the low average penalties and probabilities of inspection, there are reasons to believe that the OSHA program can achieve some of that potential. OSHA may have prevented injuries through any of a number of different mechanisms, but all of them operate through inducing compliance with the standards.

Three implications follow. First, one should not expect OSHA's effect on the injury rate to be large. Second, attempts to evaluate that effect should be designed to capture impacts that might arise from any one of the different mechanisms. Third, evaluation tests should focus on the types of accidents that compliance could prevent.

As an illustration of the second point, consider a recent study that examined injury rates for certain establishments for 1972 and 1973 and also looked at whether they had been inspected by OSHA during 1973.[1] The hypothesis was that if OSHA inspections had been effective in preventing injuries, rates at the inspected establishments should have declined relative to rates at the uninspected ones. The researcher found, however, that even when she looked only at inspections occurring in the first quarter of 1973, no evidence of declines in the 1973 rates appeared. But even if the shortcomings of this test (several of which are pointed out by the researcher) were ignored, it would not justify drawing conclusions about the total effects of OSHA's safety program.[2] Effects realized through mechanisms other than actual inspections—union pressure, manufacturers' incorporation of safety features, and so on—would not have been tested.

In order to examine the overall impact of OSHA, one would like to be able to predict what injury rates would have been in the absence of OSHA and to compare those figures with the actual rates. More precisely, those comparisons should be made only for the types of accidents that compliance with standards could prevent. Some of the pitfalls arising from a failure to disaggregate injury rates in this manner can be seen in the other major evaluation of OSHA.[3] That study argued that if OSHA's enforcement program had been effective, injury rates in the heavily inspected "target industries" should have declined in relation to other, lightly inspected industries. The research found no evidence that such a decline had occurred. Suppose, however, that, as seems likely, these target industries—which had been chosen because of their high overall injury rates—tended to have relatively small proportions of their injuries caused by detectable violations of standards (ICDVs).[4] It is easy to construct numerical examples that illustrate how such a situation could easily lead to underestimates of the OSHA inspection effect. For example, suppose that the ICDV category contains 10 percent of all injuries in the nontarget industries, but only 5 percent in the target industries. Suppose further that OSHA really has been effective, that ICDV injuries are going down by 5 percent in other industries and—because of the intense inspection effort—going down by 10 percent in the target industries. However, suppose that non-ICDV injuries are going up by 5 percent in all industries. Because of the injury mix, the calculations show that the overall target industry rate would go up by 4.25 percent, while the nontarget rate would go up by only 4.00 percent.[5] Thus the lack of impact found by this study could be consistent with an actual program impact.

By failing to establish any clear evidence of OSHA's effects, the results of these two studies certainly comport with the conclusion that OSHA's impact cannot have been very large. However, they may have failed to discern small effects, especially if they are not the direct result of compliance with citations. The first step in carrying out a test of OSHA's overall effect on injuries is to identify the types of accidents that compliance with standards could prevent; the second step is to develop a model for predicting what those injury rates would have been in OSHA's absence.

Identifying the Types of Accidents the OSHA Program Can Prevent

The same sources that we used to estimate the total proportion of injuries related to standards can also be used to identify the proportions of such injuries in each accident-type category. Table 6.1 displays the accident-type categories used in California and many other states. Data from the 1972 California study, which concluded that 18 percent of all injuries could be "controlled" by outside inspectors, were reanalyzed for this purpose. The scanty information upon which judgments of controllability were made limits their reliability, but the reanalysis showed that for the four largest accident type categories, 58 percent of the "caught in or between" (CIB) category, 26 percent of the struck by and striking against category, and 10 percent of the falls and slips category were controllable.[6] The study assumed that strains and overexertion accidents were not controllable. Rates for the other categories were based upon only a handful of controllable injuries. The eye injury category (56 percent) and the toxic substances category (55 percent) both appeared relatively controllable; motor vehicle accidents (9 percent) were less so. Other categories were too small to construct percentages.

The more reliable evidence on causation comes from accident investigation

Table 6.1 Work injuries categorized by accident type

Accident type	Fatal	Total
1. Struck by or striking against	128	71,177
Object dropped while holding	—	1,756
Hand tool or machine while using	—	10,592
Otherwise injured in handling	2	19,194
Object handled by other person	13	1,040
Falling or flying object	23	13,081
Stepping on sharp object	—	1,437
Other contact with sharp object	—	3,540
Bumping into stationary object	2	12,050
Moving equipment (except motor vehicle)	13	1,096
Other moving or rolling object	2	244
Cave-in of excavation, ditch, trench	3	69
Collapse of pile, structure, equipment	14	218
Other	56	6,860
2. Caught in or between	28	17,880
Object being handled and other object	—	3,695
Moving equipment (except motor vehicle) and other object	11	821
In machine or machine parts	8	10,160
In other mechanical apparatus	5	1,487
Other	4	1,717
3. Falling or slipping	56	57,063
Fall on the same level	6	21,280
Slip	—	12,488
From elevation	45	9,755
Into excavation, shaft, etc.	1	313
From moving equipment (except motor vehicle)	2	265
While stepping on, off, or over	2	12,630
Fall from animal	—	300
Other	—	32
4. Accident involving moving motor vehicle	214	12,435
Run over or struck by	26	2,221
Caught between moving vehicle and other object	9	719
Collision with other moving vehicle	79	4,332
Collision with object (except moving vehicle)	16	608
Overturning, running off road	75	1,263
Fall from	7	661
Struck by shifting load or object falling from vehicle	2	184
Strain or overexertion in operating vehicle	—	981
Contact with vehicle or object within vehicle	—	811
Other	—	655
5. Strain or overexertion	3	74,587
In lifting or lowering	3	39,432
In pushing or pulling	—	7,041
In holding or carrying	—	2,250
In using tool or machine	—	5,182
Other or not stated	—	20,682
6. Contact with temperature extreme	3	6,490
General heat—atmosphere or environment	1	197
General cold—atmosphere or environment	2	310
Hot object or substance	—	5,969
Cold object or substance	—	14

Table 6.1 (continued)

7. Contact with radiation, caustic, toxic, or noxious substance	38	8,424
By inhalation	25	1,813
By absorption (skin contact)	8	6,334
By swallowing	2	179
Drowning	3	3
Asphyxiation	—	—
Other contact with caustic, toxic, or noxious substance	—	95
8. Contact with electric current	40	570
Direct contact with normally energized part	12	95
Contact with overhead line through tool or equipment	20	70
Contact with normally energized part (except overhead line) through tool or equipment	3	66
Contact with object or part not normally energized	2	88
Contact with heat from arc, short circuit	3	224
Other	—	27
9. Explosion, flareback, etc.	21	601
Explosion—struck by flying object	10	163
Blasting	—	1
Flareback	2	200
Priming motor	—	50
Flywheel explosion	—	31
Explosion of combustible-material container	—	64
Other	9	92
10. Other	194	17,140
Bite, sting (including human bite)	—	1,687
Foreign substance in eye	—	12,324
Cardiovascular strain or disease	93	1,625
Plane, helicopter crash	98	117
Other accident, N.E.C.[a]	3	1,387
11. Accident type not stated	2	2,741
Total	727	269,108

Source: California Department of Industrial Relations, "California Work Injuries 1974," table 5, p. 26 (Sacramento, Calif.: 1976).

Note: The four larger categories (1, 2, 3, and 5) contain over 80 percent of all disabling work injuries in California.

[a] N.E.C. = not elsewhere classified.

reports. Minimum estimates of the proportion of 1976 California work fatalities with serious violations reached over 60 percent for the CIB category and for explosions, over 50 percent for electrical accidents, and between 16 and 24 percent for the other relevant categories. A review of the violations cited in Wisconsin accident investigations showed that over one-half involved machines, with hazards relating to falls from elevations a distant second.[7]

Discussion of these issues with safety engineers from the California Division of Industrial Safety generally confirmed that the CIB category had the largest proportion of injuries caused by violations among the four large categories; within the CIB category, the subcategories for machines and mechanical apparatus were identified as the most standards-related. It was clear that the strains and overexertion category had by far the lowest proportion of ICVs among the large groups. Among the small ones, explosions, electrical accidents, and eye injuries all ranked high. Locating the relative positions of the other categories is more difficult. Whether the struck by or the falls and slips category had larger proportions of ICVs was not clear, although safety engineers agreed that the subcategories of "falls from elevations" ranked higher than other subcategories.

Distinctions among these accident-type categories form the core of this evaluation. If OSHA has been effective, one would expect the effects to show up in the rates for the CIB, electrical, explosions, and eye injuries categories.[8]

Developing a Model of Injury Rate Determination

Predictions of what injury rates would have been in the absence of OSHA must be based on a model that can explain how injury rate levels are determined. Using multiple regression analysis, such a model can be tested on pre-OSHA data and the average effects of changes in each of the variables estimated. Then the post–OSH Act Injury rates can be predicted, based upon the levels of the explanatory variables in the post–OSH Act years. If OSHA has been effective, these predictions are likely to be too large; OSHA will have driven rates below what we would have predicted on the basis of pre-OSHA experience.

The results of this procedure can be interpreted with confidence as long as three conditions hold: first, that the model includes all of the significant factors that influence the level of the injury rate; second, that the estimated effect of a given change in a variable on the injury rate has not altered in the post–OSH Act period (unless the changes can be attributed to OSHA itself); and third, that the only significant new influence in the post-OSHA period is OSHA itself. It is not possible to prove that any of these conditions is met, but the evidence that can be brought to bear is discussed below.

In order to proceed we need to know which variables belong in the model and we need to be able to measure how they have changed over time. Unfortunately, our knowledge of occupational injury causation falls far short of these requirements.[9] Injury rates are determined on the one hand by work technology and the hazards it poses and on the other by workers and their ability to deal with these hazards. Employers can affect both of these elements. Whether they do so depends largely upon the cost of accidents and accident prevention to the firm. Some of the hazard-affecting technology is embedded in new capital equipment, so that if the new technology is safer, a firm (or industry) that introduces it may experience a sudden (more gradual for an industry) drop in injury rates.

Technological changes can increase as well as decrease hazards. The impact on hazards is only one small factor considered in the design and introduction of new techniques; other production benefits may outweigh an increase in hazards. (This is in addition to an inexperience factor associated with new equipment.) Still, since accidents do impose costs, in the long run the incentive to reduce hazards should manifest itself in safer techniques.

Given the somewhat uncertain pace at which new safety devices are likely to be invented and diffused—and the ambiguous safety impact of any particular set of innovations—it seems reasonable to assume that larger aggregates (the whole manufacturing sector rather than just the light bulb or meat-packing industry) will be more buffered against the effects of particular changes and more likely to mirror the long-run tendency toward increasingly safe production processes. If the factors that determine the course of the long run could somehow be measured, a smoother transition could be made to the second half of the model—to the workers and their capacity (because of training, maturity, and so on) to deal with the hazards. One might label this second group "demographic" factors, but the limitations of using a model based solely on demographic explanations becomes readily apparent whenever one considers some actual changes in technology. For example, it would be silly to try to explain the recent declines in the longshoring injury rates without talking about the containerization of cargoes. The model I have developed does not resolve the difficulties in an entirely satisfactory manner, but at the moment it appears to be the best we have.

Variables in the Injury Rate Model

One element in the cost of injuries is compensation for the affected worker. In one form or another, firms do have to compensate their employees for at least part of their disability losses. These losses are likely to be related to real earnings. Unless the costs of preventing injuries are increasing at as fast a rate as real earnings, employers will have an economic incentive to reduce the number of injuries.

A real earnings variable may be a satisfactory measure of the costs of injuries to the firm. If we use it without any variable for the costs of prevention, however, we just have to hope that real earnings are not systematically related to those costs. (Imagine, for example, that the bulk of prevention costs was the time in safety training. In this case real wages would be measuring both the cost of injuries and the cost of injury prevention, and changes in real wages would not affect the benefit-cost calculations of employers.) Lacking any real basis for a measure of prevention costs, this model nevertheless includes real earnings as a measure of injury costs with the expectation that real earnings will be negatively related to injury rates.

Inexperienced workers tend to have higher injury rates than workers who are familiar with the production process. Empirical studies support this commonsense view. A good measure of inexperience is the new-hire rate.[10] Because hiring expands in anticipation of booms and contracts in recessions, the rate is one of the leading indiciators of business cycles and explains much of the cyclical variation in injury rates. In addition, the new-hire rate also reflects changes in labor market structure and behavior. Thus, for any given level of unemployment, the new-hire rate tends to be higher today than it was ten or twenty years ago because workers change jobs more frequently than they used to.[11]

When an employer hires an inexperienced worker instead of an experienced one, he does have an incentive to make the workplace safer. For any given level of hazards, the former will have more injuries, and these are costly to the employer. Nevertheless, these extra efforts are unlikely to bring the injury rate down to the level an experienced worker would incur. The increase in injuries generated by inexperienced workers includes not only injuries to themselves but also injuries other workers may suffer on account of their mishaps.[12] The length of time before the injury-causing effects of inexperience wear off doubtless varies among occupations. In order not to miss part of that effect, the previous year's new-hire rate, as well as the current year's, is included as a variable. Both are expected to affect the injury rate positively.

The percentage of male workers who are young also may explain injury rate changes. Although many studies have shown that young male workers have very high injury rates, that fact alone does not justify the inclusion of this variable in the model. Part of the reason for their high rates is that young workers tend to be inexperienced, but that effect should be captured by the inexperience variable. A second reason is that at least in manufacturing, utilities, and other sectors with long job ladders, young men are generally given relatively hazardous jobs. Older men don't want them and can use their seniority to travel up the ladder into safer jobs. However, this phenomenon has no bearing on changes in injury rates over time. What does have a bearing is the apparent tendency of young males to behave more recklessly than other people and, even more importantly, to have less risk-averse attitudes than other people. The sharply higher auto insurance premiums for young males are the most prominent institutional recognition of their lack of caution. One workplace study also found that younger male workers had higher injury rates than their middle-aged coworkers on the same jobs, even after controlling for experience.[13]

The attitudinal differences may have far-reaching implications. If the supply of workers is increasingly composed of people willing to take big risks and relatively indifferent to safety concerns, then employers may become more lax about providing safe conditions. Possibly an employer will be able to recruit people to risky jobs for less money than he would have had to pay older people. More likely, once hired the young worker will value safety measures less than the older worker did and will not press as hard for the employer to provide them. The hypothesis, then, is that an increase in the percentage of young male workers will increase the injury rate.

Other variables used in some tests include the percentage of nonproduction workers and the percentage of male workers between 45 and 64. The first variable would seem almost by definition to affect injury rates, since nonproduction workers are mostly office workers and have low injury rates. Other things being equal, as the percentage of workers in this category grows, the injury rate should fall. This variable should help most in explaining injury rates for those accident types (like CIBs) office workers are least likely to suffer. Changes in this variable may also signal changes in production processes.

Adding in the percentage of male workers over 45 along with the percentage between 18 and 24 gives a measure of the effects of changing the ratio between workers over 45 and those between 25 and 44. The percentage 18 to 24 then becomes a measure of the effect of changing the ratio between workers in that age group and workers in the middle group. At least for the category of strains and overexertions, the expectation is that an increase in the percentage of workers over 45 would increase the injury rate.

Finally, many of these models include a "trend" variable and a constant. The trend variable is added to capture the effects of any excluded factors whose effects are changing in a linear fashion over time. When the data are in the form of changes between years (rather than the actual levels of the variables), the constant term acts as a trend. Otherwise, the constant simply gives the average effect of all the relevant variables not included in the regression.

In summary, the model tested here has no direct measure of any technological factors. It includes several demographic factors: more young males and inexperienced workers will generate increases in the injury rate; more older male workers will increase the injury rate in at least one category, strains and overexertions. All of these variables measure aspects of workers' difficulties in dealing with work technology. It may make economic sense for an employer to undertake preventive measures to counteract these forces, but it will rarely pay to try to push the rates back to where they were before. Other things being equal, rising real earnings increase the costs of injuries to employers, leading them to carry out more safety measures. As young male workers grow as a proportion of male workers, they may actually reduce the costs of injuries (or the costs of maintaining unsafe workplaces) to the employer. Technological factors may be reflected in the trend variable. A positive trend could indicate that we are operating in a period in which additional preventive measures have become more costly to achieve. A negative trend, on the other hand, might suggest that technological changes have reduced the costs of added safety measures.

A Test of OSHA Using Overall U.S. Manufacturing Injury Rates

The basic model I have described will be used to explain the annual changes in the U.S. injury rate in manufacturing from 1948 to 1970. The dependent variable in this regression is the year-to-year change in rate based on a Bureau of Labor Statistics (BLS) survey which used the pre-OSHA "Z-16" definition: the number of injuries involving one or more full lost workdays per million man-hours. Although the BLS survey techniques led to underestimates of the true lost-workday rates (a fact that provided the impetus to establish a new injury reporting system under the OSH Act), most observers agree that the rates provide a good indicator of injury trends.[14]

The regression explained 83 percent of the variation in the annual injury rate changes during those years. (Summary statistics are shown in the appendix.) For the individual variables, the results were[15]

a one-unit increase (for example, from 2.4 to 3.4) in the new-hire rate increases the Z-16 rate by 0.94 (t statistic = 6.84);

a one-unit increase in the lagged new-hire rate increases the injury rate by 0.26 (t statistic = 1.84);

a one-percentage-point increase (for example, from 12.2 percent to 13.2 percent) in the percentage of males who are 18 to 24 increases the injury rate by 0.30 (t statistic = 1.89);

a one-cent increase in the real hourly earnings decreases the injury rate by 0.14 (t statistic = 3.94); and

the constant term was +0.57, meaning that other factors were pushing the injury rate up by an average of 0.57 a year (t statistic = 3.44).

Table 6.2 shows that the net effect of these factors was to reduce the injury rate in the 1950s and increase it in the 1960s. The higher rate of new-hires and the slower growth in real earnings were the major factors underlying this turnaround in the 1960s, although the increasing percentage of young males also contributed. One implication of this model is that if the new-hire rate and the percentage of young workers had continued to fall as they had in the 1960s, the injury rate would have continued to decline in the 1960s, although not as rapidly.[16]

By multiplying the coefficients generated by this regression times the changes in the variables for the years since 1970, we can calculate the predicted changes in the injury rate for the post–OSH Act years. We can compare these changes with the changes reported under the new BLS survey, which is available beginning in 1972. The reported rate in 1970 was 15.2 disabling injuries per million man-hours. The regression predicts a 0.4 decrease from 1970 to 1971, followed by a 0.4 increase from 1971 to 1972. From 1972 to 1973, the predicted increase was 1.2, a rise of 7.9 percent. In comparison, the rate increase reported by BLS that year was 7.1 percent. For the following two years the changes were: 1973–1974, predicted change of +6.6 percent and reported change of +4.4 percent; 1974–1975, predicted change of −4.6 percent and reported change of −4.2 percent. Even if we ignored the sampling and rounding errors in the BLS injury rates, we would still have to deal with the prediction error of the model itself. When that error is taken into

Table 6.2 Factors underlying the U.S. injury rate for manufacturing

A one-unit (one percentage point or one cent) increase in:	(1) Led, on average, to a short-run change in the injury rate of:	(2) The average annual change in the variable was: 1950–1960	(2) 1960–70	(3) The average annual short-run contribution of the variable to the injury rate was to change it by ((1) × (2)): 1950–60	(3) 1960–70
1. New-hire rate	+0.94	−.19	+.06	−.175	+.056
2. New-hire rate lagged one year	+0.26	−.03	+.11	−.007	+.029
3. Percentage of male workers in manufacturing 18 to 24	+0.30	−.19	+.25	−.057	+.075
4. Real average hourly earnings (in cents) of production workers in manufacturing (1957–59 dollars)	−0.14	+4.80	+2.90	−.672	−.406
5. Total short-run contribution of all variables per year (sum of 1 to 4)				−.911	−.246
6. The average annual effect of excluded variables (the constant)				+.570	+.570
7. The average annual change in the injury rate (5 + 6)				−.341	+.324

Note: U.S. Manufacturing Injury Rate: 1950 = 14.7; 1960 = 12.0; 1970 = 15.2. Some discrepancies are due to rounding.

account, these differences between the predicted and reported changes are statistically indistinguishable.

A review of the findings so shows that first, the 1960s reversal of the post-World War II decline in the injury rate occurred because of the increased proportion of young workers and inexperienced workers and because real earnings apparently failed to keep pace with the costs of additional safety prevention. Second, our knowledge of the determinants of injury rate changes would lead us to expect the major increases in the injury rate that occurred between 1972 and 1974 and the decline during the 1975 recession. Third, these post-1970 injury rates are not significantly lower (or higher) than we would expect on the basis of nonregulatory factors. Therefore, we cannot reject the conclusion that OSHA has had no effect on the overall injury rate.

Using State Data to Test OSHA's Impact

Unfortunately, no national data system provides information about accident types. Consequently, a test of whether the null finding for the overall U.S. manufacturing rate would be repeated for the U.S. CIB rate is not possible. For accident type data, we must turn to the states and their workers' compensation programs. However, very few states possess the requisite time series of injury data: either the quality and thoroughness of the data collection effort have changed over the past quarter century, or the actual reporting requirements have been altered. California (along with Wisconsin) is one of the only states with a long series of injury data unimpaired either by informal changes in reporting practices or by formal changes in reporting requirements. The only pertinent changes noted by longtime participants in the data collection program have occurred during the last three years. Their effect may have been to give rates a small upward bias after 1972.[17] If that is the case, estimates of OSHA's effects for those years will be conservative.

Can California data be used to draw inferences about OSHA's effects nationally? Although some uncertainty is inevitable, several factors suggest that California findings are likely to be representative of national effects. First, the changes introduced in California by the OSHA program were qualitatively similar to those occurring elsewhere. Second, the available injury data indicate that California's rates—both before and since the OSH Act—have followed national trends.

Judging the relative effectiveness of state safety programs is not easy. California's OSH program had a superior reputation before OSHA, but that reputation was based largely on its occupational health component. As in most states, the use of financial penalties was rare in California. On a per capita basis, the size of its safety inspectorate didn't diverge substantially from other heavily industrialized states. If California possessed a somewhat larger program than the median, that remains true today as well. Like almost all other states, California maintained its preexisting safety program from 1971 through 1973, while OSHA superimposed its smaller—but much tougher—enforcement program. Having chosen to maintain an OSH program, in January 1974 California began to operate it in accord with the standards and procedures prescribed by OSHA. Federal inspections essentially ceased at that time. Under CAL-OSHA (as the state-operated program is called) penalties have been higher than in other "state plan" states but lower than in the roughly twenty-eight states where federal OSHA operates directly.

Drawing firm inferences from these facts is difficult, but there don't seem to be any strong reasons for believing that the program changes in California were atypical. California did not exchange one of the largest and toughest programs for one of the smallest and weakest—an exchange that probably would have led to underestimates of OSHA's nationwide impact—nor did it travel the opposite route, which could have produced overestimates. Extrapolations from California to national findings are also justified by the close tracking of California and national injury rate trends before and since the OSH Act. From 1947 to 1970 the correlation between changes in the U.S. and California manufacturing injury rates was over +0.90. Both rates have exhibited the same ups and downs since the OSH Act. Finally, when we turn below to changes in the critical CIB injury rate, the same downturn that causes the rate to be lower than predicted in California also appears in four of the five other states for which accident type data were reviewed. Taken together, these facts make the case for extrapolation highly plausible.

The California Evidence

Since the U.S. and California overall injury rates have shown similar trends both before and since the OSH Act, we should expect to find that the predictions for California are similar to the predictions for the United States, and we do. Figure 6.1 shows the reported and predicted overall injury rates for the model. (Some, but not all, of the explanatory variables specifically use California data. The other change is that the regression is on the absolute level of the variables rather than on first differences. For an explanation, see the appendix.) The differences between them are not statistically significant; the

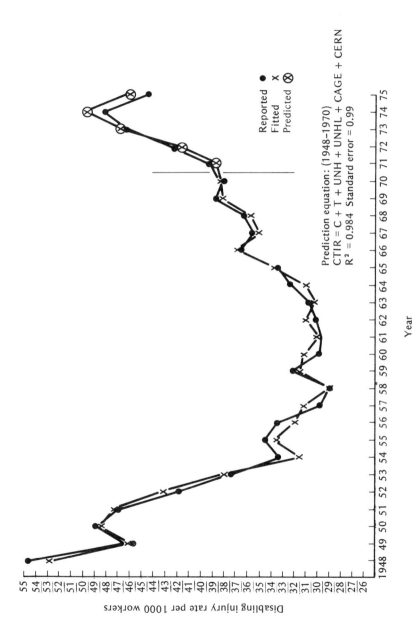

Figure 6.1 Predicted and reported overall injury rates for California manufacturing, 1948–1975

t statistic is less than 1.00 for every year except 1974, when it is 1.51. Other variants of this model gave similar results.

The regression equation was as follows:

$$CTIR = 57.02C + .86T + 2.76UNH + .11UNHL + 3.68CAGE + (-30.97)CERN + e,$$
$$\quad\quad\; (6.28) \quad (3.35) \quad (7.01) \quad\quad\quad (.25) \quad\quad (11.21) \quad\quad\quad (6.65)$$

where

CTIR = the total California injury rate for manufacturing

C = the constant term

T = the trend

UNH = the U.S. new-hire rate for manufacturing

UNHL = UNH lagged one year

CAGE = the percentage of males in California manufacturing between 18 and 24

CERN = the average hourly wage of production workers in California manufacturing (in 1967 dollars)

e = the error term,

and the numbers in parentheses are the t statistics.

These regression results differ in two major respects from the U.S. regression results: first, the coefficient for the lagged U.S. new-hire rate has slipped into insignificance; second, the coefficient for the percentage of male workers between 18 and 24 has grown disproportionately. Both of these changes probably arise from the attempt to use U.S. data as the basis for California variables (see appendix). The ensuing errors in measuring the variables for California weaken the confidence we can place in the estimates of the coefficients and in the predictions they generate.

However, these shortcomings should not be allowed to obscure the fundamental point figure 6.2 illustrates: the sharp rise in the overall California manufacturing injury rates was largely the result of increases in the "strains and overexertions" and "struck by and striking against" rates. Note that the CIB rate, even though it had roughly mirrored the trends of the other rates before OSHA, diverged markedly from them in the years after 1972. To develop estimates of the size of this divergence, we can use the same model to predict what the level of the CIB rate would have been in the absence of OSHA. Figure 6.3 shows that the downturn in the CIB rate was not predicted by pre-OSHA experience. In order to show the sensitivity of the results to different specifications of the model, table 6.3 shows the percentage differences between predicted and reported rates and the t statistics for all four

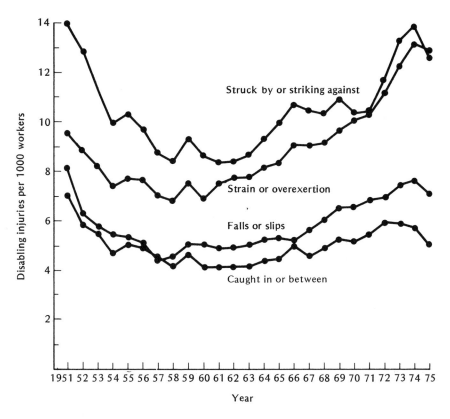

Figure 6.2 Injury rates in California manufacturing for four accident types, 1951–1975

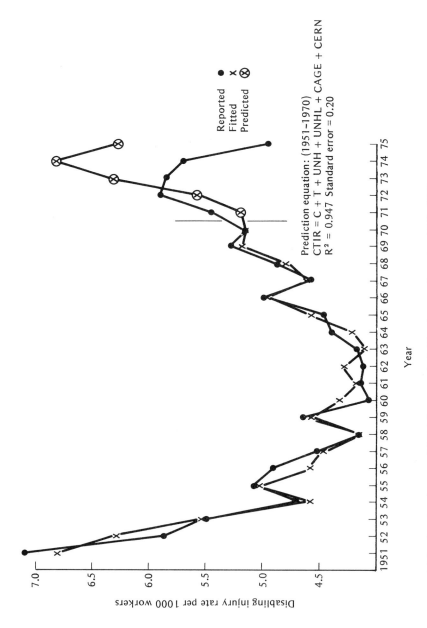

Figure 6.3 Predicted and reported CIB injury rates in California manufacturing, 1951–1975

Table 6.3 Predicted and reported CIB injury rates, 1971-1975

	Percentage by which predicted rate exceeds reported rate				
	1971	1972	1973	1974	1975
Variant 1					
Overprediction	−5%	−5%	+8%	+19%	+27%
t statistic	<1.00	<1.00	1.33	2.39	2.15
Variant 2					
Overprediction	−6%	−5%	+9%	+17%	+21%
t statistic	1.11	<1.00	1.69	1.80	2.36
Variant 3					
Overprediction	+2%	+3%	+16%	+27%	+34%
t statistic	<1.00	<1.00	3.73	3.67	3.57
Variant 4					
Overprediction	+4%	+8%	+24%	+35%	+36%
t statistic	<1.00	1.13	1.90	2.97	2.41

Source: Based on regression equations in appendix.

variants that were tested. (The regression shown above is the first variant. The other three are described in the appendix. For a one-tailed test at the .05 level, the critical t statistic is 1.76 for the first two variants and 1.77 for the other two.) These figures reveal a clear swing toward overprediction in 1973, although it attained statistical significance in that year for only two of the variants. In 1974 and 1975 the size of the overpredictions grew, although by decreasing amounts, and achieved statistical significance in both years for all variants.

Except for California, no attempts were made to predict the levels of the CIB rate for the post–OSH Act years. However, simpler comparisons reveal that similar changes were occurring in other states. For all California sectors covered by workers' compensation, the CIB rate comprised 7.4 percent of all injuries in 1970 but only 6.6 percent in 1974. An examination of WC data from five other states—Ohio, Florida, Wisconsin, Nebraska, and Iowa—shows that all except Iowa experienced similar drops.[18] For example, in Wisconsin (for all industries) the percentage of all compensable injuries that were CIB was 10.1 in 1971 and 1972, 9.8 in 1973, and 9.1 in 1974. In Ohio the figures were 11.5 percent in 1970, 11.8 percent in 1971, 12.0 percent in 1972, 11.8 percent in 1973, and 10.5 percent in 1974.

Having shown that the CIB rate decreased more than would have been predicted on the basis of pre-OSHA experience, and that there is some evidence that this phenomenon is not confined to California, it becomes critical to consider whether any other factors aside from OSHA could explain these findings. We might begin by looking at the model and asking what, if anything, changed in the post-1970 years to produce these overpredictions of the CIB rate. If we reestimate the model by including data through those years, we find that one of the coefficients does change markedly: the trend coefficient becomes much smaller.[19] It is possible, although not necessarily correct, to interpret that change as a result of OSHA. The trend variable has been presented as a possible proxy for the cost of injury prevention activities. The shrinking of that coefficient could mean that employers are behaving as if the costs of complying with the relevant safety standards had declined, which is exactly what we would expect to see if OSHA has been successful.

However, the overprediction of the CIB rate could also have resulted from other factors which made injuries more expensive to employers or injury prevention less expensive. The most obvious candidate for the first role is the growth in workers' compensation premiums, the result of a wave of benefit increases in the early 1970s. In California, for example, benefits were raised in April 1972 and again in April 1974. The chief difficulty with this explanation is that premium increases would provide incentives to prevent all types of injuries, yet the rates have declined only for the accident types most clearly related to standards.[20]

The other explanation could be that some non-OSHA factor has made it easier or cheaper for employers to prevent CIB injuries. For example, breakthroughs in machine guarding technology or technological changes that reduce workers' exposures to the hazards that cause CIB accidents (such as the increased number of computer-operated machines) could conceivably explain the overprediction. However, interviews with California safety engineers uncovered no awareness of technological breakthroughs, and the growth in computer-operated machines is far too small to account for the overprediction.[21]

Another possible rival explanation would be that the CIB rate has declined because the number of machines in the manufacturing sector has declined. That explanation receives no support from a survey of the metalworking industries, which found that the number of machine tools used in California grew by about 15 percent from 1968 to 1973.[22] Moreover, if it were true, we would expect that the rate for non-CIB machine injuries (such as bumping into machines or falling from them) would have declined at the same time; however, the rate for these types of machine injuries followed a different pattern and increased after 1972.

A more precise alternative would be that the decline in CIB accidents resulted from a relative decrease in the number of the particular types of machines (presses, power saws) that are especially likely to cause CIB accidents. However, this cannot explain the CIB decline because for each major machine category the proportion of CIB accidents declined after 1971 or 1972. For example, for mechanical punch presses and shearing presses, the percentages of CIB accidents were as follows: 1966, 74.7; 1967, 75.7; 1968, 74.7; 1969, 74.2; 1970, 71.9; 1971, 75.5; 1972, 75.6; 1973, 73.9; 1974, 69.7; 1975, 67.0.

If OSHA is really responsible for a reduction in the CIB rate that reached more than 20 percent by 1975, why hasn't the impact shown up in predictions of the overall rate? CIB injuries comprise only a little over 10 percent of the overall manufacturing rate, so that a 20 percent reduction amounts to only a 2 percent reduction in the overall rate. Has this effect simply been obscured by the prediction error of the overall rate? We can construct a better explanation by examining the predictions for rates for the other major accident types.

The two major components of the injury rate are the "struck by" and the "strains and overexertions" accident type categories. As table 6.4 indicates, the rate for the former can be accurately predicted on the basis of pre-OSHA experience; none of the differences between predicted and reported rates is statistically significant. For the latter, however, the rate becomes significantly underpredicted in 1972 (at the .05 level with two tails) and again in 1973 and 1975. Thus it appears that OSHA's impact on the CIB injury rate has been masked by the higher-than-predicted rate for "strains and overexertions"—the accident type category with by far the smallest proportion of injuries caused by violations.

Could OSHA be responsible for this unexpected increase in strains? Some plant safety directors do complain that OSHA diverted them from their regular safety programs and forced them to spend more time complying with physical codes. However, most of the ones I have spoken to claim that the diversion was a temporary one. Another explanation for the underprediction could be that because strains and overexertions are the easiest injuries to fake (along, perhaps, with eye injuries), any boost in the proportion of fraudulent injury claims triggered by improvements in WC benefits would show up in this category.

Blaming OSHA for the higher-than-predicted strains rate, although conceivably correct, seems far-fetched; hence the conclusion that OSHA has caused a reduction in the overall rate remains tenable. Like the rate for CIB injuries, the rate for "falls and slips" also was lower than predicted; however, many of

Table 6.4 Predicted and reported injury rates for three accident types, 1971–1975

Accident type	Percentage by which predicted rate exceeds reported rate				
	1971	1972	1973	1974	1975
Struck by	+2%	0%	−3%	−2%	−5%
t statistic	<1.00	<1.00	<1.00	<1.00	<1.00
Strains	−2%	−8%	−11%	−14%	−14%
t statistic	<1.00	2.69	2.26	2.08	2.47
Falls and slips	+6%	+12%	+19%	+31%	+34%
t statistic	<1.00	1.15	1.31	1.94	2.07

Source: Based on regression equations in appendix.

the coefficients in the "falls and slips" regression were not statistically signifi-cant, indicating that an extra dose of skepticism is needed in interpreting the results. Within the falls and slips category, it did turn out that "falls from ele-vations" had declined relative to all other falls and slips, a finding consistent with the hypothesis that OSHA has been effective.

Evidence of OSHA's impact can also be discerned in the trends in injuries caused by explosions and electrical contacts. Because these two categories together contain less than 1 percent of all disabling injuries, their trends can-not have a great impact on the overall injury rate; however, since along with CIB injuries and perhaps eye injuries they have the highest proportion of standards-related injuries, their trends are important for the evaluation. Ex-cept for the CIB and motor vehicle accident rates, they are the only cate-gories whose rates actually declined before the 1975 recession. The rate for explosions dropped sharply after 1972; for electrical contact injuries, the drop occurred after 1971. In neither case did these declines merely continue previous trends.

Not all of the evidence supports the view that OSHA has decreased the in-jury rate. In at least one study, safety engineers argued that many and per-haps most eye injuries could be prevented by outside inspectors. From 1971 to 1974 the rate for eye injuries in manufacturing leaped over 50 percent, the largest percentage increase of any category. One resolution of this discrep-ancy could be that the assumption that tougher enforcement would be effec-tive in this area is incorrect. Indeed some inspectors believe that OSHA-style enforcement is not very effective in getting workers to comply with standards requiring personal protective equipment. The evidence on eye injuries cer-tainly supports that contention and is also consistent with the claim that OSHA has failed to decrease the injury rate.

Finally, a brief look at data on fatalities may provide some additional insights. Again, I will focus on the accident types most likely to be caused by violations. Even a loose screening procedure (one that omits deaths from heart attacks, assaults, airplane crashes, and highway motor vehicle accidents) excludes well over one-half of all deaths reported under the California workers' compensation program. Of the remaining categories, we saw in chapter 5 that CIB, electrical, and explosion fatalities were much more likely to involve violations than were fatalities in other accident type categories.

If we look at numbers of deaths for the accident type categories in which a pre-OSHA trend was discernible, we find that most of the post-1970 California figures are fairly well predicted, and none are much above the trend line. In three cases, however, the post-1970 experience has been considerably better than one would have predicted simply by extrapolation: explosions, electrical, and rollovers of earthmoving equipment.[23] Although the CIB category was not among the overpredictions, the fact that the other two categories were seems to support the view that OSHA has had some effect. Attemps to quantify the estimated effect of safety regulation on fatalities is obviously highly speculative and very crude. If we take the difference between trends and actual post-OSHA figures, the net reduction is about 35 to 40 in each year after 1971. If the actual effects attributable to OSHA were even one-half that number, the result would be a 2 to 3 percent reduction in the overall workers' compensation death toll.

Evaluative Conclusions and Their Limitations

The evaluation I have presented was designed to be both broad and narrow: broad in the sense of capturing all of the possible mechanisms through which OSHA might prevent injuries and narrow in the sense of focusing on rates for the types of injuries that compliance with standards is likely to prevent. The central findings are the following:

1. Most of the accident type categories with high proportions of injuries caused by violations (ICVs) experienced declines relative to other injury rates, declines not predictable on the basis of pre-OSHA experience.

2. Attempts to account for these declines without invoking OSHA have not been very successful, although some portion of the decline could be attributed to non-OSHA developments.

3. If we exclude the possibility that the higher-than-predicted rate for strains

and overexertion can be attributed to OSHA, we can conclude that OSHA has reduced the injury rate in California by a few percentage points.

4. Nationwide extrapolation of these California findings would be speculative but quite plausible. The degree of change introduced by OSHA in California's safety program mirrors changes elsewhere. Changes in injury rates in California before and after the OSH Act have followed national patterns. Finally, four of the five other states examined, show a decline in CIB injuries similar to California's.

The model of injury rate determination has increased our understanding of injury trends, but it cannot by itself provide the critical test of OSHA's impact. On the national level, there are relatively good data on the explanatory variables in the model, but rates for specific accident types are lacking; on the state level, the accident type rates are available, but the explanatory variables are poorly measured. Thus the econometric analyses play a mainly corroborative role; the defects in the data and the model weaken but do not cripple the evaluation.

Several other problems with this interpretation of the findings should also be noted. First, not all of the results were consistent with the hypothesis of OSHA's effectiveness. Neither eye injuries nor CIB fatalities were overpredicted. We should also consider the negative conclusions of other evaluations of OSHA, although their findings do not necessarily contradict the assessment that OSHA has had a small impact.

Second, the timing of the effects found here is perplexing. The simplest assumptions were that OSHA would either have immediate effects (owing to the efforts of safety directors or corporate law-abidingness) or gradually increasing effects (as the cumulative effects of postinspection compliance grew). One of the high-ICV categories (electrical accidents) did exhibit declines after 1971, but the CIB category showed no sign of declining until after 1972. If the CIB decline were the result of OSHA, why didn't it begin to show up earlier? (Or, alternatively, if it were the result of the CAL-OSHA program, why didn't it begin in 1974, when that program began?) Possible explanations can be constructed, but they tend to be convoluted and speculative.

If we resolve these issues in OSHA's favor and also absolve it of responsibility for the increase in the strains rate, what quantitative estimate of its impact seems reasonable? Again, precise answers can't be given. The CIB overpredictions amount to about 2 to 4 percent of the overall manufacturing rate for 1974 and 1975. Perhaps some of this amount can be attributed to non-OSHA causes (such as rising WC benefits, more computer-controlled machines), but other accident types besides CIB have been effected by OSHA. Perhaps the total effect of OSHA on the manufacturing rate has been to reduce it by 3 to 5 percent. For the construction industry the range might be similar, but for most sectors the effects would almost certainly be smaller, both because of smaller proportions of ICV injuries and because of less frequent inspections. For the entire private sector, the reduction might be on the order of 2 to 3 percent—approximately 40,000 to 60,000 out of the two million disabling injuries that occur nationally each year. The percentage drop in fatalities has probably been similar or a little larger.

The casual quality of this discussion of the quantitative estimates arises not only because greater precision would be misleading but also because greater precision would not really be of any benefit to policymakers. However, before exploring the conclusions that *can* be helpful, it is worthwhile carrying the numbers a step further, if only to show that despite all of OSHA's shortcomings a case can be made that the social benefits of its safety program exceed the social costs.

First, we can use the findings to pick a plausible point estimate of OSHA's effect on the overall injury rate during the years through 1975. I will choose 2 percent, or approximately 40,000 injuries prevented a year. The second step is to estimate the social losses imposed by the average nonfatal disabling injury. The third step is to determine how the severity of the particular injuries prevented by OSHA compares with the average severity of all injuries.

To develop a minimum estimate of the losses from injuries we can add up the lost productivity of injured workers, their medical expenses, and the other costs of accidents to employers. This estimate will be a low one, because a "willingness to pay" approach would certainly also include the costs of pain and suffering and of incapacity for nonwork activities. If we employ lost wages as a measure of lost productivity, we can use studies of the proportion of lost wages supplied by WC benefits to calculate that component. Then, along with estimates of medical expenses from WC sources, we can add in crude estimates that employers' noncompensable losses (like downtime or damaged equipment) are between 50 and 100 percent of the wage losses. The resulting minimum estimates of the average social losses of disabling injuries range from $6700 to $10,200 (in 1975 dollars.)[24]

Data on the average compensable losses of disabling injuries by accident type are available from Florida.[25] They show that the average CIB injury cost slightly more than the average for all injuries. Several of the accident types with high proportions of ICVs also had above-average compensable losses (for example, falls from heights, electric contact, explosions); however, the very severe but laregly unpreventable category of motor vehicle accidents provided a strong counterweight. Overall, categories with high ICV proportions appear to have average compensable losses that are roughly the same and perhaps a little higher than the average for all injuries. Consequently, it seems reasonable that the $6700 to $10,200 range would apply to injuries prevented by OSHA. For 40,000 injuries the annual losses prevented by OSHA would range from $268 million to $408 million, not counting the more subjective injury losses or any losses from fatalities.

How do these figures compare with estimates of the costs (public and private) attributable to OSHA's safety program? So many uncertainties beset any estimation of the private costs that the plausible range includes figures that vary by a factor of five or six. The important point here is that a review of the available data suggests that the low end of the range for the total costs could be under $400 million.[26] A bigger cost figure is probably more plausible, but the major purpose of this exercise is to suggest that the true state of affairs is not really known.

Even if we had the information needed for a benefit-cost analysis, precise estimates of the magnitude of OSHA's effect on the injury rate would not be very helpful. One important reason, of course, is that legislators have few incentives to care whether programs have met their stated objectives (much less whether they have met them at a reasonable cost) unless the dominant political interests insist that the program be judged on such a basis. For union leaders, however, several other criteria are more important for judging OSHA than its effects on injuries. Preventing occupational disease epidemics is one of them, but even in the safety field there are potent rivals. These include (1) increasing the power of unions, especially at the local level, by allowing them to invoke the newly toughened enforcement procedures against violators of standards; and (2) removing issues on which unions are weak from collective bargaining forums to a national forum, where the public bureaucracy (adhering to the intent of the OSH Act) will ensure that the unions will be stronger.

Program administrators—quite apart from the lack of interest in policy outcomes in general and efficiency outcomes in particular that some of them share with legislators—will also not find estimates of the number of injuries OSHA has prevented very helpful. Retrospective evaluations about overall program impacts are mainly useful when the decision being contemplated is of the "go or no go" variety and when the expectation is that the same pattern of effects will continue if and only if the program is continued. These conditions are rarely met. An evaluation of this kind does not provide answers to practical questions like, How would the injury rate be affected (if at all) if inspections were increased by 10 percent or penalties raised by 5 percent?[27]

This evaluation of OSHA's effects does in fact have value for policymakers, but as is so often the case the value inheres more in the evaluation's by-products than in its end products. The most important insight it offers grew out of two observations. First, contrary to many arguments, the small size of OSHA's average penalty and the infrequency with which the typical establishment is inspected do not preclude extensive compliance with OSHA standards. Not only might OSHA induce compliance through other means than direct inspections, but even on the basis of inspections alone a noticeable impact could be expected because of their concentration at large establishments in hazardous industries and because of the substantial threat that noncompliance with citations will be heavily penalized. This argument suggests that other explanations for OSHA's small impact must be sought. An important part of that explanation can be found by lowering the usual estimate of the proportion of injuries that OSHA inspections can prevent. The estimate must be lowered because most OSHA inspections are limited to preventing the 5 to 15 percent of all injuries that are caused by detectable violations.

These observations raise the intriguing possibility that despite its small impact the OSHA program may be approaching the limit of its potential. But regardless of whether that inference is correct, the critical point is that significant increases in OSHA's effectiveness will require redesigning its enforcement strategy to apply to a broader set of injuries. In chapter 7 I present enforcement alternatives that not only have a broader scope but also promise to reduce injuries at a lower average social cost.

Although significant gains are unlikely under the current inspection policy, some improvements can be made. This evaluation provides several hints about how to proceed within the current framework. First, if detecting violations that cause injuries is the objective, then rates for these types of injuries should be developed and used instead of overall injury rates as the basis for targeting inspections. Second, the size of "first instance" penalties does not seem to be very consequential. More important is that the workplaces of a large proportion of workers facing serious hazards be inspected and that employers realize that noncompliance with citations will be costly. OSHA should not worry whether initial penalties for nonserious violations (or general violations, as they are now called) average $50 or $10. Instead, in its monitoring of its area offices or of states operating their own OSHA-approved programs, it should focus on penalizing noncompliance with citations and inspecting a larger proportion of the work force.

If OSHA were to adopt an experimental approach toward enforcement strategies—trying different ones in different areas, for example—then evaluations such as this would become relevant to the marginal choices that policy-makers really do confront. Decisions about individual standards make even clearer demands for evaluations, both prospective and retrospective, in the form of cost-effectiveness and benefit-cost studies. As we have seen, however, OSHA has preferred to consider costs and effects separately and to refrain from any explicit valuations. Taking account of these constraints, chapter 8 sketches some changes in the process that might be both feasible and helpful.

7
OSHA's Safety Program: A Policy Analysis

The preceding chapters have shown that OSHA's safety program has had, at most, a small impact on injuries and that it probably does not prevent them in an economical fashion. The small impact appears to be less a result of small fines and a paucity of inspections than of the limited proportion of injuries caused by violations inspectors can detect. The main reasons for the relative costliness of the prevention effort are (1) the standards have never been reviewed to see whether the benefits would exceed the costs; and (2) the injury losses that can be prevented most cheaply may not be the ones that compliance with standards can prevent; and even if they are, compliance with those (or any) standards may not be the least costly preventive approach.

Confronted by evidence of limited effectiveness and a costly approach, several analysts have argued for "taking the S out of OSHA," focusing the organization's entire energies on health problems and perhaps creating an "injury tax" if new incentives for enhanced injury prevention were thought worthwhile.[1] Without additional knowledge about the benefits and costs of preventive measures, it is not possible to adopt an unambiguous judgment about the desirability of preventing more injuries. Yet political realities ensure that OSHA's safety enforcement is here to stay; thus it becomes important to explore how it can be improved. This analysis accepts as a given that greater effectiveness in preventing injuries is one criterion by which alternatives must be judged. Preventing injuries at a lower average social cost is another.

For OSHA to have substantially greater effectiveness would require widening the scope of enforcement beyond the subset of injuries caused by detectable violations of current standards. To make OSHA more socially cost-effective, two strategies could be employed: (1) to focus enforcement more narrowly on violations whose abatement is especially likely to be worthwhile; or (2) provide general incentives to prevent injuries rather than specific incentives for compliance with certain standards, mainly dealing with equipment.

Of course, the policy that these requirements most clearly evoke is the injury tax, which would increase the cost of all injuries and allow employers to determine which safety measures were worth adopting. Yet the injury tax lacks political support; moreover, even if such support were forthcoming, implementing an injury tax would be extremely difficult.[2] Nevertheless, the injury tax can still serve as a touchstone for this analysis: when a tax approach might be preferable to standards but lacks political appeal, one response can be to redesign the program for enforcing standards to capture some of the virtues of a tax. Several variants of this strategy will be developed after a fuller description of the criteria for assessing policy alternatives and a brief review of a broad set of alternatives.

The Criteria

Five criteria play a prominent role in this analysis. Three of them—effectiveness, cost-effectiveness, and fairness—can be called "substantive" criteria because they determine the intrinsic desirability of a proposal. The other two—adoption and implementation feasibility—force us to evaluate the likelihood that we can attain what we desire.

Public Cost-Effectiveness (Effectiveness)

By public cost-effectiveness I refer to the capability of a government safety agency with a given budget constraint to prevent injuries. An agency with a budget of $5 million that prevents 1,000 injuries has the same public cost-effectiveness as an agency with a budget of $10 million that prevents 2,000 injuries. Because this analysis takes existing budgets as given, this criterion basically means simple effectiveness in preventing injuries.

Effectiveness can be seen as a function of two characteristics. The first is the potential scope of the program. For example, a program that can only affect injuries caused by violations that inspectors can detect has a much narrower scope than one that penalizes all injuries. The second characteristic is the extent to which the potential of the program can be realized by means of the various mechanisms—deterrence, actual detection of hazards, dissemination of information—composing the regulatory effort.

If two programs have a similar scope and use the same mechanism, the one with the more forceful use of that mechanism—such as bigger deterrent, more inspections to detect violations—will usually be more effective.[3] Generally, however, we can't answer questions like, Will a weak deterrent or detection effort in a program with a broad scope be more effective than a strong effort in a program with a narrow scope? We also lack information about the marginal effects of different alternatives needed to design the package of programs with the greatest public cost-effectiveness. For example, devoting all enforcement resources to Alternative A may prove more effective than devoting all of them to Alternative B, but it might also turn out that a program comprised of 90 percent Alternative A and 10 percent Alternative B would be better than Alternative A alone.

Social Cost-Effectiveness

The budget of the public safety agency constitutes a small part of the resources used in the effort to prevent injuries. The largest component of these social costs is the compliance costs incurred by employers. The objective of a safety program is to prevent injuries at the lowest social cost per injury (or, more precisely, per dollar of injury loss). If a program has a better public cost-effectiveness ranking, it will always have a better social cost-effectiveness ranking as well, provided that it does not impose greater social costs. However, often additional injuries can be prevented only by raising the average cost of prevention.

Fairness

The proposals should not violate widely shared norms of what constitutes fair treatment. The bases for treating one employer differently than another should be acceptable. For example, deterrence mechanisms that impose costs on randomly chosen employers are acceptable only up to a certain point. Attempts to compensate for the small probability of inspection at small establishments by burdening them with especially heavy penalties could easily stray beyond that point.

Procedural rights accorded to workers by the OSH Act should not be abridged without very strong reasons. On a quite practical level, since any major program changes in this labor-management field are likely to be challenged in the courts, they should be designed to respect constitutional requirements of procedural due process. (I do not include vertical equity as a criterion here because I don't feel it is an issue in the choice among the alternatives considered.)

Adoption Feasibility

Regardless of its virtues, a policy proposal serves little purpose if it is too politically unattractive to be adopted. Adoption feasibility obviously depends on shifting political currents. While legislative action is normally more time-consuming than administrative action, the actions that agencies take on their own tend to be more timid and incremental, yet discretion gives agencies that wish to act boldly ample room to do so.

The alternatives I present are ones whose basic components can be set in place by administrators without legislative action. Fortunately for would-be reformers, OSHA is so beset by troubles that its leaders, forsaking some of the usual agency resistance to change, are seeking policy changes that could still some of the criticisms threatening the agency's basic programs.[4] The

Senate Labor and Public Welfare Committee has steadfastly refused to hold hearings on or report out any bills amending the OSH Act because Senator Harrison Williams and the unions fear that hostile amendments could be adopted on the Senate floor.[5] This is another practical reason for the analyst to examine administrative rather than legislative channels.

Implementation Feasibility

The decision to adopt has little meaning if the policy cannot be implemented. Ignorance about "what works" creates difficulties in the implementation phase just as it does in the design phase. Similarly, political problems are no less common in implementing policies than in designing them. For example, suppose a particular alternative requires a 50 percent increase in the number of clerks in a particular unit. The existing budget has no room for them, so they can only be obtained by shifting them out of another unit in the agency. While outsiders might think that such reallocations can be made easily, insiders know that the agency's top leadership will have to be very strongly committed to force the other unit, which may have its own constituency, to give up staff. A similarly strong commitment would be needed to win this kind of nonincremental budget increase from the legislature for the following year.

A major problem in the injury field is that any safety program based upon employers' reports of injuries must devise mechanisms to guard against underreporting. Some of these mechanisms may be politically unpopular. Frequently the most serious political problems arise not when the original idea is proposed but only much later (often after "adoption") when all of the steps required to implement the program are discovered.

The Policy Alternatives

Efforts to reform OSHA's safety program can follow many paths. Choosing among them depends on many interrelated factors: how the policy problems are defined, which political constraints are accepted as binding, and what time perspective is adopted. Figure 7.1 presents one way of categorizing a far from exhaustive list of alternatives. The alternatives developed in this chapter fall within C1a. Why are other alternatives not pursued here? Neither the alternative of gutting the safety program (B) nor the approach (BD) of replacing the safety program with new safety incentives is politically feasible. The strategy of adding such incentives to the status quo (AD) does contain some

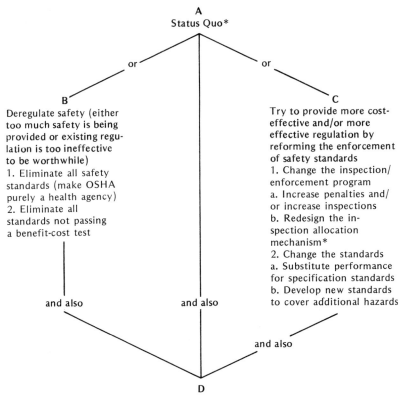

A
Status Quo*

or

or

B
Deregulate safety (either
too much safety is being
provided or existing regulation is too ineffective
to be worthwhile)
1. Eliminate all safety
standards (make OSHA
purely a health agency)
2. Eliminate all
standards not passing
a benefit-cost test

and also

C
Try to provide more cost-
effective and/or more
effective regulation by
reforming the enforcement
of safety standards
1. Change the inspection/
enforcement program
a. Increase penalties and/
or increase inspections
b. Redesign the in-
spection allocation
mechanism*
2. Change the standards
a. Substitute performance
for specification standards
b. Develop new standards
to cover additional hazards

and also

and also

D
Try potentially more cost-effective and
perhaps more effective alternatives to standards
1. Use taxlike mechanisms
a. Adopt an injury tax*
b. Increase WC benefits and premiums
2. Restore tort liability for work injuries

*Discussed in text.

Figure 7.1 Relationships among safety regulation alternatives

feasible alternatives, and trying to deal with the existing OSHA program (C or CD) has a certain appeal: given that an OSHA safety program will continue, it would be unfortunate if opportunities to improve it were overlooked. More pertinent to officials in OSHA and the Labor Department, some of the changes in OSHA (especially those relating to redesigning enforcement procedures) can be carried out without new legislation and without substantial new funds.

A few of the alternatives within C appear to fare very poorly by some of the criteria or to run head-on into constraints. For example, a major increase in the size of fines for violations would probably induce some added compliance and thus prevent at least a few more injuries, but the average social cost of preventing a given injury or injury loss would probably tend to rise.[6] More inspections would have similar effects but would also require larger budgets for expanding the inspectorate.

Transforming specification standards into performance standards, a process that OSHA has already begun, may facilitate the choice of less costly hazard abatement measures. The size of the potential savings from these changes is unclear; in any event, I lack the technical expertise needed to assess them.[7] The same reason rules out consideration of the potential for gains in effectiveness from developing new standards.

What kinds of alternatives are left to explore? The proposals I will develop take several forms, all of which can be characterized as performance-based inspection programs. One relies upon making the frequency of inspection a positive function of each establishment's overall injury rate relative to the rate for its industry. This design uses the enforcement of standards as a lever to give employers an extra incentive to prevent all of their injuries, not just those related to standards. Two other alternatives both rely upon a much heavier use of accident investigations (AIs), which have the unique property of allowing investigators to cite retroactively violations that caused injuries— modestly expanding the scope of OSHA's impact from injuries caused by *detectable* violations to *all* injuries caused by violations. One of the accident investigation options is designed to be very cost-effective, while the other ranks higher on the effectiveness scale. Since inspections are triggered by injuries, the programs provide an incentive to prevent injuries. *Performance* rightly refers to injury experience, not merely to compliance with standards— which does not necessarily show a high correlation with injury experience.

A full understanding of these three alternatives requires a review of the inspection practices that OSHA currently employs. In calendar 1976, 60 percent of federal OSHA inspections were scheduled inspections; 19 percent were inspections in response to a complaint; 18 percent were follow-ups to determine compliance with earlier citations (mostly issued during scheduled inspections); and 2 percent were accident investigations.[8] The figure for AIs is small because OSHA adopted regulations requiring employers to notify it only in the case of deaths or accidents hospitalizing more than four workers. In most states where OSHA oversees state-operated enforcement programs, the proportion of scheduled inspections is somewhat larger.

During OSHA's first two years, the bulk of OSHA's scheduled inspections were performed in five target industries, chosen because they had the highest injury rates. Area directors had great discretion about where to schedule the others. More recently, OSHA has tried to formalize its guidance to area offices, but the newer rules still rely almost entirely on choosing establishments because they are in high-rate industries. Within those industries, inspectors are encouraged to visit the larger establishments. No logical basis is provided for deciding how frequently to inspect a given workplace. One proceeds down a list, from one industry to another, until resources are exhausted, or an arbitrary decision is made to begin again at the top. The assumptions underlying this emphasis on high-rate industries are not readily apparent. The assumption that inspections will reduce injuries by some constant proportion would lead to an emphasis on workplaces with the largest total number of injuries, but OSHA seems to assume that greater gains can be made (or perhaps greater efforts should be made) in the more hazardous workplaces.

The central point is that OSHA's enforcement program emphasizes scheduled inspections, which are carried out in a manner that basically limits them to preventing only those injuries caused by detectable violations. Within this small subset, several steps could be taken to improve OSHA's effectiveness in reducing injuries. For example, the priorities of an inspection program limited to detectable violations should be shaped by the rate of injuries caused by such violations rather than by the overall injury rate.[9] However, more fundamental alterations require redesigning the enforcement system to widen its scope and improve its cost-effectiveness.

Accident Investigations

Except for its accident investigation program, OSHA does not penalize employers retroactively for injuries that result from violations of standards. Consequently, OSHA's impact has been largely limited to preventing injuries caused by violations that inspectors can detect. Since a large proportion (probably at least one-half) of the injuries related to standards involve the sort of momentary violations that inspectors are unlikely to detect, this limitation is substantial, although various methods exist for transcending it. One is the accident investigation program; others work through state WC programs. Examples of the latter include the provisions found in many statutes for extra indemnity payments to the injured worker when the injury was caused by "serious and willful" misconduct by the employer; there is also the Wisconsin practice of adding a 15-percent surcharge to the benefits when any safety code violation contributed to the accident.[10] To a large extent, OSHA's accident investigation program gives similar incentives to employers—although the costs it imposes take the form of fines paid to the government rather than benefits paid to workers.

Although OSHA only requires employers to report by telephone about fatalities and catastrophes, some states have imposed broader reporting requirements and, proportionately, make many more AIs. For example, in addition to the OSHA categories, California also requires telephoned reports of amputations, permanent disfigurements, and hospitalizations (except for observation) over twenty-four hours; consequently, 7 percent of CAL-OSHA's inspections were AIs in 1976, compared with less than 2 percent for federal OSHA. OSHA has the authority to establish reporting requirements that equal or exceed California's.[11] The possibility of even further expansion is demonstrated by Wisconsin, where AIs have comprised from 20 percent to over 50 percent of all inspections.

More accident investigations increase the probability that a given injury will be investigated and thus increase the incentive for employers to abate violations likely to cause injuries. Since (based on 1976 California data) over 20 percent of the AIs cite serious violations, which carry fines of $500 to $1,000, the incentive may not be paltry. Yet since OSHA has only a limited number of inspectors, it ought to use them efficiently, making sure they conduct most of their investigations where violations are involved. Here one faces a familiar trade off. As employers come to feel that any accident with a violation will be investigated, the deterrent will increase, but as the net is spread wider and larger numbers of accidents are investigated, the investigations tend to become less discriminating. Consider the following evidence. In 1969, Wisconsin investigated 15 percent of all compensable injuries and found violations 21 percent of the time. In 1974, investigations in Wisconsin dropped to 2.7 percent of all compensable injuries, and the percentage finding violations rose to 32.4 percent. Finally, in 1976, California investigated only 0.7 percent of all compensable injuries and found violations in about 39 percent.[12] However, despite the drop-off, these data still suggest that, for example, in California a tenfold increase in AIs would probably increase the number finding a causal role for violations six- or seven fold.[13] Those figures would imply about 13,000 AIs and 3,000 to 3,500 injury-causing violations in California, with ten times those numbers nationwide.

For federal OSHA, the first step might be simply to adopt a reporting requirement like California's. As the AI program becomes more prominent, the importance of complete reporting mounts; employers who underreport are unfairly spared inspections. One remedy could be to require employers to post a prominent notice about their reporting requirement and, after each reportable injury, to post the date on which the enforcement agency was contacted. In this manner, employees could help to detect underreporting in some cases.

Any substantial expansion of the AI program—for example, beyond 10 percent of all inspections—demands more thorough measures. One promising route is to use the "doctor's reports," which almost all states require physicians who treat injured workers to submit. In California, for example, this report tells whether the worker was hospitalized, whether any amputation occured, and more (such as the estimated period of disability). The reports also have some (but not much) information about the accident type, enabling some judgments to be made about the possible relevance of violations. In California, doctors' reports are used as a backup system for triggering AIs and for monitoring employers' compliance with the reporting requirement.[14]

Finally any AI program would be complemented by dissemination of information about which violations of standards actually have contributed to injuries. Previous AIs provide by far the best source of this information. Enough of them have already been conducted by OSHA and by state agencies to provide the basis for a guide to employers and workers, and—not least—to the enforcers themselves.

A greatly expanded accident investigation program could use either of two options. In the first—the pure accident investigation option—the investigator would examine only violations related to the accident, refraining from any "wall-to-wall" inspection of the workplace. In the second option—the accident investigation with wall-to-wall inspection—the inspection would include this component. (Currently, most AIs take this latter form.) Although the difference may appear to be minor, the consequences may be substantial. Each of the options is analyzed in relation to the five criteria for policymaking described at the opening of the chapter.

Option 1: Pure Accident Investigation

Public Cost-Effectiveness Some aspects of pure AIs suggest that their substitution for scheduled inspections would lead to a reduction in injuries. Other aspects, however, suggest the result would be the opposite. Only a carefully controlled field experiment can resolve the issue.

AIs have a broader scope than scheduled inspections, although not as broad as the injury tax's. They can retroactively penalize employers for all violations causing injuries, not just for the subset of detectable violations. AIs give up the detection mechanism that scheduled inspections employ; in exchange, they gain a deterrent more strongly focused on the types of violations that cause injuries. The effect of these gains and losses cannot be determined a priori.

The effectiveness of expanding the AI program depends upon two factors. First, the smaller the ratio of injuries caused by detectable violations to all injuries caused by violations, the more effective AI expansion would be relative to the status quo. Second, the smaller the probability that inspectors will get to workplaces with detectable violations, the more effective AI expansion would be. In other words, the gain from expanding AIs is an inverse function of the status quo's potential.[15]

Social Cost-Effectiveness Accident investigations function like a tax on injuries to which violations contributed. Because the AI program focuses the employers's attention on the probability of injuries rather than on the probability of detection, it does promise to prevent injuries at a lower cost than the status quo. First, employers may discover that another method can be used to reduce the hazard and prevent an injury, a method that is cheaper than correcting the violation. Second, because inspectors will not be conducting wall-to-wall inspections, employers will not be forced to spend money to comply with standards they think are not relevant to injuries (except for any violations cited in the accident investigation). The tax operates through penalties, which are transfer payments, not actual costs to society.

Nevertheless, compared with an injury tax, the AI program still inefficiently biases employers' choices in two ways. First, even though another method may provide a socially cheaper abatement strategy, the expected penalty of an AI citation may still lead the employer to choose to abate the violation. Second, because the AIs are confined to standards-related injuries, they may induce him to forego correcting other equally great hazards that are socially less costly to remove.

Fairness The major problem with an expanded AI program by this criterion is to assure that employers are not rewarded for failing to report injuries.

Adoption Feasibility This proposal may encounter considerable political opposition. Unions may complain that it shuts the barn door after the cows are gone. It is true that AIs lack the protective image of inspectors stepping in to shut down dangerous operations. A particularly sore point would be the absence of accompanying wall-to-wall inspections. After all, it will be asked, if the inspector is already there, shouldn't he at least look around for other obvious violations?

Yet as long as the complaint program was not curtailed, the unions would be unlikely to oppose strongly some expansion of this AI option. They would balk, however, at attempts to replace scheduled inspections completely. Business groups would generally applaud the gains in social cost-effectiveness (or, more pointedly, the likely reductions in their own compliance spending).

Some of OSHA's current problems make an expansion of the AI program especially attractive. The prospect that the Supreme Court may uphold a string of lower-court decisions requiring OSHA to have special reasons or "probable cause" to inspect an establishment could be faced with greater equanimity if AIs replaced scheduled inspections.[16]

Criticisms of the paucity of serious violations also make AIs attractive. Twenty percent of the AIs in California cite serious violations. (By telling inspectors to ignore the probability that a violation would cause an injury and to focus only on the severity of the injury that might result, OSHA has recently managed to get its percentage of serious violations up to 20 percent, but most state-operated programs still have only 1 or 2 percent in that category.)

Implementation Feasibility This option is not terribly difficult to implement, but administrative measures to encourage complete reporting are needed. If some employers came to believe that other employers were "getting away with something," the whole program could be jeopardized. A major expansion of the program should include some provisions for auditing the accuracy of the reporting. The use of WC data for that purpose would require negotiations to assure OSHA access to them in states where it runs the enforcement program. Because of differences in data availability, a uniform national approach would probably not be feasible.

Option 2: Accident Investigation with Wall-to-Wall

The second option differs from the first primarily with regard to public cost-effectiveness and social cost-effectiveness.

Public Cost-Effectiveness Since wall-to-wall inspections would accompany the AI, firms would have a considerably greater incentive to prevent accidents that could lead to investigations than they would under option 1. The increase in the number of AIs, however, would not be as great if inspectors' time had to be devoted to these wall-to-wall inspections. Whether this increase in deterrence along with the restoration of the detection mechanism would offset the reduced number of AIs is not certain, although I suspect that option 2 would be more effective. Although I also think, with less confidence, that it would be more effective than the status quo.

Social Cost-Effectiveness Because it would require compliance with all standards at the inspected workplaces, more expenditures on inefficacious standards are likely with option 2 than with option 1. I suspect that the cost differential would be large enough to make option 2 less socially cost-effective than option 1. However, because option 2 puts more emphasis on inury prevention relative to compliance than the status quo does, I think option 2 would be slightly more cost-effective than the status quo.

Fairness Both options are the same under this criterion.

Adoption Feasibility This option would encounter little political opposition. OSHA could argue that now its inspections would be targeted on the firms with accidents (although, the AI options are of course only crudely responsive to injury rate differentials).

Implementation Feasibility Both options are the same.

Other Options

Other AI options are possible. One of the most important could be a variation on option 2, which still attempted to choose accidents in which violations were implicated. As long as the program can impose costs only when a violation contributed to an accident (as in option 1), this selectivity is clearly desirable. But once the AIs include wall-to-wall inspections and costs may be imposed for violations unrelated to the accident, it may become preferable to select accidents randomly from a pool that includes all accidents. If a back sprain could trigger an inspection as surely as an amputation, the potential scope of the program would expand. Employers would have an added incentive to prevent all types of accidents. This option is the crudest sort of injury tax imitation. The problems it would encounter become apparent in the analysis of the much more sophisticated THIRE alternative. Once again, minor administrative changes can have significant consequences.

Targeting Inspections of High Injury Rate Establishments (THIRE)

THIRE presents a possible method of extending the effects of inspections beyond the reach of standards without having to resort to any direct sort of injury tax. THIRE relies upon (1) developing overall injury rates (frequency or severity) for establishments and ranking them within detailed industry categories; (2) establishing and publicizing the policy of making the frequency of inspection depend upon the ranking of the establishment within its industry; and (3) relying upon the costs entailed by inspections (time, penalties, and compliance) to serve as a rough form of injury tax. High injury rate establishments are put on notice that unless they can reduce their rates, they will be subject to intensive inspection efforts. Although inspectors will still be able to cite only for violations of standards, the policy provides incentives for employers to reduce all types of injuries, regardless of whether they are related to standards, and does not constrain them from doing it in the least costly manner.

Politically, THIRE could get enforcement agencies out of a difficult spot. Currently, employers frequently complain that they are cited for a long list of violations of standards even though they have an excellent record of injury prevention. Such criticisms underscore the apparent irrelevance of many standards and make OSHA (or the state agencies) look as if it were harassing employers rather than preventing injuries. If the agency were able to explain that the inspected firms were the "bad apples," the ones with the highest injury rates in their industries, then criticism of this sort would recede.

THIRE would largely supplant the general inspection program, but it would still be accompanied by complaint and accident inspections as well as follow-ups. Unions would maintain their right to request an inspection and thus would not oppose firm-specific targeting. Because THIRE would probably lighten the inspection probability for about half of all firms, employers would have no reason to unite against it. The firms that would be hurt, those with the highest rates in their industries, would have such a poor image that they would have trouble garnering sympathy for their oppsition.[17]

The Logic and Operations of THIRE

The fundamental assumption upon which injury prevention programs are based is that an employer can influence the level of injury losses at his workplace. This assumption does not deny that differences in technology and in the demographic composition of the work force (age, marital status, inexperience) play an important role in explaining variations in injury rates. Nor, of course, can it be denied that chance accounts for a large chunk of the variation. However, the evidence indicates that even after controlling for these factors differences in management policy and practices have an impact on the level of injury rates.[18]

The crucial operating principle of the targeting program is that it imposes incremental costs on employers for each additional injury or injury loss. Many different methods of implementing that principle are feasible. For example, frequency of inspections could be tied directly to changes in the injury rate at a workplace, ignoring the whole issue of whether the workplace had a good or bad injury record. However, it might seem fairer to tie the initial allocation of inspections to each establishment's record, so that bad establishments were inspected more often than good ones. Note, however, that the key principle would remain unchanged—for each increase in its injury rate, the frequency of inspections would increase.

Linking the frequency of inspection to relative safety performance may have an analytic rationale as well. Poorly performing establishments may plausibly carry out injury prevention more cheaply *at the margin* than high-rate establishments.[19] Under a system based on changes in rates, a high-rate firm would not be inspected at all unless its rate worsened. Under a THIRE system, in contrast, it would be inspected frequently unless its rate improved.

If we do want to target establishments where management has given little emphasis to safety, we need to control for the other factors that influence relative injury rates. However, since information about the demographic composition of each establishment's workforce is unavailable, the only controls that can be applied are for differences in production technology. (Of course, to some degree demographic and technological choices can be determined by management. There may be more than one method for sawing lumber or baking bread.) Four-digit SIC industries will probably serve well enough, but the classification used by WC programs (categories designed expressly to group workplaces with similar levels of risk) would probably be preferable.[20]

Table 7.1 has been constructed as an illustration of how to develop an inclusive system for ranking the comparative performance of all establishments. The ranking is based upon how many fewer (or more) injuries the establishment would have experienced if its injury performance matched the

Table 7.1 Ranking safety performance

Establishment	(1) Employment	(2) Establishment injury rate (%)	(3) Industry injury rate (%)	(4) (2) − (3) Rate gap (%)	(5) (4) × (1) Injury gap
Sawmills					
S1	50	12	10	+2.0	+1
S2	100	6	10	−4.0	−4
S3	200	11.5	10	+1.5	+3
Bakeries					
B1	50	6	4	+2.0	+1
B2	100	9	4	+5.0	+5
B3	200	1	4	−3.0	−6

average for its industry. (If information on dollar losses is available, the rankings could be made in terms of "excess" losses rather than injuries. With this system, establishment B2 would get top priority even though its rate was lower than the rates for two of the sawmills. Note, however, that a pure performance ranking would be based upon the "rate gap" rather than upon the "injury gap." The latter is created by adjusting for the number of workers at the establishment, an adjustment made because the number of injuries prevented by a given rate reduction is greater at a larger plant. For the same reason, the rankings in column 5 should be further adjusted to account for the average severity of injuries in each industry. Thus if the average sawmill injury is 50 percent more severe (in terms of days lost or compensable losses per injury) than the average bakery injury, the injury gap for all of the sawmills could be increased by 50 percent. Finally, another adjustment for size might be appropriate because inspections at larger firms tend to require more time.

Once we have decided how to rank establishments, the next question is how to allocate inspection resources among them. The alternative bearing the greatest similarity to an injury tax would make the frequency of inspection a continuous function of safety performance. No matter where they ranked, establishments would always have an incentive to improve, which might not be the case if, for example, the worst 20 percent of all establishments were inspected three times a year and all others were left alone. (The actual number of inspections the enforcement agency is capable of conducting must also be considered.) On political grounds, however, it might be preferable to exempt better-than-average establishments from THIRE inspections. That step would clearly demonstrate the intention of going after the bad apples and would increase support from safety-conscious managements. Analytically such an exemption would probably not be desirable, but the damage is unlikely to be great.[21]

To illustrate the allocation process and to show how it simulates an injury tax, two further stipulations are needed. Assume first that the average cost an inspection imposes upon an employer is $1,000, and second that the enforcement agency will increase the annual frequency of inspection by 0.2 for each "excess" injury—that is, each injury above what the establishment would have had if it had experienced the average rate for its industry. Under this stipulation, establishments S2 and B3, in table 7.1 would not be inspected at all. Establishments S1 and B1 would each have a one-in-five chance of being inspected during the year. S3 would have a one-in-three chance, and B2 would be certain to be inspected. (Follow-ups to check on compliance would take place in a high percentage of cases.) The marginal cost per injury imposed by this program (an implicit injury tax) would be $200.

The greatest practical difficulties with THIRE are (1) whether the costs the targeting system imposes on firms are large enough to influence their safety behavior; (2) whether the threat that employers will respond to THIRE with underreporting of injuries can be countered and (3) whether the shortcomings of THIRE for very small establishments pose insuperable problems.

Inspection Costs: Will THIRE Provide Enough Incentive?
One potential problem under the THIRE program is that the marginal costs imposed by inspections may not be large enough to induce employers to prevent injuries. If an inspection costs the employer only $100, for example, extensive programs to lower injury rates and avoid the inspection become unlikely. What are the costs of inspections to employers? First is the actual time involved in dealing with the inspector at the workplace. This cost is largely a function of the length of the inspection. California data suggests that the time spend at the inspection site averages about five hours for all nonconstruction inspections.[22] Using this figure and assuming that two management representatives (at $12 an hour) are involved the entire time and one union representative (at $8 an hour) is involved for three hours gives a total cost of $144.

One way to increase employers' incentives to prevent injuries would be to assess higher fines for violations at workplaces with relatively high injury rates. The OSH Act does explicitly require that penalties should be calculated ". . . giving due consideration . . . to the good faith of the employer, and the history of previous violations," as well as to the size of the firm.[23] Although

OSHA currently allows a maximum of 20 percent off for "good faith," a larger amount could be established. However, levying different penalties for the same violation would not be politically acceptable beyond a certain point. Recently the average OSHA penalty per inspection has risen to over $200. Under THIRE the average figure could be increased somewhat.

The third component of the monetizable costs to employers is the cost of compliance. Rather than relying on higher fines, THIRE relies chiefly on increasing the probability of detection at poorly performing workplaces. To avoid almost certain detection and fines, in many cases these firms will abate the violations before inspections. Whether undertaken before or after inspections, the cost of correcting violations is likely to stand as the employer's largest expense.

The potential weakness of THIRE is that the number of violations detected and their costliness may tend to decline sharply after the first one or two inspections.[24] Once railings, machine guards, and ventilation equipment have been installed, they are unlikely to require replacement for several years. Consequently, firms inspected in one year may have relatively little fear of being inspected the next year. Continually recurring violations—those due to inadequate maintenance, bad housekeeping, and worker resistance—do not usually require major abatement expenses.

A rough (and probably conservative) guess is that the costs to a firm with 100 to 200 workers would average about $1,000 per inspection, including $600 or $700 for compliance costs. The profit-maximizing firm should be willing to pay up to $1,000 to avoid a near-term threat of a certain inspection. Whatever the actual magnitudes are, the costs per worker would almost certainly be larger for small establishments than for big ones. Since small establishments currently have relatively weak incentives for safety (at least to the extent that they tend to be part of small firms and subject to only a limited degree of experience rating under workers' compensation), that bias may be advantageous. The precise targeting formula can be adjusted to give the desired emphasis, whether on small, medium, or larger establishments.[25]

No description of the costs of OSHA inspections to employers would be complete if it included only financial costs. Employers don't like to post citations which remind employees about the violations. They don't like inspectors to order them around, and they don't like the uncertainty surrounding inspections. They also would not like any publicity attendant upon having a high injury rate. Safety directors generally share these sentiments, with the additional problem of professional embarrassment at getting a citation.[26] All of these factors—most of which are present in the current enforcement program—operate in THIRE and help augment the purely financial incentives for firms to reduce their rates.

The Threat of Underreporting

Under any plan where an outside authority penalizes employers for workers' injuries, firms may respond either by reducing actual injuries or by reducing reports of injuries. For this reason, the main criterion for choosing the measure of safety performance has to be its susceptibility to underreporting.

Unfortunately, the only national reporting system, the one established by the OSH Act, performs poorly by this criterion. Not only are employers still uncertain about the meaning of the reporting definitions, but more importantly, the reports aren't used for any purpose that would encourage full reporting. In contrast, most firms do have something to lose by failing to report injuries to their workers' compensation insurers. Consequently, the best measure of safety performance derive from reports filed under state workers' compensation programs. While use of these reports can limit underreporting, it cannot halt it.

One problem arises with self-insured firms (which employ about 10 to 20 percent of all workers), which lack any financial incentive to report. More generally, consider the situation with an inspection program that imposes a marginal tax rate of $200 per injury. The financial incentives would favor reporting only when $(I-X)L>\$200$, where L is the amount of losses compensated by the insurer of medical expenses and losttime indemnity, and X is the percentage of those losses that will be added to the employer's future insurance premiums—a figure that depends upon the extent of experience rating for that employer, which, in turn, partly depends upon the size of the firm's payroll. For a large firm, X might be 80 percent; in that case the firm would have an incentive to report only when the compensable loss exceeded $1,000. Even for an employer too small to be experience rated (and thus for whom $X=0$), the expected payments by the insurer would have to exceed $200 before an injury became worth reporting. Clearly, in order to guarantee full reporting, the financial incentives to report injuries that workers' compensation provides must be supplemented.

Fortunately, tools are available within most state WC programs for combating most of the forms that underreporting can take. However, effective use of these tools will probably require additional staff and, in some states, legislative increases in penalties for underreporting.[27] The need for a substantial auditing effort to enforce the reporting requirement should not be surprising. After all, if a system is designed to work like a tax, it will need an auditing arm as surely as the Internal Revenue Service does. Precautions may be unnecessary, but unless such an auditing program exists when inspections based on establishment data begin, we will have no way of knowing the nature of underreporting. Evaluationg the effects of these plans on safety performance also requires having a way to measure the extent of underreporting.

Inclusion of Small Establishments

Because the costs imposed by inspections will loom larger for small establishments than for large ones, THIRE can have its greatest effect on smaller ones—but only if they are large enough to be included in the program. The problem under THIRE is that very small establishments simply have too little injury experience to allow valid rankings to be established.

Most establishments are small. Even in manufacturing, where they tend to be larger, two-thirds of California establishments have fewer than 20 employees.[28] However, even though the large establishments are few in number, they include the great bulk of workers and injuries. With an average injury rate of 5 percent and with one year of injury data, it is probably reasonable to restrict a THIRE scheme to establishments with 50 or more employees. In California manufacturing, that would include about 5,000 establishments (17 percent of the total) and about 80 percent of the workers. In other sectors with lower rates and fewer large workplaces, a smaller proportion of workers would be covered.

One way to increase the coverage is to base the performance rankings on more than one year's injury experience. This step would have the drawback that firms would not be able to change their rankings as quickly and thus might not respond as much to the incentives for change, although the difference would probably not be great enough to outweigh the advantages of more injury experience. Consequently, although states may begin with only one year's injury data, they should try to add one or two more as they proceed.

Perhaps for the very small firms, those with fewer than 10 or 20 employees, a system of random inspections should be used to maintain a deterrent. An alternative would be to rely upon an intensive program of accident investigations so that small firms would learn that serious injuries bring inspections. If he found that the employer had a poor safety program, the inspector could recommend that the employer seek help from the state's consultation program.

Assessing THIRE

How THIRE compares with the status quo depends partly upon which variant of THIRE is examined. I will choose one in which establishments with better-than-average safety performance are exempted from inspections.

The status quo relies almost entirely on detection of violations that cause injuries, along with a very small deterrent from the threat of inspection. For THIRE the treatment depends upon the establishment's ranking within its industry. For establishments with injury rates above the industry average, THIRE adds the implicit tax to the detection program. For establishments below the average but not so far below that they don't need to worry about exceeding it, detection is eliminated, but the new incentive is introduced. Finally, for establishments so far below the average that exceeding it is very improbable, neither actual inspections nor the threat of inspections will be present (except that complaint and accident investigations will continue).

Effectiveness Very likely THIRE would be less effective than the status quo among the lowest injury rate establishments in each industry. Inspectors would no longer be searching for the small class of violations that cause injuries, while the incentives created by the taxlike component of THIRE wouldn't extend to these workplaces. For the establishments below the average but still in danger of exceeding it, it is uncertain whether the addition of incentives to reduce all injuries would outweigh the loss of the detection mechanism. For establishments with above-average rates, THIRE will certainly be more effective. First, the overall number of inspections made at these establishments will grow, increasing the detection effect. Second, the taxlike mechanism gives an added incentive to prevent all injuries. The overall result will almost surely be an increase in effectiveness, especially since the very low rate establishments presumably have relatively good safety programs and thus relatively few injuries caused by detectable violations.[29]

Cost-Effectiveness Compared with the status quo, the cost-effectiveness of THIRE for the lowest-rate establishments is uncertain; the effects will probably be smaller, but the costs of compliance will undoubtedly shrink as well. For the middle group, the substitution of incentives for detection means that whatever injury reductions occur as a result of OSHA will be achieved at a lower cost per injury. For the poorer-performing establishments, the cost-effectiveness will also be greater because the current detection program will be combined with the more efficient taxlike incentives. Overall, it is very likely that THIRE would be more cost-effective than the status quo.[30]

Fairness Part of THIRE's appeal is that the treatment that firms are

accorded by OSHA will be partly determined by their own safety performance. As in any administrative scheme, arbitrary decisions are legion (like
choosing the cut-off points for inspection probabilities), and some mistakes
are inevitable (like placing a firm in the wrong industry group for comparative
purposes.)

Adoption Feasibility THIRE promises to be a politically popular proposal
because it concentrates inspections on the firms with poor safety records.
Firms will no longer be able to complain that OSHA cited them even though
they had not had any injuries in ten years. Politicians, as well as administrators, should appreciate the broader scope and increased potential impact
THIRE provides. As long as complaint inspections are not curtailed, labor
unions will have no reason to oppose THIRE. Firms with good safety records
will benefit relative to firms with bad ones. The poor public image of the
latter will hamper any attempts to oppose the adoption of THIRE.

One drawback of THIRE from the perspective of OSHA's administrators is
that it must be established in a piecemeal fashion, requiring more administrative work, and depends upon the cooperation of various state officials, restricting OSHA's freedom of maneuver. Outright opposition could come
from some state workers' compensation and statistical agencies, which might
oppose the use of employers' or doctors' reports for enforcement purposes.
Lower-level enforcement officials also might object to a system that deprives
them of discretion about which workplaces to inspect.

Implementation Feasibility Because it depends upon a well-functioning
injury reporting system, THIRE can only be implemented in states that
already have one. The current status of these systems would probably prevent
more than about twelve to fifteen states (including California, New York,
Wisconsin, and the seven states with monopolistic WC systems) from having
operational THIRE programs within the next two years.

In "state plan" states, OSHA can probably only encourage states to adopt
THIRE, not order them to do it. But since most state agency officials face
pressures similar to those OSHA officials face, THIRE should be attractive to
most of them for the same reasons. In states where OSHA runs the enforcement program, it must negotiate with the states to gain access to the injury
data, a process that could be full of pitfalls.

The work of calculating rates and auditing reports will require additional
funds, presenting a potential stumbling block. The need for extra funds gives
outsiders (members of congressional appropriations committees or their state
legislative counterparts) an opportunity to exert leverage on OSHA. Another

hurdle related to the auditing effort would be the attempt to seek legislation to allow higher penalties for nonreporting.

Conclusion

Assessing the potential effects of the alternatives I have described involves considerable uncertainty. For example, the effectiveness of a deterrence mechanism depends upon how employers perceive it, but the relation between perception and reality is not clear. Despite this kind of problem, it does seem worthwhile to rank the proposals that have been discussed. In the following evaluation matrix, the rankings on the substantive criteria (public cost-effectiveness, social cost-effectiveness, and fairness) are based upon a comparison with the status quo. Thus = indicates that the ranking is the same as the status quo, + that it is better, ++ that it is better yet, and so on (see table 7.2).

The matrix shows that, on the substantive criteria, accident investigation with wall-to-wall inspection (option 2) is dominated by THIRE. Pure accident investigation (option 1) appears to be the most socially cost-effective because it wouldn't require compliance except for violations that contributed to injuries, but the magnitude of its potential effect on injuries remains unclear. Option 2 dominates the feasibility criteria. THIRE, while popular, would face substantial implementation difficulties. Option 1 would be easy to implement, but skepticism about its effectiveness makes its adoption more problematic.

How should OSHA and state enforcement agencies proceed to make the best use of this analysis? Since the assessments are uncertain, the procedures should be experimental. Although effectiveness is hard to pin down, estimates of social costs are even harder to make. Because of this difference, it makes sense to assume that the social-cost rankings are accurate and to test the effectiveness judgments. For example, as the matrix shows, the analysis indicated that option 1 would be more cost-effective than the status quo. If field

Table 7.2 Evaluation matrix for safety alternatives

Alternative	Public cost effectiveness	Social cost effectiveness	Fairness	Adoption feasibility	Implementation feasibility
AI: Option 1	?	++++	=	Low	Med.-High
AI: Option 2	+	+	=	Med.-High	Med.-High
THIRE	++	++	=	Med.-High	Med.-Low

experiments show that it is no less effective than the status quo, then it should be preferred. Of course, when no alternative is preferable to another on all criteria, policymakers must choose what weights to assign the criteria.

While only a field test can resolve questions about the effectiveness of the alternatives, further study can go a long way toward refining the assessments of feasibility. For example, THIRE must overcome the serious threat of underreporting, its limitations for small establishments, and the need to co-ordinate OSHA's use of state data. Success depends largely on the quality of state WC data systems and the willingness and ability of enforcement agencies to use them. These factors should be the subject of an implementation study.

Even a finding that one proposal dominated all the others would not neces-sarily justify the total exclusion of the alternatives. However, in view of the miniscule effects OSHA has had in the past, it would be optimistic to expect field experiments to tell us what the ideal mix of inspection types would be. Regardless of the field experiment results, it would probably be wise to main-tain at least a small capability to carry out every type of inspection—accident investigations, seeking out certain detectable hazards, and putting pressure on the bad apples.[31]

Evaluation and Research with Establishment Injury Data

Despite their pretensions, none of these proposals is guaranteed to work. Un-less they are evaluated in the field, no one will know whether they do work. The assumption that evaluations can be helpful clearly requires them to be designed to ward off major threats to the validity of the findings. Carrying out such powerful evaluations is not easy. Certainly, the alternatives should be implemented in a manner that facilitates the evaluation. In practice, this means trying certain plans in some geographical areas but not in others.

As an alternative or supplement, time-series models like the one developed in chapter 6 can be used to generate predicted injury rates. If the inspection policy deals only with standards-related injuries (the AI options), the test would compare the actual and predicted number of standards-related injuries. If the policy focused on establishments with high overall injury rates (THIRE), then the evaluation would be more complicated. First, any fall in injury rates could be due to underreporting, which must be either stopped or measured. Second, no simple comparison of targeted and nontargeted establishments can be relied upon because there is no way to measure the size of the regres-sion effect (which ensures that firms chosen because of their high rates will tend, on average, to have relatively lower rates the next year). The evaluation must rely first on seeing whether the targeted district's injury rate is lower than predicted (or lower than that of a control district) and second on whether the reduction has come from a compression in the high-rate tail of the distribution of establishments. Only if both conditions were met could we have real confidence that the policy of targeting high injury rate establishments deserved credit for any reduction in injuries.[32]

8
Reforming Standard Setting

How satisfactorily OSHA policymakers set standards depends on the quality of information available to them and on the strength of their incentives to give balanced consideration to both benefits and costs. In this chapter I will explore whether any politically feasible procedures could be adopted that would be likely to lead to better OSH standards. My discussion is guided by five major points.

First, OSHA policymakers should acknowledge that standards have costs as well as benefits and that a standard should be adopted only if in some sense the benefits exceed the costs. Any sound decision involves trade-offs. If these trade-offs are not made explicitly, they will be made implicitly.

Second, OSHA is not set up very well for giving balanced consideration to benefits and costs. Its legislative mandate, the professional backgrounds of its top officials, and the institutional and political milieux in which it must operate all draw attention away from costs and focus it on effects, but they oppose efforts to put a price tag on them.

Third, the lack of data about the potential costs and effects of compliance with standards introduces great uncertainty into the decision process. When formal benefit-cost analysis is considered, additional problems appear: the analytic difficulty of finding an operational method for determining the value workers (and others) place upon risk reduction on the job and the political and moral opposition to setting any value upon the saving of a life.

Fourth, the same lack of information that perplexes standard setters also hampers anyone who tries to evaluate their output. Thus no one knows for sure whether OSHA standards have actually generated net benefits or net costs. One is left only with the strong hunch that the factors cited in the second point, along with the procedures OSHA has adopted, are likely to create overly protective standards. For example, consensus standards are likely to present some of the most flagrant cases of overprotection simply because they were adopted without any attempt to assess their costs and effects.

Fifth, OSHA's concern with costs appears to vary considerably from one standard to another. The variation is related to distinctions between safety and health, fatal and nonfatal effects, small affected groups and large ones. While these distinctions can find some justification in either analytical or popular thinking, it is difficult to know exactly how much of the variation is justified.

These five points do not necessarily imply that OSHA's standard-setting behavior has been irrational. Even if we agreed that we would be materially better off if decision makers applied a strict benefit-cost criterion, we might find the process of applying it so distasteful that we would prefer to forego the advantages. The act's legislative mandate and the views of OSHA's administrators do appear to express this sort of feeling. The aversion to valuing lives has special force in the OSH area for three main reasons: first, the worker is not perceived as choosing his risks as freely as the typical consumer does; second, often the potential victims are in a relatively small, identifiable group; and third, organized labor is ready and able to make a political issue out of the valuation question.

Certainly OSHA policymakers should be encouraged to weigh the costs and benefits, but practically that must be done through procedures that are acceptable to them and to the other central actors. Proposals to improve standard setting should emphasize benefit-cost as a way of thinking rather than trying to give it a formal and prominent role. In practice, this means that formal procedures should, I think, be limited to a more thorough and explicit treatment of costs and effects but not benefits. Before specifying how this should be done, I will review some of the alternatives to this modest change.

First, we might consider what sort of changes in OSHA's political and bureaucratic environment would be necessary to alter the way in which trade offs are considered. Changing the congressional committees with jurisdiction over OSHA to ones less closely tied to organized labor would be one example of a step toward changing the political climate in which the agency operates. A shift in the partisan balance in Congress might lead to adoption of some of the proposed OSH Act amendments requiring the explicit use of a benefit-cost criterion, yet in the absence of detailed rules for carrying out these analyses such a change in OSHA's mandate would leave its discretion almost intact.

Organizational shifts might also lead to changes in behavior. If OSHA were transferred into the Commerce Department, its concern with safety might well be sacrificed to that department's dominant interest in economic growth as well as to its political ties to business. Somewhat less plausibly, if other safety agencies were transferred into the Labor Department, its leaders might feel more need to develop methods to rationalize decision making and develop common criteria to ensure that the agencies behaved in a similar fashion.[1]

Certainly neither the bureaucratic nor the political changes are at all likely—nor are they necessarily desirable—but they indicate the kind of steps that would be required to alter the present constraints on OSHA's behavior.

Another approach would be to replace OSHA's top officials, most of whom have backgrounds in the health and safety professions, with economists who have been benefit-cost practitioners and who are more likely to believe that the valuation of death and disability represents progress. I do not think, however, that it would be wise to enshrine efficiency in too preeminent a place. Any attempt to shift the professional balance would also meet strong political opposition from the labor movement as well as from the other professions displaced.[2]

It would also make little sense to have OSHA adopt decision rules like those used in the water resources field. Under the terms of the Flood Control Act of 1936, the benefits of all approved projects must exceed their costs. That stipulation meant relatively little until the early 1950s, when federal task forces specified the exact methodology to be used for calculating benefits and costs. With regard to OSHA, there is no analytical consensus on a workable method for valuing lifesaving, and even if there were, it would encounter withering political attack. An explicit benefit-cost requirement may help restrain the excesses of political logrolling in the water resource field, but it won't work for OSHA.

Several less extreme alternatives remain: the status quo; requiring benefit-cost studies for advisory purposes; and requiring cost-effectiveness studies for advisory purposes. The status quo is characterized not only by the absence of any explicit decision rules, but also by the failure to set out data in a way that would help clarify the issues involved. Each standard's project officer does try to gather information about its effects, but he rarely presents any judgment about the likely potential impact on injuries or illnesses of the proposed change in the standard. Similarly, for health standards NIOSH estimates whether any health effects will occur (such as at what exposure levels rats or humans become ill), but it never tries to gauge the impact in terms of lives saved or diseases prevented. Although the dearth of data does severely crimp attempts to assess the impact of standards, more could be done with the information that is available.

The Office of Standards Development (OSD) does carry out some studies of costs and has contracted for cost and cost-effectiveness studies, usually when industry has complained loudly about costs. Since inflationary impact statements have been required, consultants have been producing more elaborate studies of costs and of the impact of compliance on the industry and the economy. Most of these cost studies give point estimates rather than indicating the uncertainty that besets any calculation of this type.

Another option is for OSHA to contract for independent benefit-cost studies of its standards. This step would take the heat off the agency, and it would also allow economists to compete in figuring out new and better ways to measure benefits. For the same reason, however, it would make comparisons among standards more difficult. Such benefit-cost studies also might focus attention on the controversial valuation techniques rather than on the underlying figures about costs and effects. Moreover, unless the techniques are understood and the numerous assumptions they make are acceptable, the benefit estimates are unlikely to be taken seriously.

A more straightforward approach would be for OSHA officials simply to announce that each life saved would be valued at X amount and each day of disability prevented at Y amount. Yet such a valuation procedure would not only be politically dangerous, it would also be much too crude. Neither economic reasoning nor popular values condone placing the same value on lifesaving under all circumstances; known individuals facing high risks rate higher than "statistical" individuals facing low risks; thirty-year-olds facing imminent death probably rate higher than sixty-five-year-olds facing death in ten years.[3] But for OSHA to try to specify the rules for making these comparisons would lead even deeper into the political and analytical thickets.

Cost-effectiveness studies also must make questionable assumptions, of course, so that the analytical difference is one of degree rather than of kind. The complaint that can be lodged against cost-effectiveness studies is that they don't provide sufficient grounds for making decisions, but neither do benefit-cost studies, unless all of the relevant considerations can be satisfactorily expressed in dollars. Since this is not the case, the objection loses much of its force.

What needs to be done is to encourage decision makers to acknowledge the trade-offs they are making on standards and give outsiders a way of intelligently appraising their decisions. Even though the X and Y valuation formula would be rigid and obviously imperfect, we don't really know whether the resulting decisions would be inferior to those reached under a more flexible, discretionary cost-effectiveness approach. Yet since the latter would encounter less (although still substantial) political opposition, it presents a more promising framework for reform. Specifically, the most reasonable practice would be to require OSHA to publish its estimates of the range of costs over time and of effects over time in both its proposals and promulgations (or revocations) of standards. The use of ranges, rather than point estimates, acknowledges the uncertainty inherent in these calculations;

one would hope that when the range is large some estimate of the probabilities for different parts of the range could be included.[4]

Better decision making requires better data as well as the incentive to make use of it. One potential source of better information about the potential effects of safety standards is the data generated by some state workers' compensation programs. For example, the main source of information cited in OSHA hearings on safety standards is frequently the State of California. However, the data cited are often not helpful to standard setters because they are not precise enough to identify the impact of particular marginal changes. Since standard setting is primarily a federal responsibility, no state has the incentive to develop such a precise information base. An obvious case exists for federal subsidy for the expansion of data collection and analysis in some of the states that already have a good base from which to work.[5] Such a subsidy, whether it involved contracting with the states or setting up federal units to work with them, seems preferable to establishing a totally new data system.

Each year NIOSH and OSHA could determine which safety measures would be likely to come up for review during the upcoming year or two. An interdisciplinary team "piggybacked" on a state WC data system could then decide how to compile the precise information needed. For example, suppose a standard would require a certain hood for grinding operations. Using a review of WC reports on grinding injuries, site visits, telephone interviews, and other methods, the team could provide much better answers to questions like, Did injuries occur at any of the machines already meeting the contemplated standard? How many of the injuries would have been prevented if all grinders had such equipment? What were the costs of installing the equipment? A survey of employers could also lead to estimated injury rates for grinders with and without the equipment.

One reason for the importance of the development of these units is that no counterpart to NIOSH currently exists in the area of safety. OSHA is much more dependent on industry in the area of safety than in health for information about both costs and effects. Even though firms usually have better incentives to provide proper safety measures than they do with health measures, the "public goods" dimension of safety research and information practically guarantees that private-sector research into these issues will be undersupplied to society.

What would it take to get these recommendations implemented? Does OSHA have any incentive to adopt them? For the proposal to gather more information about safety standards from the states, the answer is almost surely yes. Other things being equal, standard setters would prefer to know more about the potential effects of their actions. Better information from this source would reduce OSHA's dependence on industry and enable it to give a better technical justification for its decisions on safety standards.

However loosely it is done, explicit treatment of costs and effects would facilitate the development of an OSHA policy for valuing safety and health measures and for choosing among them. The advantages are that OSHA's reputation as a responsible regulator may be enhanced and that its officials will not have to start from scratch with each new standard. Under the new system, if a standard with a certain set of costs and effects was rejected (or accepted) last year, and another one with a similar set comes up this year, then OSHA will have some guidance about how to act. (It could, of course, still rule differently in the two cases.)

Such greater explicitness has its disadvantages. By requiring OSHA officials to clarify some of the key issues, it may subject their decisions to more informed criticism, forcing them to justify their exercise of discretion. In addition, to the extent that the security of the agency or its leaders requires that decisions be made on essentially political grounds, the figures on costs and effects may hinder attempts to mask political influence. However, the political pressures on OSHA have been indirect, and the range of discretion open to OSHA officials would almost certainly allow a necessary modicum of political responsiveness. Probably the most important difference that emphasis on costs and effects would make is that business and labor groups would be forced to pay more attention to the trade-offs in their own arguments.

In the absence of any strong push, OSHA officials are, I think, not likely to become more explicit about cost-effectiveness. Aside from their concern about discretion, they would be wary of organized labor's reaction. Labor leaders would correctly perceive such a move as potentially reducing OSHA's tendency to view any significant lifesaving measure as worthwhile. Union influence over the congressional labor committees makes the legislature an unlikely source for the needed push. That leaves the White House. For OSHA it would be salutary to exchange the executive order requiring inflationary impact statements for one requiring cost-effectiveness statements to be prepared for each standard.[6] Although standards whose impacts are likely to be greater should receive greater attention, it seems unwise to exempt any decision on a standard from this scrutiny.

9

Analyzing OSHA: A Summing Up

No one appears to be very happy with the Occupational Safety and Health Administration. Business groups deride it for enforcing picayune or irrelevant safety standards. Large firms direct most of their criticisms at OSHA's alleged failures to look at the costs as well as the benefits of compliance with its regulations. Organized labor chides OSHA for not providing adequate enforcement—for penalties that are too small and inspections that are too infrequent—and for setting new standards at so slow a pace that millions of workers are left unprotected.

Some OSHA officials have tried to dismiss this cross fire as the normal product of any controversial labor-management legislation; some have even interpreted it as a tribute; "If both sides are complaining, we must be doing something right." But even if these defenses do have some validity, a serious assessment of OSHA's performance must probe much more deeply. How strong is the rationale for the government invervention authorized by the OSH Act? To what extent have choices about how to implement the act kept it from fulfilling its potential? What has OSHA actually accomplished in terms of preventing injuries and illnesses, and how has it performed by other criteria? All these questions lead up to the practical issues of how safety and health policy can be improved.

Arguments for Federal Action

The economic case for public intervention rests mainly on the grounds that employers are not forced to bear all the costs of injuries and hence will not consider all the benefits of injury prevention. Economic theory relies on workers to force the employer to bear the full cost of injuries by requiring him to pay them higher wages for accepting greater risks. While evidence exists that risk premiums are often paid, there is no particular reason to believe that the labor market works so well that the premiums accurately measure the value workers place on risk reductions. Moreover, even if there were such a reason, it would still not justify an acceptance of market results. Only the most extreme individualist would deny that a worker's family and friends should be considered (and they will not necessarily be fully taken into account by the worker himself). A more difficult issue is posed by the value placed on safer work conditions by people who have no direct or material relation to the affected workers. Certainly these people exist. We would not see charitable contributions or "public-regarding" voting patterns if they did not. Business leaders realize that the argument that consumers would not be willing to pay higher product prices to make workplaces safer is not credible;

partly for that reason, they make their pitch about compliance costs along a different line, emphasizing plant closings and the loss of jobs.

Some economists view "public-regardingness" with a wary eye. Substantively, it smacks of paternalism; methodologically, it pushes the almost impossible task of deducing the social willingness to pay over the brink of rational analysis. The preferences of the workers themselves must not be casually overridden, but as Arthur Okun has pointed out, laws like the OSH Act appear to be based on the view that "anyone who takes an . . . extremely risky job must be acting out of desperation. That desperation may result from ignorance, immobility, or genuine lack of alternatives, but it should be kept out of the marketplace. . . . With these bans, society assumes a commitment to provide jobs that are not excessively risky. . . ."[1] The assumptions underlying this view are, at most, only partly valid. Although it may be true in some cases, desperation is almost certainly not the main cause of risk taking at work. Of course, even if these cases of subtle coercion are few in number, we might be willing to restrict risk taking as a means of protection.[2]

The assumption about ignorance certainly has some validity. In dealing with health hazards, workers (and their employers) frequently don't know what they are working with or whether it can be harmful; if they do know that, they often don't know at what exposure levels it becomes harmful, and even if they do, they will usually not know what their actual exposures are. Of course, rather than requiring compliance with standards, the government could substitute a purely informational strategy, providing workers and employers with all the pertinent information and letting them work out their own solutions. However, even if we were willing to let the level of protection be determined partly by the distribution of bargaining power, government standards might be preferred in the belief that the losses from overriding preferences at some workplaces would be smaller than the losses at others from failing to convey information properly. Legal standards, like telegrams, are more likely to be read.

Many writers have argued that because workers know more about safety hazards than about health hazards, the case for public standards is greater for the latter. This conclusion is right, but the reasoning is wrong. Although many safety hazards are recognizable, calculating that a given hazard will cause an accident is likely to be no easier for workers than calculating the probability of contracting lead poisoning or asbestosis. The relevant difference for regulatory purposes is that experts know a great deal more about health hazards than workers do but not much more about safety hazards. One implication is that if safety researchers were able to make any breakthroughs in the study of accident causation, the arguments for safety standards would be as strong as those for health standards.

A persuasive rationale for new public action depends upon a display not only of defects in the private market but also of inadequacies in the existing public programs established to remedy those defects. The effect of workers' compensation on safety incentives depends on assumptions about the incidence of the insurance premiums. Under the most realistic assumptions, higher premiums do create the potential for added safety, but the size of the premiums makes a difference only if the employer can reduce them by preventing accidents. Probably the most important shortcoming of workers' compensation is the limited extent to which premiums are experience-rated, adjusted to reflect each employer's actual loss experience. For smaller firms, large reductions in losses will reduce their premiums by only a small amount. Another major fault with WC programs in many states is that occupational diseases are not fully covered.

The state OSH programs that existed before OSHA are easy to criticize. Eight lacked any health component, and many others had very skimpy ones. Many and probably most failed to apply tough penalties even against firms that failed to correct serious violations. Generally, state programs failed to allow workers to participate in the enforcement process. They were not allowed to accompany the inspector and not informed of the inspection results, even those bearing on their own exposure to hazardous materials. Finally, neither the states nor the federal government had conducted substantial research into workplace hazards despite the socially inadequate incentives for private sponsorship of research.

By 1970 some labor union leaders had become worried about the possibility of occupational disease epidemics. They feared that unions had neither the technical capability nor the bargaining power to deal with this threat. They wanted a national program because they believed that state agencies would always wilt under the threat that industry would leave and also because they felt that it made better sense for standards to be set nationally and enforced uniformly. Moreover, the unions had more clout in Washington and could do a more effective job of monitoring the program's performance. They also wanted procedures that would allow local unions to monitor the enforcement. And although they certainly wanted tough enforcement, they also wanted to protect workers for whom enforcement could entail plant shutdowns, unwanted personal protective equipment, or job-threatening medical exams.

But these interests in policy change did not lead to legislative action until certain catalysts had begun to work. Ralph Nader began to hammer at union leaders for their failings. A new coal mine disaster and the grass roots movement to win benefits for the victims of black lung disease sensitized legislators to the potential public costs of occupational disease and union leaders to the issue's capacity to spur rank and file insurgency. Finally, the decision of the president of the Steelworkers Union to assert his leadership guaranteed that the issue would become a top legislative priority.

Most of the issues I have referred to were mentioned in the legislative hearings and debate on the OSH Act, but almost always in a superficial, cursory style. Instead, the debate focused upon whether greedy employers or careless workers deserved the blame for most injuries and illnesses. The most heatedly debated provisions of the act dealt with the location of authority. The unions and most Democrats wanted standard setting, enforcement, and the authority to rule on employers' appeals all to be vested within the Labor Department. Business groups and most Republicans wanted both the first and third functions assigned to independent commissions. Although their arguments were couched in terms of separation of powers and due process, the desire for separation rested largely on a fear of organized labor's influence in the Labor Department.

The Legislative Process: The Choice of Standards Enforcement as a Safety Strategy

The failure of legislators to grapple with the more complex analytic issues can perhaps best be illustrated and explained by examining the reasons for the legislative choice of the enforcement of standards as the method for reducing workplace injuries. The standards-enforcement strategy has several weaknesses as a method for preventing injuries. First, most workplace injuries are not caused by violations of standards, and even fewer are caused by violations that inspectors can detect. Consequently, the potential impact of a standards-enforcement approach is quite limited compared with one (like taxes on injuries) that offers general incentives to prevent injuries.[3] Second, good standards require an enormous amount of information about the value of a certain safeguard in thousands of different circumstances; the employer will often understand the risks involved as well or better than OSHA does. Third, even when accidents are standards-related and the standards are worthwhile, compliance with them may not be the cheapest means of preventing injuries. Perhaps more training or some other physical safeguard would be preferable.

Despite these disadvantages, the standards approach was adopted without any hestiation. No one suggested that it shouldn't be, and no one suggested any alternative. One reason was that the first bills had originated in the federal agency with responsibility for enforcing most existing federal safety standards. Even though the enforcement of those standards had relied on education rather than penalties—and thus had really not demanded compliance at all—the agency was committed to standards as the means of regulation, as were all the state enforcement agencies. Labor unions as well as Nader's group saw standards as necessary components of an OSH program and criticized only their weak enforcement and the industry domination of the standard-setting process. The unions were not uninterested in directly altering the costs of injuries to employers. They simply saw it as something to be achieved by federal pressure on state workers' compensation programs to raise their benefit levels.

Some writers have suggested that the absence of economists on congressional committee staffs helps explain why efficiency is rarely considered, but the real question is why economists are absent in the first place. The political environment usually accords efficiency concerns little weight; neither economists nor efficiency are in great demand. Thus the recent suggestion from some economists that an injury tax be substituted for the enforcement of safety standards was never put forward during the legislative debate. The injury tax idea has some attractive analytic features. It applies to all injuries and allows firms to find the cheapest means to reduce them. But if an injury tax had been proposed during that debate, it would have come under devastating attack, both for the methods it employs and for those it fails to employ.

For unions, a tax is too automatic. It would fail to provide them the opportunities to make special cases to the secretary of labor about the particular problems in their industries. Replacing the hearings on standards would be a single critical decision—how high to set the tax rate. Unions correctly fear that in that context emotional arguments would tend to lose out to financial arguments. A substitution of a tax for standards would also deprive unions of their ability to call in an inspector or, equally important, threaten to call in an inspector. Since the standards are so detailed, violations are commonplace, and the threat of inspection can give a local union extra bargaining leverage with management, whether in the safety area or in some other. Finally, some of the cheap methods the tax might encourage employers to adopt might be viewed as antiworker—firing workers for violations of safety rules or transferring workers who have had several accidents.

Politicians also see tax approaches as too automatic. Those involved with OSHA, especially the subcommittee chairmen (who, of course, have the most to say about it), play important roles in communicating union or management views on standards and in serving their grievances about enforcement. Popular perceptions also must weigh heavily in legislative thinking, and it is clear that just as the effluent tax got tagged by opponents as a "license to pollute," so an injury tax would raise the specter of a license to maim. The public often views tax mechanisms as too passive; the legislators should "do something" about bad practices, namely stamp them out rather than merely discourage them.

More fundamentally, one should not expect the Congressional decision-making process to accord with the analytic ideal of reviewing policy options to see which rank highest in achieving specified objectives. Politicians are more interested in finding issues that meet their political needs than in finding policies that meet analytic needs. As Mayhew and others have persuasively argued, for politicians the costs of analytic failure are very low.[4] Thus the task of constructing policies designed to meet the stated objectives is left in the hands of the private or public organizations who are the chief advocates of action. But these organizations usually care as much or more about the methods used to pursue the objectives as they do about the objectives themselves.

Business leaders might have been expected to think up or at least support an injury tax proposal, since it would free firms from the obligation to comply with standards they felt were irrelevant. However, the fact remains that all of the initial tax burden would be placed on business without, for example, any offsetting reduction in other business taxes. Although the social costs of prevention would probably be reduced with an injury tax, the costs to firms would probably not be. Finally, firms may fear that the tax mechanism might metamorphose from a way to prevent injuries into another handy source of public revenue.

The choice of the standards-enforcement strategy was only one of the legislative decisions that established the framework of regulation. In a departure from the usual bill-writing process on labor bills, outsiders to the labor movement—representatives of Ralph Nader—joined in with the unions and the committee staff. The Nader people helped to give the law its "get tough with employers" aura. The government was allowed to cite employers for violations, placing the burden of appeal on them and making it administratively feasible to levy frequent fines. The Nader influence also appears in the emphasis given to asserting workers' rights to information.

The standard-setting function was placed in the Labor Department along with enforcement, but a separate three-member commission (the OSH Review Commission) was set up to hear appeals. The law allowed OSHA to start off by adopting all the occupational safety and health standards promulgated under other federal laws or produced by private consensus standard-setting organizations. It was intentionally vague about the criteria for choosing how protective new standards should be; there was no explicit mention of the proper role of economic considerations.

The Implementation of the OSH Act

Legislation may set the framework of regulation, but almost invariably enough discretion is left to the administrators to allow them to decide what the edifice will look like. The economist's traditional marginal social cost and benefit curves, which delineate the potential net social benefits, need to be supplemented by a set of lines that represent the universe of regulatory choices. The following discussion of key issues and choices in the implementation of the OSH Act provides some tentative answers to questions like, Do regulators have enough information to distinguish good choices from bad ones? What incentives do they have to make the good ones? In standard setting, the issues are the en masse adoption of the preexisting consensus standards without any examination of their worth and, more generally, the treatment accorded to economic concerns in setting new standards. In the enforcement process, the issues are the emphasis on safety inspections despite the stronger case for government action on health hazards, the inadequately thought-through system of targeting inspections, and the rigid requirement that costly engineering controls always be the method used to abate health hazards. These issues all bear upon the effectiveness and efficiency of the OSHA program. They are examined here because any attempts to rectify their defects must be based upon an understanding of the political and organizational pressures that determined the choices that were made. Although effectiveness and efficiency are not the only criteria for evaluating the OSH Act, they are especially likely to be neglected in the political process.

Adoption of the Consensus Standards

OSHA's adoption of all the privately established consensus standards, without any review of their efficacy of costs, forced employers to comply with thousands of provisions that had been developed as models of the "best practice" in safety engineering. The choice to adopt all of them was a product of the statutory language, the administrative impossibility of examining the cost-effectiveness of more than a handful of standards, and a political environment that made compromise very difficult.

The statute required the adoption of all the standards unless OSHA could show that they were not needed to protect particular groups of workers. Business leaders had opened themselves up to this provision by proclaiming almost unanimously that consensus standards were already widely accepted by industry. Instead of deflecting the pressure for regulation, that proclamation made the adoption of the consensus standards seem like a reasonable *minimum* step.

The statutory language was drafted expressly to extirpate any potential for administrative delay or omissions. As Gary Sellers, one of the drafters, stated, "We tried to squeeze out every drop of discretion."[5] Lacking the staff or the data to build cases against many standards, OSHA chief Guenther chose to adopt all of them with thirty days, rather than use the two years the act allowed. He hoped to use whatever goodwill his promptness created to win a delay in the actual date at which the standards became effective. Faced by the prospect of political and legal opposition from the unions, Guenther probably could not have chosen a fundamentally different course.

The Treatment of Costs and Benefits in Standard Setting

During OSHA's first five years, the promulgation of new standards has been so infrequent that the agency's basic impact has derived from its enforcement of preexisting standards. However, the effects of new standards will obviously grow.

Congress was silent on the question of what weight to give economic considerations in the standard-setting process, with only an unelaborated reference to the criterion of "feasibility." The unions had not wanted any clearer reference, but in any event congressmen were not anxious to take responsibility for this morally and politically controversial issue. Court decisions and the White House have since made it clear to OSHA that the economic impact of standards must be considered. But the import of these messages is blunted, first by the uncertainty that pervades all estimates of these matters and second by the unwillingness of either intervenor to tell OSHA how it should calculate the benefits. The reluctance of politicians to get caught "playing politics with safety" leaves OSHA officials with considerable discretion, but they must still be wary of going too far in one direction or another and upsetting the delicate political support the agency enjoys.

How have OSHA officials used that discretion? When dealing with carcinogens, they have chosen to set the lowest exposure limit that was technically feasible, without much regard for the costs. OSHA has usually accepted the exposure levels suggested by NIOSH, which determines them purely on the basis of health criteria. However, on nonfatal hazards—punch presses, noise—OSHA had demonstrated a much greater concern for costs.

The stated views of OSHA officials (like those of most politicians, labor leaders, and businessmen) are contradictory. They acknowledge that costs must be considered but deny that they would ever sacrifice lives for economic reasons. In part this paradox is a shallow one, put forth for political protection, but it appears to have deeper roots as well. It is hardly surprising that the officials who must make decisions affecting the fates of thousands or millions of citizens find the process discomforting. Although everyday experience demonstrates that people don't act as though risk reduction has infinite value, many people appear to derive satisfaction from the thought that they are unwilling to make these trade-offs, and they like to think that their government won't make them either. To indulge these preferences, people are willing to accept decreases in output. There is nothing necessarily irrational about calling some values "absolute" and declaring them off limits to economizing procedures. While it may be paradoxical that the same people don't observe these "absolutes" in their daily behavior, it would hardly be the first time people wanted public policy to preach better behavior than they practice themselves.

The tension between economic and noneconomic thinking gets resolved differently in different contexts. Thus a number of government agencies have in fact used economic analyses to determine what values they should place on their lifesaving activities. Both the Federal Aviation Administration (FAA) and the National Highway Traffic Safety Administration (NHTSA) fall in this category. Several factors explain these differences.

First, the social willingness to spend money to save lives seems to depend upon the identifiability of the people at risk. This correlation implies that the value of lifesaving is situationally specific. At one end of the spectrum is the trapped miner; millions of dollars may be spent for his rescue. At the other end are such large, amorphous groups as car riders, cigarette smokers, and pedestrians. Compared with the FAA and NHTSA, OSHA faces many more choices that affect only a few hundred or thousand people at a handful of known workplaces. Thus to talk about a single value for lifesaving is wrong; to talk about an average value is likely to be very misleading.

Second, although standard setters drive cars and ride airplanes, they don't operate punch presses or work in asbestos plants. Although the idea may run counter to some preconceived notions, it seems plausible that decision makers are more likely to be protective when the do *not* share the risks. Without being easily able to rely on their own personal appraisal of the risk, they are placed in a more paternalistic position.[6]

The third and most important factor is the different political environments of the agencies. Organized labor's influence with OSHA is unmatched by any consumer or passenger group's influence with NHTSA or the FAA. The relatively noncontroversial role of safety in the FAA means that decision makers there are freer to ignore popular distaste for valuations of lifesaving. NHTSA, although beleaguered by Ralph Nader, has also been under constant pressure from the auto companies, who have presented their own benefit-cost studies of auto safety regulations. The auto companies are publicly wiling to set values on the lives of anonymous consumers, but when it comes to the workers in their foundries (for example), they too back off.

Since union leaders play such an important role in triggering OSHA activities, their views deserve a more thorough examination. Unions' experiences with collective bargaining have obviously sensitized them to the existence of trade-offs among bargaining objectives. But the unions would hardly have sought government intervention if they had not thought they could achieve special advantages by it. A union might be willing to give up $10 million in other benefits to get rid of a hazard, but the company or industry might have demanded $20 million. Depending on market and bargaining structures, a government order to eliminate the hazard can make it more likely that some of the costs will be passed forward to consumers. Price increases induced by the cost increases are more likely to limit growth in the affected firms' employment than to reduce current employment. For all unions, long-term contracts and firms' needs to maintain internal wage relativities and to remain competitive in the external labor market provide some protection against short-term shifting of the full costs to workers. When the union does fear severely adverse effects from a standard, it can negotiate with both OSHA and the firms. As with any organization, the cost to the union is what counts, not the social costs. Indeed, the very idea of social costs is totally foreign to political thinking.

Many of the distinctions that OSHA leaders apparently make in setting standards are consistent with a willingness-to-pay approach. Faced with imminent death, the trapped miner would give up almost anything to escape. The most plausible assumption about attitudes toward risk suggests that workers facing high probabilities of death would value each decrement in risk more than workers facing low risks. To the extent that small, identifiable groups tend to face relatively high risks, greater protectiveness toward them would be warranted on these grounds. Yet the consistency of economic reasoning with these other modes of reasoning is largely fortuitous. Like most people (including most economists) OSHA standard setters don't believe that you can find out how much value workers place on safety. Unlike economists, they aren't sure that such a valuation would even be relevant, but in any event they feel sure that other factors matter too.

Yet these attitudes do not guarantee strict regulation. As a hundred years of public regulation of occupational safety and health in America reveal, there is nothing intrinsic to the issue that ensures protective action. Moral issues can often be skirted unless someone is there to keep pointing them out and legitimizing them. The basic differences between pre-OSHA and post-OSHA regulation are the more prominent position of the regulators within the bureaucracy, the statutory language that makes it difficult for them to tolerate continuous noncompliance, and the higher priority that organized labor has placed on monitoring their activities. Although still dependent upon the unions for political support, OSHA can now be depended upon by them to establish and routinize their concerns within the bureaucracy.

Emphasizing Safety over Health

With so many safety standards, OSHA's interpretation that the act required inspectors to cite every violation they saw naturally led to a predominance of safety violations. Despite all the picayune violations this policy forced OSHA to cite, it possessed the great administrative virtue of making it easier to control the exercise of discretion. In contrast to the exhortation to "use your judgment," the "cite what you see" rule promised more uniform results. Moreover, with many untrained inspectors, neither OSHA nor the unions had great faith in whatever judgments would be exercised.

But a more important determinant of the imbalance between safety and health was the dearth of industrial hygienists. Unless the agency's leaders were willing to keep it small, most of its work had to be devoted to safety, not health. That conclusion held to the extent that the enforcement of health violations required the skills of hygienists. OSHA, under pressure from the review commission that rules on appeals from its citations, decided that the evidential standards used by the commission prevented the use of less well trained staff.

Inspection Strategies in Safety

OSHA began its life by concentrating its inspections in the five industries with the highest injury frequency rates. The implicit reasoning was that the good OSHA could do would somehow be proportional to the injury rate. Hoping for dramatic evidence of its impact on injuries, OSHA thought these industries were the places to begin.

Unfortunately, the issues involved in allocating inspections properly are much more complex. Along with equity and procedural fairness, OSHA should consider how its allocation can achieve the greatest reduction in injury losses for a given compliance cost. As a first step, OSHA needs to know (regardless of the compliance costs) what type of inspections at which workplaces will do the most good. This step requires hard thinking about the ways OSHA can affect employer behavior. It also requires injury data that provide more information than the current BLS survey of employers can supply.

Only a minority of work injuries are caused by violations of safety standards and many of these are momentary violations which inspectors could rarely detect. OSHA's inspection program should be designed to deal with all classes of injuries: those caused by detectable violations, by "nondetectable" violations, and by no violation. In practice OSHA has focused almost exclusively on the first category, practically ignored the second, and totally ignored the third, apparently in the belief that only education and training—not enforcement—could address those injuries. Recently, in part because of a policy change (triggered by the criticism it received for failing to investigate an informal complaint about what turned out to be a major health hazard), OSHA has experienced a large increase in complaint inspections. Although these certainly have some value, the increase has concentrated OSHA's enforcement more heavily at larger, unionized workplaces—leaving others less protected—and has sapped the agency's capacity to initiate programs.

Engineering Controls versus Personal Protective Equipment

The method of abating hazards has enormous consequences for the costs of complying with health standards. The difference in compliance costs between a standard with low exposure limits and one with high exposure limits could be vast if engineering controls were required, but trivial if personal protective equipment were allowed.

OSHA adopted a regulation requiring engineering controls except where they were "infeasible." The crucial definition restricted infeasibility to cases in which the cost of engineering controls would put a firm out of business. Neither the policy nor the exemption made much economic sense. Personal protection can sometimes provide equal protection at much lower cost. And when engineering controls are worthwhile, firms that can't afford them should not be subsidized. Politically, however, the policy allows OSHA to assure unions that no workers would have to lose their jobs because of health standards.

OSHA officials maintain that personal protective equipment can be as effective as engineering controls only if it is carefully implemented (for example, to assure proper fit and maintenance) and that since such care cannot be assured, engineering controls are preferable. When pressed, however, OSHA officials admit that the distinction is one of degree, because engineering controls require careful maintanance too.[7] OSHA has not commissioned any studies to investigate the cheaper methods; the agency has both political and organizational reasons for standing pat, workers generally dislike wearing equipment like respirators and earmuffs. (After all, if they liked wearing them, employers would usually have every reason to make sure they had them and wore them.) Unions don't want to allow personal protection as a long-term solution to health problems in part because they fear that rank and file support for health enforcement would erode. OSHA, in turn, has little reason to jeopardize its relations with its chief supporters.

However, if OSHA strictly enforced the engineering requirement, the cost increases would generate a fierce reaction from business groups. In practice, OSHA has found a middle road, chosen largely because of its administrative practicality. OSHA maintains the engineering requirement but grants very lengthy abatement periods during which personal protective equipment must be worn. The unions' concern with the ultimate use of engineering controls is preserved, but employers are essentially granted as many extensions as they ask for. A seemingly more sensible policy would be to make case-by-case determinations of the costs and effectiveness of the two methods. But such a policy would require far more people with technical expertise than OSHA has to spare. Even more importantly, to implement that policy, OSHA would have to confront the dilemma that its present approach allows it to avoid—

how to weigh costs and benefits. A recent OSH Review Commission decision that OSHA must indeed carry out that weighing poses the prospect that OSHA will be forced to change.

Evaluating OSHA's Impact

While the exploration of the policies and procedures that influence the costs of compliance and their effects on injuries and illnesses can be revealing, it is important to try to go on to estimate what OSHA's effects and costs have actually been. In addition, we should examine how well OSHA performs under the criteria of vertical equity and procedural fairness.

Effectiveness

No confident conclusions can be drawn about OSHA's effects on occupational diseases; evaluators suffer from the same lack of information that plagues standard setters. For injuries, however, an econometric model can be used to test the hypothesis that injury rates are no lower than one would have predicted on the basis of pre-OSHA experience. This test shows no OSHA impact on the overall U.S. or California manufacturing injury rates. However, disaggregation of the California rate by accident type shows that the rate for the category that OSHA enforcement is most likely to affect ("caught in or between" injuries), according to the judgment of safety engineers, has been significantly lower than predicted since 1973, while the category least related to standards ("strains and overexertions") is much higher than predicted. Thus OSHA's apparent lack of impact on the overall rate probably results from the swamping of the true effect by the unrelated (but unexplained) growth of injuries that enforcement cannot affect. A conservative conclusion appears to be that by 1974 OSHA had reduced the manufacturing injury rate by about 4 percent and the rate for the private sector as a whole by about 2 percent. A much cruder anlaysis of fatalities in California suggests that 20 to 30 deaths a year may have been prevented by OSHA. Because California had one of the better safety and health programs before OSHA, the extrapolation of these figures to the country as a whole appears plausible.

These conclusions about OSHA's effects are not supported by other studies that have tried to test for the effects of inspections on injuries. For example, one test compared establishments that had been inspected with others that had not to see whether rates at the former showed a relative decline from the previous year. In one sense, this study does a better job of controlling for outside influences that may have coincided with OSHA's development. However, for that very reason it cannot capture any of OSHA's effects attributable to mechanisms other than inspections. Also, since this test and others fail to disaggregate the overall injury rate, they lose a great deal of the power they might have had.

Several writers have attributed the failure to find a specific "inspection effect" to the puny size of OSHA's fines (averaging only about $25 per violation) and the paucity of its inspections (about 170,000 in 1974 for over five million covered workplaces). However, once the size of the establishments that OSHA inspects and the industries in which the inspections are concentrated are taken into account, it appears that each year OSHA is inspecting workplaces employing a substantial proportion of all workers who suffer the types of injuries OSHA can prevent. Once cited for a violation, employers have strong incentives to comply to avoid the heavy penalties for "failure to abate."

But if these assertions are correct, then other reasons must be sought to explain the failure of studies to find an inspection effect. One reason, of course, could be the failure to disaggregate injury rates. A second reason could be that OSHA's effects are mainly attributable to mechanisms other than inspections. These include union threats to call in inspectors; the efforts of safety directors, who have a limited authority to spend money on their own and can justify spending more because of their companies' desire to be law-abiding; and the selfinterest of equipment manufacturers, who will usually incorporate OSHA's requirements as "standard equipment." Finally, a third explanation could be that OSHA really hasn't had any effect; that is, that the models from which the more optimistic results are derived are misleading. We can never be positive that a model captures all the relevant variables.

The most important insight to be derived from an examination of OSHA's effect on injuries does not pertain to the estimate of its quantitative impact, but to its potential scope. Several studies indicate that only a small minority of all injuries are caused by violations; moreover, perhaps only about one-half of them (amounting to 5 to 15 percent of all injuries) are caused by violations that inspectors could detect on scheduled inspections. OSHA may actually be achieving a substantial part of its potential; the problem is that the potential of its present program is so small. Although small improvements are possible within the current emphasis on seeking detectable violations, the more important gains to be made require expanding OSHA's scope and preventing injuries more cost-effectively.

Social Cost-Effectiveness

The reason the quantitative estimates are not very useful is that even if information about both costs and effects were available, retrospective judgments may not have much relevance to future choices. In this case, however, we have information about only one side of the equation, the effects on injuries. Thus it is possible to identify a range of likely minimum benefits for the nonfatal injuries that appear to have been prevented. The resulting estimates are substantial—several hundred million dollars in 1974, for example—but the corresponding estimates of the safety costs attributable to OSHA are based on too many arbitrary assumptions to merit serious attention. The same judgment applies to costs for complying with health standards. Despite this uncertainty about costs, the arguments about the methods OSHA uses suggest that the benefits OSHA generates can be won more cheaply.

Vertical Equity

The chief beneficiaries of OSHA are workers in industries with many injuries caused by hazards that compliance with OSHA standards could reduce. This category of injuries is concentrated in construction and most manufacturing industries; the health benefits flow to workers in industries like petrochemicals with heavy use of toxic substances. Since there is no reason to believe that these workers are particularly low-paid, OSHA does not appear to pass muster as an instrument for redistributing income.

Procedures Fairness

Finally, OSHA's effects include the establishment of a new set of rights for workers and corresponding obligations and restrictions on employers. OSHA's procedures make it easier for workers to participate in the enforcement process and to keep informed of workplace hazards. Worker participation encourages inspectors to behave more evenhandedly than they did before OSHA, when they usually dealt only with management representatives. Providing more information to workers not only seems fair but may also foster greater efficiency by helping the market for risk taking work better. From a more critical perspective, OSHA subjects employers to heavy sanctions without eliminating significant elements of arbitrary administrative behavior; for example, variations among inspectors, districts, and regions in citing policy. In addition, the OSH Act placed the burden of initiating quasi-judicial proceedings (to appeal citations) on employers rather than on the government. While as in the case of traffic citations, this procedure has overwhelming administrative advantages, it hardly conforms to the highest ideals of due process.

Designing Improvements in OSH Policy

Remedial work has already begun on several of OSHA's shortcomings. Task forces are at work eliminating some of the consensus standards that are ineffective or unnecessarily rigid, although the dearth of information continues to hamper that effort severely. Part of the reform strategy has been to replace specification standards (which specify, for example, that ladder rungs must be one inch in diameter) with performance standards (which require, for example, that the rungs be capable of supporting 500 pounds). The latter allow employers to seek out less expensive methods of providing safety; they also make it more difficult for inspectors to determine violations and force them to exercise more discretion.

An attempt to shift more enforcement activity to health, rectifying the imbalance of OSHA's early years, progresses slowly, still hindered by the limited number of hygienists.[8] Exactly how additional enforcement resources should be used in the health field remains uncertain, but evidence from past inspections suggests that the most serious hazards are still the ones that are least well controlled. A rethinking of the appropriate policy for choosing when to allow personal protective equipment as the method for abating health hazards remains to be carried out. Many undoubtedly oversimple rules present themselves—allowing the use of personal equipment when noise is the hazard or for exposure lasting less than a certain period (depending on the toxic substance) or for exposures in plants with some sort of certified industrial hygiene program—but this politically sensitive and economically important issue deserves a careful study.

The chief areas in which the analysis I have presented can contribute to improving OSHA policy are targeting safety inspections and improving standard setting. Despite its humdrum image, the targeting issue can have significance not only for OSHA's effectiveness in preventing injuries but also for its social cost-effectiveness.

The proposals I have presented are based on an evaluation of OSHA's performance and on an understanding of the political and administrative constraints that policymakers face. Thus, for example, since OSHA will not stop doing safety enforcement (as some analysts have suggested it should), the relevant question becomes how to improve its performance. The injury tax, which has many desirable features, is simply not going to be politically acceptable. It is also very likely to be administratively unworkable because of the data requirements it poses. By contrast, adjustments in inspection priorities are largely within the control of administrators, and they can design inspection systems that capture some of the advantages of the injury tax. While minor improvements could be made in the current inspection program—so that inspectors would be a little more likely to get to workplaces with detectable violations that caused injuries—major improvements must rely on extending the proportion of injuries that enforcement can affect and on achieving injury reductions at lower cost.

One proposal would replace many or most of the current scheduled inspections with an expanded program of accident investigations. (For political reasons as well as for reasons of fairness, all the proposals presented here would still allow workers to request inspections.) Accident investigations allow penalties to be assessed retroactively for violations that contribute to injuries. They penalize all violations related to injuries, not just the ones inspectors can detect on scheduled inspections. Aside from expanding the potential scope of effectiveness, this proposal would have several other advantages. By essentially putting a tax on standards-related injuries, it allows employers to reassess whether the probability that an injury will occur at their workplace is great enough to justify incurring the added cost. If accident investigations only dealt with violations related to the injury, compliance with other standards would not be compelled.

This plan has several drawbacks: first, whatever injury-prevention benefits scheduled inspections had generated would be lost. Second, it would still create added safety incentives only for the minority of injuries related to violations of standards. While this proposal would probably be an improvement over the status quo, a more ambitious plan might be even better. Such an improvement requires an inspection policy that more directly simulates the effects of an injury tax.

That simulation can be achieved by making the frequency of inspection for an establishment depend upon its relative safety performance (that is, comparing its overall injury rate with the overall rate for its industry.) In this manner, the enforcement of standards can be used as a lever to give firms added incentives to prevent all injuries, regardless of whether they are related to violations. The employer is left free (but only until he is inspected) to choose what methods he will use to prevent injuries. This proposal is not a perfect simulation of the injury tax because it relies on the costs imposed by inspections (the costs of complying with violations that are cited) to serve as the "tax"; some employers who are inspected may still be forced to spend money for safety measures that are not worthwhile (though this will occur substantially less frequently than under the status quo).

Politically, this proposal—called THIRE, for "targeting high injury rate establishments"—has great political appeal because it focuses on the poorest performers, the "bad apples." It is in the administrative realm, in implementing this plan, where great care would have to be taken. The THIRE policy would require injury data for individual establishments, data that are not readily available in many states.[9] The use of rates for individual establishments could also foster widespread underreporting of injuries, a threat that necessitates extensive "auditing" efforts. In consequence, the implementation of the THIRE proposals would have to proceed piecemeal. In one respect, a piecemeal procedure is desirable, for it can facilitate evaluation and allow for "debugging" before wider applications are tried. Unless OSHA experiments with these alternatives and carries out evaluations, we will never know for sure which of them is the most effective. It is likely that some mixture of these alternatives would comprise the best overall enforcement strategy.

For standard setting, I recommend changes in procedures that acknowledge the political and analytic difficulties in following any simple decision rule based on an efficiency criterion. It seems that the most sensible way to ensure that efficiency concerns are considered is to require standard setters to present judgments about the range of costs and effects (but not monetized benefits) for each proposed standard.

However, these ranges will frequently have to be nothing but admissions of ignorance. Probably the greatest aid to rational decision making would be better information about costs and effects. Except perhaps in cases involving carcinogenic substances, it seems likely that OSHA policymakers would in fact be willing to consider evidence bearing on cost-effectiveness. To get the precise data on effectiveness that it needs for safety standards, OSHA should create interdisciplinary teams to make intensive reviews of state workers' compensation injury reports, supplemented by visits to employers. Each year OSHA and NIOSH could list the hazards to be considered in the following year or two, providing the agenda for these research teams. For health, getting better information is more difficult, but one useful step would be to increase OSHA's own industrial hygiene and engineering capacity, so that at least on the cost side uncertainties could be reduced.

In summary, the method of enforcement enshrined in the OSH Act is a relatively costly way to prevent injuries. It has not proved a very effective method either, although it appears to have achieved some gains. How many of these gains would be lost if the program were ended is unknown. The measures to keep workers informed represent a substantial gain in procedural fairness, one that I believe outweighs the encumbrances placed on employers. In health, the method is sound, and its most important contribution has been the construction of a framework for faster and more comprehensive national action to combat occupational disease. That framework needed to be built. Whether or not, on balance, the standards that ensue will prove beneficial remains to be seen. In the face of that uncertainty, it seems preferable to maintain the capacity to intervene rather than to abjure it. However, unless program changes are made that allow injuries and illnesses to be prevented at lower cost, the burden that OSHA imposes will be far greater than it needs to be.

Appendix
Econometric Issues in the Injury Rate Models

The more confidence one has in the explanatory power of an econometric model, the more likely one is to trust predictions based upon it. My interest here, however, is in the predictions themselves. The only other econometric model that has been proposed for this field gives similar predictions.[1] Robert Smith tested a model that states (in first-differences terms)

$$I = B_0 + B_1 A + B_2 H + B_3 C + B_4 W + E,$$

where I is the Z-16 manufacturing injury rates for the U.S., and

B_0 = a constant term
A = the U.S. manufacturing accession rate
H = average overtime hours worked per week in manufacturing
C = the capacity utilization rate in manufacturing
W = the average real hourly earnings of manufacturing production workers
E = the random-error term.

For 1948-69 (N = 21), Smith found the following results:

I	=	B_0	+	A	+	H	+	C	+	W
		+.650		+.602		+.556		+.071		−16.53
		(2.84)		(1.89)		(2.25)		(2.03)		(3.67)

(t statistics in parentheses), where

$R^2 = .72$ S.E. = .469   D−W = 1.74.

His estimates of the constant term (trend in this case) and the earnings variable are quite similar to mine. (See equation 1 in the list that follows.) The new-hire variable is somewhat larger and more significant than the accession rate, an expected result since the former reflects inexperience more precisely.

For my present purpose, the important point is that the Smith model seems to give very similar predictions to equation 1. The predictions from Smith's model, from equation 1 (the analogous regression reported in the text), and the reported rates were, respectively, as follows: 1969-70: (−2.4%), (N.A.), (+2.7%); 1970-71: (−3.6%), (−2.6%), (N.A.); 1971-72: (+1.6%), (+2.5%), (N.A.); 1972-73: (+7.4%), (+7.9%), (+7.1%); 1973-74: (+5.0%), (+6.6%), (+7.4%).

The tests of OSHA's impact use comparisons of the predicted and reported rates for each year rather than a dummy variable for the post-OSH Act years because the reasoning presented in chapter 5 included the possibility that

OSHA's effects would grow over time and the dummy variable measures only the *average* effect during these years.[2]

The most troubling aspect of my basic model is the instability of the coefficient for its most innovative feature, the variable for the percentage of male manufacturing workers between 18 and 24. Its coefficient appears to be quite sensitive to the specific years chosen. For all the models cited in the text (see equations 1 through 12), the coefficient is positive and always significant. However, the coefficient is much larger in the California regressions than in the U.S. regression, about four times larger in percentage elasticities. Since the variable was constructed using national data and only benchmarked for California for the census years, the latter coefficient is much more plausible.

National data on the number of employed males in each age group for each year can be constructed from table 3 and table 6.1 of the 1975 BLS *Handbook of Labor Statistics*. The census volumes on *Characteristics of the Population* provide the decennial figures for the manufacturing sector. For both 1950 and 1960, it turned out that the proportion of employed males 18 to 24 in the U.S. was the same as the proportion in the manufacturing sector (13.3 percent in 1950 and 11.4 percent in 1960). I made the assumption that the year-to-year changes in manufacturing in the intervening years followed the same pattern as for all employed males. For 1970, however, the census figure for manufacturing was 13.9 percent, while the figure for employed males was 14.6 percent; thus the ten-year change was 2.5 percent, not 3.2 percent—78 percent as much. Therefore, for each of the years after 1960, I multiplied the change for employed males 18 to 24 by .80 to get the manufacturing sector percentage. The same procedure was followed for the California data and for the older age group.

The procedure appears to work well for the U.S. manufacturing sector; it is reasonable to think that national age-sex trends in overall employment and in the manufacturing sector will be similar. However, as we move to other comparisons, the correlation is likely to weaken. For example, the apparent reason the youth coefficient was so much larger for California manufacturing was that the percentage of young males changed very little in California from census to census. Thus, although the direction of change was the same as in the U.S. Census, in the regression more influence is attributed to each increment of change because of the compression in the variable.

The resulting instability of the CAGE coefficient is illustrated by CCIR equation 6. When regressed from 1952 to 1970 instead of 1951 to 1970, the youth coefficient is transformed from a highly significant +.41 to −.24, with a t statistic of 1.60. For many other regressions, that particular one-year shift also changes the sign, although the t is usually small. Some instability is apparent at the national level as well. Although the Chow test for the homogeneity of the coefficients for two subperiods of the U.S. regression did not reject the hypothesis that the coefficients were the same in both, the coefficient for the youth variable did become insignificant in both and had the "wrong" sign in one.

Another problem, noted in the text, is that the lagged new-hire rate fails to perform as expected in the California regressions. It is often negative, although almost always insignificant. This finding may reflect some differences in timing between U.S. and California business cycles, although, if so, the unlagged new-hire rate would probably be affected as well. In fact, however, the relative magnitude of the unlagged new-hire coefficient is very similar for the U.S. and California. The lagged new-hire variable did contribute to better Durbin-Watson statistics and to higher R^2's.

In retrospect, one way to avoid the problems of the lagged new-hire rate may have been to use a model in natural logarithms. For example, in the following model, all variables except C and T are logged.

$$LCITR = \quad C \quad + \quad T \quad + \quad LUNH \quad + \quad LCAGE \quad + \quad LCERN \quad + LCOAGE \quad + \quad LNP$$

	C	T	LUNH	LCAGE	LCERN	LCOAGE	LNP
	+.302	+.02	+.13	+.69	−1.57	+.77	−.87
	(1.03)	(1.98)	(2.39)	(6.84)	(4.51)	(1.09)	(2.11)

$R^2 = .9857$ S.E. = .0138 D−W = 1.96
N = 24 1947-70.

(The predictions of this model are 1971 = 38.68; 1972 = 41.06; 1973 = 44.85; 1974 = 46.82. None of the predicted values is significantly different from the reported WC rates.)

For all the California regressions, the Durbin-Watson (D-W) statistics are in the inconclusive range, leaving it uncertain whether autocorrelation is present. Serial correlation of the errors does not bias the coefficients; conceptually, therefore, even if autocorrelation is present, the predictions made with these coefficients should not be affected.

However, because autocorrelation does bias the variances, I reestimated several of the regressions using the standard two-step procedure based upon first-round estimates of $\hat{\rho}$.[3] For the two regressions on the overall California rate, the results were that the coefficients were essentially unchanged, the standard errors were slightly smaller, and the D-W statistics were the same or worse. (One explanation for the poor performance of the D-W statistic is that the correlation takes a more complex form than first-order serial correlation.) The "corrected" results appear in equations 14 (a "correction" of equation 2) and 15 (a "correction" of equation 5). In both cases, the predictions of these new equations for 1974 were somewhat smaller than the originals, but again they were not significantly different than the reported rates.

The one "caught in" model for which I carried out the two-step procedure also failed to improve its D-W statistic. In addition, the youth coefficient changed from positive and significant to negative but insignificant. As a result of that change, the predicted injury rates shrank dramatically, so that instead of overpredicting the actual rates, they underpredicted them. However, as I already noted, the same change in the sign of the youth variable occurred when we ran an uncorrected regression for the same period (1952–1960, instead of 1951–1970 in the "uncorrected" model). Since we don't know whether autocorrelation is present or not, my response is to reject this "correction." However, this exercise again points out the instability of the age coefficient and the important consequences it can have for the predictions of the "caught in" rate.

Another point to note is that the new-hire rate has been estimated for the years 1947–1950. Confronted by the alternative of using the less precise "accessions rate," I took advantage of the fact that the correlation between them approached +0.90 and extrapolated the new-hire rate back four years in step with the accessions rate changes during those years. Since a California manufacturing new-hire rate was not available for most of this period, the California regressions use the national new-hire rate.

The new-hire rates and accession rates used are taken from tables 53 and 54 of the 1976 BLS *Handbook of Labor Statistics*. The average hourly earnings of production workers in manufacturing are found in table 98 (for the U.S.) and table 106 (for California). [4]

Regression Equations

1. $FUSIR =$ C + FUNH + FUNHL + FUAGE + FUERN
   +.57   +.94   +.26   +.30   −14.37
   (3.44)   (6.84)   (1.84)   (1.89)   (4.17)
   $R^2 = .83$ S.E. = .405   D−W = 2.05
   N = 22   1949–70

1a. $USIR =$ C + UNH + UNHL + UAGE + UERN +   T
   24.80   +.69   +.28   +.31   −14.16   +.56
   (4.67)   (4.62)   (1.63)   (3.75)   (3.94)   (3.67)
   $R^2 = .95$ S.E. = .383   D−W = 1.40
   N = 23   1948–70

2. CTIR = C + T + UNH +UNHL+ CAGE +COAGE+ CERN + NP
+50.25 +.84 +1.86 −.20 +3.63 +.73 −28.08 −.83
(2.05) (2.02) (3.22) (.42) (11.86) (.84) (5.82) (1.48)
$R^2 = .9881$ S.E. = .916   D−W = 2.41
t statistic for prediction was less than one for each year from 1971 to 1975
N = 23   1948-70

3. CTIR = C + T + UNH + UNHL + CAGE +COAGE+ CERN
+28.35 +.48 +2.47 −.26 +3.68 +1.27 −31.25
(1.40) (1.37) (5.91) (.54) (11.67) (1.57) (6.98)
$R^2 = .9864$ S.E. = .950   D−W = 2.12
t for 1971 = < 1.00; 1972 = 1.65; 1973 = 1.26; 1974 = 1.29;
1975 = < 1.00
N = 23   1948-70

4. CTIR = C + UNH + UNHL + CAGE +COAGE+ CERN
+2.55 +2.37 −.24 +3.70 +2.06 −27.18
(.34) (5.61) (.50) (11.45) (3.48) (7.92)
$R^2 = .9848$ S.E. = .974   D−W = 1.91
t for 1971 = < 1.00; 1972 = 2.25; 1973 = 2.29; 1974 = 4.14;
1975 = 3.39
F (Chow test) = 6.90   1948-74
N = 23   1948-70

5. CTIR = C + T + UNH + UNHL + CAGE + CERN
+57.02 +.86 +2.76 +.11 +3.68 −30.97
(6.28) (3.35) (7.01) (.25) (11.21) (6.65)
$R^2 = .9843$ S.E. = .990   D−W = 1.91
t for 1974 = 1.51; < 1.00 for all other years
F (Chow test) = .5321   1948-74
N = 23   1948-70

6. CCIR = C + T + UNH + CAGE + CERN + UNHL
+11.06 +.16 +.45 +.41 −5.25 −.12
(5.64) (2.82) (4.66) (2.91) (5.42) (1.19)
$R^2 = .9466$ S.E. = .197   D−W = 2.33
F (Chow test) = 5.88   1951-74
N = 20   1951-70

7. CCIR = C + T + UNH + CAGE + CERN + NP
+11.12 +.14 +.20 +.49 −3.65 −.20
(6.68) (3.18) (1.34) (3.42) (4.41) (1.74)
$R^2 = .9517$ S.E. = .187   D−W = 2.36
F (Chow test) = 5.75   1951-74
N = 20   1951-70

8. CCIR = C + T + UNH + UNHL + CAGE + CERN + NP
13.83 +.21 +.20 −.18 +.51 −4.56 −.25
(6.63) (3.89) (1.44) (1.91) (3.90) (5.09) (2.32)
$R^2 = .9622$ S.E. = .171   D−W = 2.63
F (Chow test) = 7.425   1951-74
N = 20   1951-70

9. CCIR = C + T + UNH + CAGE + CERN + NP +COAGE
+16.3 +.23 +.20 +.49 −3.65 −.26 −.18
(3.11) (2.52) (1.35) (3.45) (4.41) (2.03) (1.05)
$R^2 = .9554$ S.E. = .186   D−W = 2.45

F (Chow test) = 4.61   1951–74
N = 20   1951–70

10. CSIR =   C +   T   + UNH + UNHL + CAGE + CERN +   NP

+20.33   +.27   +.72   +.007   +.77   −5.77   −.42

(5.83) (3.01) (3.17) (.04)   (3.52) (3.86) (2.33)

R^2 = .9747   S.E. = .286   D–W = 2.40

F (Chow test) = 0.41   1951–74
N = 20   1951–70

11. CEIR =   C +   T   + UNH + UNHL + CAGE + CERN +COAGE

+3.54   +.20   +.48   −.11   .43   −6.00   +.38

(.67) (2.07) (3.75) (.78)   (2.52) (5.23) (1.84)

R^2 = .9599   S.E. = .233   D–W = 2.57

F (Chow test) = 1.93   1951–74
N = 20   1951–70

12. CFIR =   C +   T   + UNH + CAGE + CERN +COAGE + NP

+16.27   +.29   −.04   +.95   −6.52   −.10   −.22

(1.76) (1.86) (.16)   (3.79) (4.49) (.34)   (.99)

R^2 = .8975   S.E. = .328   D–W = 1.83

F (Chow test) = 1.19   1951–74
N = 20   1951–70

13. A Series of First-Difference Models for CTIR (1948 or 1949 to 1970):

FCTIR = +C + FUNH +FUNHL +FCAGE+ FCERN+FCOAGE + FNP

a.   −.28   +2.81

(.66)   (4.36)

R^2 = .53   S.E. = 1.81   D–W = .78

b.   −.91   +3.16   +2.90

(2.26) (5.56) (2.37)

R^2 = .71   S.E. = 1.85   D–W = 1.30

c.   −.75   +2.95   +.65   3.36

(2.07) (5.47) (1.26) (3.04)

R^2 = .75   S.E. = 1.65   D–W = 1.71

d.   +.54   +2.79   +.03   3.44   −25.75

(1.09) (6.34) (.06)   (3.84) (3.23)

R^2 = .85   S.E. = 1.34   D–W = 2.56

e.   +.01   +2.77   −.08   +3.68   −23.87   +1.45

(.02)   (6.35) (.17)   (4.00) (2.93) (1.07)

R^2 = .86   S.E. = 1.33   D–W = 2.52

f.   +.16   +2.38   −.10   +3.50   −22.73   +1.62   −.58

(.22)   (3.21) (.20)   (3.60) (2.69) (1.16) (.66)

R^2 = .86   S.E. = 1.35   D–W = 2.57

California Regressions "Corrected" for Autocorrection:

CTIR =   C +   T   + UNH + UNHL + CAGE + CERN +COAGE+ NP

14.   +33.42   +.85   +2.00   −.41   +3.07   −26.77   +.90   −.88

(1.84) (1.83) (3.33) (.91)   (6.40) (5.14) (1.01) (1.45)

R^2 = .96   S.E. = .92   D–W = 2.95   N = 22 $\hat{\rho}$ = .31

(a "correction" of equation 2)

15.   57.22   +.95   +2.82   −.10   +3.44   −31.70

(6.65) (3.71) (7.50) (.23)   (9.63) (6.98)

R^2 = .98   S.E. = .94   D–W = 2.09   N = 22 $\hat{\rho}$ = .05

(a "correction" of equation 5)

Glossary of Variables

When F begins the variable name, it is in first-difference form. C at the beginning indicates California, W Wisconsin, and U the United States. L preceding these geographic markers indicates the variable has been transformed into natural logarithms.

USIR   U. S. manufacturing injury rate

CTIR, WTIR   Overall manufacturing injury rates, California and Wisconsin

CCIR   California "caught in" injury rate—manufacturing

CSIR   California "struck by or striking against" injury rate—manufacturing

CEIR   California "strains and overexertions" injury rate—manufacturing

CFIR   California "falls and slips" injury rate

(U, C, W)ERN   Real hourly earnings of manufacturing production workers in that polity (in 1967 dollars, except for UERN 1957–59 dollars)

(U, C W)AGE   Percentage of all male workers in manufacturing who were 18-24 years old in that polity

(U, C)OAGE   Percentage of all male workers in manufacturing who were 45-64 years old in that polity

UNH   U.S. new-hire rate for manufacturing

UNHL   U.S. new-hire rate lagged one year

NP   U.S. percentage of manufacturing employees who were nonproduction workers

Notes

Notes to Chapter 1

1. Section 6(b)(5) of the act.

2. The figure on federal OSHA inspectors was provided to me by Larry Pagels of the OSHA San Francisco Regional Office. The figure on inspectors in "state plan" states was calculated from OSHA Report No. SP03 (December 5, 1977), which describes the total number of inspections and the number of inspections per inspector for fiscal 1977.

The number of states running their own programs continually varies as states lose or acquire OSHA approval. As of 1978, only two (California and Michigan) of the ten largest states conducted their own programs.

3. OSHA's enforcement policy changed significantly after 1975. Through 1975 only about 2 percent of all violations were cited as serious, with an average proposed penalty of about $650. The bulk of penalties were for nonserious violations. Then two changes occurred. First, OSHA cut back on fines for nonserious violations. Second, by changing the definition of "serious," it raised that proportion of violations to about 20 percent. Although the average penalty per serious violation declined, the average penalty per inspection rose from about $100 in 1975 to over $230 in the quarter ending in September 1977.

4. *Congressional Record,* December 2, 1975, pp. H 11663–11664.

5. The earlier episode is described in Bureau of National Affairs, *Occupational Safety and Health Reporter,* January 23, 1976, pp. 1140–1141 (hereafter Bureau of National Affairs *Reporter*). For the 1977 clash, see *Wall Street Journal,* July 18, 1977, p. 11.

6. For example, in 1944 Robert Lane found only three instances of federal regulation that most moderate-sized businessmen were likely to encounter: wages and hours laws, the Wagner Act, and the Robinson-Patman Act regulating trade practices. See his book, *The Regulation of Businessmen: Social Conditions of Government Economic Control* (Hamden, Conn.: Archon Books, 1944).

7. For an excellent discussion of these issues, see James Q. Wilson, "The Politics of Regulation," in *Social Responsibility and the Business Predicament,* ed. James W. McKie (Washington, D.C.: Brookings Institution, 1974). Also see Wilson's article, "The Dead Hand of Regulation," *The Public Interest,* no. 25 (Fall 1971), pp. 39–58.

8. The traditional lack of attention to consumer and environmental issues has been explained as a typical problem in the theory of public goods. Almost everyone benefits from cleaner air, but no one benefits very much. For any individual, the costs of initiating the organizational action needed to affect public policy exceeds his potential benefits. Moreover, if an organization does emerge, he will benefit from its victories whether he actively supports it or not. Consequently, organizations will not emerge unless some actor appears with a lot to gain. See Mancur Olson, Jr., *The Logic of Collective Action* (New York: Schocken, 1965).

Two developments appear to alter the political implications of that conclusion. The first is the growth in political entrepreneurship, the seeking out of issues that command widespread but latent support, which has been described by Wilson in "The Politics of Regulation." By 1970 this reservoir of support appeared to have developed in both the consumer and environmental areas for reasons that are only partly clear. Factors fostering entrepreneurship were media attention, presidential ambitions, and the independence allowed Democrats by the Republican control of the White House. In an important sense, Ralph Nader showed the way, and Nader also figures in the second development. Legislators are not the only ones who have been able to turn their jobs into careers. The "public interest" advocates (legal and nonlegal) have also developed a reasonably stable and rewarding profession. This "professionalization of reform," to use Daniel Moynihan's phrase, can create political action even in the absence of traditional interest groups.

Notes to Chapter 2

1. Robert S. Smith, *The Occupational Safety and Health Act: Its Goals and Its Achievements* (Washington, D.C.: American Enterprise Institute, 1976), p. 25 (hereafter referred to as *Health Act*).

2. Guido Calabresi popularized this phrasing in *The Costs of Accidents: A Legal and Economic Analysis*, student ed., (New Haven: Yale University Press, 1970), p. 26.

3. Testimony of Dr. Irving J. Selikoff in U.S., Congress, Senate, Committee on Labor and Public Welfare, *Occupational Safety and Health Act of 1970: Hearings*, 91st Cong., 1st and 2d sess., 1970, p. 1080.

4. For a good description of workers' lack of understanding of the asbestos hazard, see Paul Brodeur, *Expendable Americans* (New York: Viking Press, 1974), pp. 73-107. In theory what is important is not the average worker's understanding but the marginal worker's, for he is the one whose preferences affect the wage. If the theory describes reality well, the prognosis is a gloomy one, since the marginal worker—usually unfamiliar with the operations—will tend to be relatively uninformed. However, since wages are often at least partially determined through more complex institutional arrangements, the significance of this point is moot.

5. Probably the best of these studies is by Richard Thaler and Sherwin Rosen, "Estimating the Value of Saving a Life: Evidence from the Labor Market" (University of Rochester, Department of Economics, 1974), mimeo. Its superiority derives largely from its use of risk data for occupations rather than for industries. (The uniformity in risk faced by workers in the same occupation is probably much greater than for workers in the same industry.) The authors found that, other things being equal, workers in occupations with annual risks of death 0.001 above the sample mean received about $200 a year more in wages. The authors interpret this finding to mean that one thousand workers would value the saving of one life at approximately $200,000. In the regressions, the coefficient for the size of the risk premium has, at best, borderline statistical significance.

Several qualifications to their findings should be noted. The authors themselves observe that their sample of occupations was restricted to high-risk ones, which may tend to attract workers who are less risk-averse than the average worker; in that event, the premiums would understate the value that the average worker would place on lifesaving. Another qualification is that the measured valuations don't necessarily include the value that family and friends place on the risk reduction. Also, the risk of death is the only nonpecuniary factor the study includes; however, there is some evidence that hazardous jobs also tend to have other unpleasant characteristics (dirty, noisy, tiring) which may require risk premiums in their own right. This correlation implies that the $200,000 may overestimate the value placed on lifesaving alone. Perhaps most importantly, it isn't known how well informed workers were about the actual risks. For a more extended discussion of these issues, see John Mendeloff, "Costs and Consequences: A Political and Economic Analysis of the Occupational Safety and Health Act" (Ph.D. diss. University of California, Berkeley, 1977), chap. 2, appendix A.

6. For definitions of "hazard" and "surroundings" factors that ignore disease problems, see the *Job Description and Classification Manual* published by the United Steelworkers of America and Coordinating Committee Steel Companies (August 1971), pp. 25-26.

The economists who are most convinced that the labor market generates risk premiums may have missed this clear-cut source precisely because it is a product of institutional practices, whose importance they often tend to denigrate. Yet market forces are not irrelevent to job evaluation schemes. Part of the reason they are used is to balance the supply and demand for jobs with certain characteristics (such as high risk). Even more clearly, though, they are used to satisfy management's need for a routinized wage-setting mechanism that is perceived as fair by employees. See Peter B. Doeringer and Michael

Piore, *Internal Labor Markets and Manpower Analysis* (Lexington, Mass.: D. C. Heath, 1971), and George Strauss and Leonard R. Sayles, *Personnel: The Human Problems of Management*, 2d ed. (Englewood Cliffs, N.J.: Prentice-Hall, 1967), for a discussion of job evaluation. The former assigns somewhat more importance to job evaluation relative to wage surveys and other more direct market guides than the latter.

7. Strauss and Sayles, *Personnel*, p. 567. Within a company, the net advantages of jobs for equally skilled workers are not equal, which provides incentives not only for seeking and accepting promotions but also for remaining with a firm. However, viewed from the perspective of two firms—one with a job evaluation plan and long job ladders and one without them—poorer initial job packages in the first firm can be compensated for by opportunities for promotion. Professor Lee Friedman suggested this comparative perspective to me.

8. Union leaders may be equally resistant to initiating changes. For example, when I worked with unions on health and safety issues, we offered to run an educational program for the members, but the president of one union declined, noting that since hazardousness was one of the factors used to set wages, new information might create new dissatisfactions. He preferred to leave well enough alone.

9. Smith, *Health Act*, p. 30.

10. This example is taken from *Report of the National Commission on State Workmen's Compensation Laws* (Washington, D.C.: Government Printing Office, 1973), p. 95.

11. U.S., Congress, House, Committee on Education and Labor, *Occupational Safety and Health Act of 1969: Hearings*, 91st Cong., 1st sess., 1969, pp. 881–882.

12. Actually, the act only required the federal government to pay for claims filed through 1973; after that the coal firms were required to pay, although some states have offered to subsidize part of their payments. See J. David Cummins and Douglas Olson, "An Analysis of the Black Lung Compensation Program," *Journal of Risk and Insurance* 51, no. 4 (December 1974). The authors rightly criticize the limitation on federal jurisdiction, since most of the claims filed in the 1970s and even the 1980s will relate to conditions in the fairly distant past. If company payments were based upon the number of former employees who had died or been disabled by a disease, then marginal costs would not be affected. If financing took the form of a surtax on current WC premiums, then they would be.

13. For a discussion of these issues and others, see Richard Zeckhauser, "Procedures for Valuing Lives," *Public Policy* 23, no. 4 (Fall 1975).

14. Raymond A. Bauer, Ithiel De Sola Pool, and Lewis Anthony Dexter, *American Business and Public Policy*, 2d ed. (Chicago: Aldine, 1972), p. 405.

15. Author's interview with Tony Mazzocchi, legislative director of the Oil, Chemical, and Atomic Workers' Union, Washington, D.C., October 1975.

16. U.S., Congress, House, Committee on Education and Labor, *Occupational Safety and Health Act of 1968: Hearings*, 90th Cong., 2d sess., 1968.

17. Interview with the author. Sheehan is the legislative director of the United Steelworkers of America.

18. The following account of the legislative history draws upon several sources. *Bitter Wages*, by Joseph Page and Mary-Win O'Brien (New York: Grossman, 1973) was very helpful. So were sections of *The Occupational Safety and Health Act of 1970* (Washington, D.C.: Bureau of National Affairs, 1971). In addition to the interviews cited in the text, I learned about this period from interviews with Congressman William A. Steiger,

Senator William Hathaway, Gary Sellers, Leo Teplow (formerly of the American Iron and Steel Institute), and George Taylor (head of the AFL-CIO's standing committee on OSH).

19. Sellers's work is described in Charles McCarry, *Citizen Nader* (New York: New American Library, 1972), pp. 196-219.

20. Richard F. Fenno, Jr., *Congressmen in Committees* (Boston: Little, Brown, 1973), p. 34.

21. Page and O'Brien, *Bitter Wages*, p. 178.

22. Senator Spessard Holland is quoted in U.S., Congress, Senate, Committee on Labor and Public Welfare, *Legislative History of the Occupational Safety and Health Act of 1970*, 92d Cong., 1st sess., June 1971, p. 476. For a good description of clientelism in federal agencies, see Harold Seidman, *Politics, Position, and Power: The Dynamics of Federal Organization* (New York: Oxford University Press, 1970).

23. Section 6(b)(5) of the OSH Act.

24. For a description of the phrases used in other safety legislation, see Joseph Page, "Toward Meaningful Protection of Worker Health and Safety," *Stanford Law Review*, 27, (May 1975): 1350-51.

25. Interviews of Robert Nagle and Daniel Krivit with the author.

26. U.S., Congress, Senate, *Congressional Record*, 92d Cong., 2d sess., December 18, 1973, p. 42151.

27. The recognition that congressmen will shy away from acknowledging trade-offs, much less set values for saving a life, led one proponent of more protective standards to propose an unlikely scenario in which "at the very least, the law should be amended to spell out the precise factors OSHA must take into account in balancing the economic burden imposed by a standard, as well as the relative weight to be given each factor. It is crucial that congressional feet be put to the fire in delineating the exact circumstances under which worker health is to be sacrificed for economic reasons." Page, "Meaningful Protection," p. 1355.

28. Senate, Committee on Labor and Public Welfare, *Hearings*, 1970, p. 88.

29. House, Committee on Education and Labor, *Hearings*, 1969, p. 137.

30. Ibid., p. 1324.

31. Ibid., p. 642.

32. Smith, *Health Act*, p. 75.

33. At the urging of Senator Javits, the OSH Act did provide for the establishment of a National Commission on State Workmen's Compensation Laws, whose work and report have spurred substantial improvements in benefits in most states. Another element in the labor union strategy in the health area is the Toxic Substances Control Act, which requires pretesting of substances before they can be used in the workplace.

34. Allen V. Kneese and Charles L. Schultze, *Pollution, Prices, and Public Policy* (Washington: Brookings Institution, 1975), pp. 113-120.

35. A. Myrick Freeman and Robert H. Haveman argue that the reason politicians have failed to adopt effluent taxes is, paradoxically, because they would work. See their article, "Clean Rhetoric, Dirty Water," *The Public Interest*, no. 28 (Summer 1972), pp. 63-65. I find their argument unsatisfying because it relies upon the view that politicians

automatically serve business interests. While business obviously wields great power, it does not always win its fights. Until some groups seriously push for an effluent tax, no one can test whether business opposition plays such a dominant role. Certainly local officials like the current emphasis on building municipal treatment plants; so do construction unions. Environmentalists prefer standards to effluent taxes on ideological grounds. Thus politicians' opposition to effluent taxes may not be solely the result of business opposition. Support for the effluent tax choice is not unanimous among economists; see Susan Rose-Ackerman, "Effluent Taxes: A Critique," *Canadian Journal of Economics* 6, no. 4, pp. 512–528.

36. See chapter 5 for a discussion of this assertion.

37. This conclusion is somewhat oversimplified; other preventive methods are available. For example, almost all the excess incidence of lung cancer found among asbestos workers occurred among smokers. Some synergistic effect puts smokers at great peril when they work with asbestos; nonsmokers' chances of getting lung cancer appear to be unaffected, although they are still vulnerable to other asbestos-caused diseases (e.g. asbestosis). If cases arise where nonsmoking totally removes any risk from exposure, then screening out smokers becomes a possible alternative.

38. For a discussion of these conditions, see Russell Settle, "The Welfare Economics of Occupational Safety and Health Standards" (Ph.D. diss., University of Wisconsin, 1974), pp. 248 ff. They include the assumptions that firms are cost minimizers; that adjustment times until an equilibrium is reached are the same under the two methods; that the costs required to calculate the proper tax amount are not significant; and that enforcement costs are lower under the tax approach. Of course, even if these are not at all true, the tax approach may still be superior.

39. Robert Smith has grappled with some of these issues. For his views on the optimal size of a tax, see *Safety and Health Act*, pp. 80–82. For his estimate of the effect on the injury rate for a tax of a given size, see "The Feasibility of an 'Injury Tax' Approach to Occupational Safety," *Law and Contemporary Problems*, 38 (Summer-Autumn 1974): 730–744. He concluded that a tax of $250 per lost-workday injury would reduce the lost-workday injury rate in manufacturing by about 1 percent. That result depends upon a figure for the value of lifesaving, calculated by Smith, which is about ten times larger than the value reported by Thaler and Rosen. If the latter valuation is substituted in Smith's calculation, the elasticity of the injury rate increases tenfold. We don't know what the real effects would be, but plausibly they are somewhere between 1 and 10 percent. (In practice, levying the tax as a flat amount per injury could be a mistake if employers directed their efforts at preventing relatively minor injuries; however, focusing only on severity could impose an unfair burden on some unlucky employers. For a discussion of the relative attractiveness of frequency and severity measures, see Mendeloff, "Costs and Consequences," chap. 8, appendix A.

40. Even if a $250 tax reduced the injury rate by 10 percent, 1,800,000 injuries would still occur (90 percent of two million), and the tax payments would be $450 million. Ideally, the size of an injury tax should be set to equal the amount by which the social costs of injuries exceed the private costs to employers. The tax raises the firm's cost curve for injuries. With the addition of the tax, the firm will add resources to injury prevention in order to reduce its tax payments. Preventive measures will be added until the point at which the net private cost of preventing another injury equals the tax payment. The tax payments on the remaining injuries are transferred from private to public coffers.

41. Any proposal to reverse the transfers and pay employers for each extra injury they prevented would, of course, be laughed out of Congress.

42. The Union's leverage depends upon the expected marginal cost to the employer of the threatened inspection. If the employer is inspected frequently anyway (for example, because the plant is a large one in a hazardous industry) and if the expected costs decline

with successive inspections which are less than a certain time period apart (that is, because violations have been abated as a result of the earlier inspections), then the union's leverage begins to slip away. See chapter 7 for further discussion.

Interestingly, the provision of the OSH Act that authorizes "complaint inspections" [Section 8(f)(1)] did not appear in the Daniels bill. Instead that bill included a rather complicated procedure allowing a worker to "absent himself" if, following a determination of toxicity by HEW, the employer either didn't reduce exposures to within safe limits or didn't provide personal protective equipment. This procedure was eschewed by the Senate committee in favor of allowing employee complaints. House criticism that the bill allowed "strikes with pay" finally led Daniels to follow suit. See Senate, Committee on Labor and Public Welfare, *Legislative History*, p. 1009.

43. Fenno, *Congressmen in Committees*, p. 103.

44. David Mayhew, *Congress: The Electoral Connection*, (New Haven: Yale University Press, 1974), p. 122.

45. Ibid., p. 138.

46. Only under two conditions could workers, in theory, pay all the costs. One is where workers valued the risk reductions at an amount equal to or greater than the cost of the reductions to the firm. In such a case, however, it would have paid the firm to correct the hazards in the absence of OSHA. Thus, almost by definition, measures fostered by OSHA don't meet that criterion. Under a competitive model, a firm could not reduce wages by more than the amount the worker valued the risk reduction, or it would suffer a competitive disadvantage in the labor market. Only if the per-worker cost of compliance for all firms were equal could firms shift all of the cost onto labor, for then OSHA would act like a payroll tax. (Even that conclusion depends upon a number of other assumptions about the mobility of labor and capital, the relative capital intensity of risky and nonrisky industries, and the elasticity of substitution between labor and capital.) See Wayne Vroman, "The Incidence of Compensation Insurance Premium Payments," in *Supplemental Studies for the National Commission on State Workmen's Compensation Laws*, ed. Monroe Berkowitz (Washington, D.C.: Government Printing Office, 1973), 2: 241–270.

47. In theory, this discussion need not be limited to unionized workplaces, but since the crucial issues are that workers be well informed and that some mechanism for bargaining over wages exists, workers in a union are assumed to be more competent than those in a nonunion workplace.

48. The New York income data for occupations in 1949 are from the 1950 census. The data on injury and fatality rates (for events compensated in 1951 and 1952) are from New York State Department of Labor, "Age and Sex Differences in Work Injury Rates," Special Labor News Memorandum no. 125 (September 1, 1969). I was able to match 57 occupations or occupational groups from the two sources. For the 1967 data, see Thaler and Rosen, "Estimating the Value of Saving a Life," p. 31. Settle, "Welfare Economics," pp. 36–37, calculated the correlations between an injury frequency–severity index and the wage for three-digit SIC *industries;* he found a positive relation for nonmanufacturing industries and no relation for manufacturing. Industry is a less relevant measure than occupation.

The steel industry data are from the 1971 edition of the *Job Description and Classification Manual*. Other correlations were as follows: Job Class (J) and Surroundings (S) = +0.04; J and Physical Effort (P) = −0.29; P and S = −0.33; P and Hazards = +0.34; S and Hazards = +0.38.

49. But to say "largely symbolic" is to concede that it is partly material. For someone greatly concerned about these status inequalities, the meager contribution of the OSH Act may nevertheless surpass those of other possible governmental actions.

Notes to Chapter 3

1. The Walsh-Healey standards included "threshold limit values" (TLVs) for about 400 toxic dusts and gases as well as a 90-decibel noise exposure limit (for an eight-hour day).

2. Bureau of National Affairs, *Job Safety*, (Washington, D.C.) p. 222.

3. Interviews by the author with Robert Nagle and William Steiger in Washington, D.C., October 1975.

4. U.S., Congress, House Committee on Education and Labor, *Occupational Safety and Health Act (Oversight and Proposed Amendments): Hearings*, 92d Cong., 2d sess., 1973, pp. 236-237.

5. Interviews with Leo Teplow and Frank Barnako, October 1975.

6. See, for example, Robert Moran, "Occupational Safety and Health Standards as Federal Law: The Hazards of Haste," *William and Mary Law Review* 15: 777-797. Moran was a member of the OSHRC.

7. Joseph Page and Mary-Win O'Brien, *Bitter Wages*, (New York: Grossman, 1973) pp. 199-203.

8. Ibid.

9. In response to questioning by the Senate labor subcommittee, the Labor Department wrote that "Section 9(a) of the Act provides that 'If, upon inspection or investigation, the Secretary or his authorized representative believes that an employer has violated a requirement of [the Act] . . . he shall with reasonable promptness issue a citation to the employer.' Pursuant to this Congressional mandate, the Secretary has established the firm and unequivocal policy of citing *all* violations to which employers are, have been, or could be exposed, and which have a direct or immediate relationship to safety and health." Reprinted in U.S., Congress, Senate, Committee on Labor and Public Welfare, *Occupational Safety and Health Act Review, 1974: Hearings*, 93d Cong., 2d sess., 1975, p. 1115.

10. The implications of this step are actually quite complex. Standards whose violation never involves a serious hazard could be revoked, but that would address only a small part of the problem. Usually a particular violation will be hazardous in some situations but not in others. Discretion really is needed.

11. For calendar 1973 and 1974, the total number of OSHA inspections is given in the 1974 *President's Report on Occupational Safety and Health*, (Washington, D.C.: Government Printing Office), table 5, p. 17. For the first two quarters of 1975, I took the figures from OSHA worksheets provided by Peter Bouker of OSHA. The figure for the total number of health inspections was calculated by adding up the number of inspections for each toxic substance listed on OSHA Report 27N for the period covered.

12. Nicholas Ashford, *Crisis in the Workplace: Occupational Disease and Injury* (Cambridge, Mass.: MIT Press, 1976), pp. 444-445.

13. A memo from OSHA chief Guenther to Labor Undersecretary Silberman describing the agency's responsiveness to the president's electoral needs in 1972 came to light during the Watergate investigation. While hardly an admission that standards were being deliberately held back for political reasons (as some have charged), the memo did reveal that Guenther was checking the political party affiliation of all OSHA area and regional directors and planned to have the Republican National Committee and the Committee to Reelect the President propose applicants for the major OSHA jobs. A copy of the memo appears in the Bureau of National Affairs *Reporter*, July 25, 1974, p. 215.

14. This example of the language used is taken from the "Notice of Proposed Rulemaking on Asbestos," *Federal Register*, October 9, 1975, p. 47661.

15. This Walsh-Healey standard is reprinted in Bureau of National Affairs, *Job Safety*, p. 325. "Administrative" controls refer to personnel policies that would, for example, limit the hours of exposure by splitting a hazardous job between two workers. In practice employers very rarely resort to administrative controls.

16. U.S. Department of Labor, Occupational Safety and Health Administration, *Compliance Operations Manual* (Washington, D.C., January 1972), p. X-10 (date of issue November 15, 1971).

17. B. F. Goodrich, 2 OSHC 3035 (1974).

18. The cases, in which mobility of capital and of labor skills is very limited, might include geographically isolated workplaces, those with quite elderly workers, and those employing skills for which there is very limited demand.

19. Penn-Dixie Industries, 4 OSHC 1209 (1976).

20. In 1972, the average initial abatement period for unionized firms was 17 months (3 cases); for nonunion firms, 26 months (4 cases). In 1973, the average for unionized firms was 22 months (6 cases); for nonunion, 29 months (4 cases). The means were compared with both years together: unionized, 20.4 (9); nonunion, 27.6 (8). The difference was significant at the .05 level with a one-tailed test. For 5 of the 23 noise violation cases I was unable to ascertain the abatement date from the case file; in one case, it was not apparent whether the firm was unionized. The *COM* gives a list of factors that the area director should take into account in determining the abatement date: "the seriousness of the violation, the number of exposed employees, the availability of needed equipment or personnel, the estimated time required for delivery and installation of needed equipment, and any other relevant circumstances" (p. X-8).

21. In an interview, Baruch Fellner, deputy associate solicitor for OSH in the Department of Labor, stated that OSHA has refused to grant extensions in only 11 out of every 1,000 cases. Since 1974, OSHA has tended to grant initial abatement periods of only one year and then rely on extensions.

22. The cases on the burden of proof for technical feasibility were Reynolds Metals, 3 OSHRC 2051, and Love Box Co., 4 OSHRC 1138 (4/7/76). The two-to-one decision to require the weighing of costs and benefits came in Continental Can Co., 4 OSHRC 1541. Continental Can had argued that it would cost over $30 million to meet the noise standard at its plants with engineering controls. With personal protective equipment it stated that it could control exposures for only a few hundred thousand dollars. OSHA presented no evidence about the costs of compliance, arguing that it was irrelevant except in cases of financial jeopardy. Thus OSHA could not carry the burden that the OSHRC placed on it.

23. Interview with Ben Mintz, associate solicitor for OSH in the Department of Labor.

Notes to Chapter 4
1. Boyd is quoted in U.S. Department of Labor, Occupational Safety and Health Administration, *Job Safety and Health* (Washington, D.C., 1975), pp. 24–25. The Mintz quotation is found in *Health Politics*, (published by New York University and the Committee on Health Politics) 5, no. 3 (Spring 1975): 22. Schaffer is quoted in Peter Sheridan, "Toxic Substances Control: Congress Prepares to Act," *Occupational Hazards*, July 1975, p. 43. Samuels's statement appears in David Kalis, "Cost Impact: How and Where It Fits into OSHA's Standard Setting Scheme," *Occupational Hazards*, February 1975 p. 37.

2. Interview with Daniel Boyd, October 1975. All the interviews cited in this chapter were carried out in Washington, D.C., during that month.

3. Religious language does indeed provide appropriate expressions for describing this

phenomenon, as Aaron Wildavsky has argued in the case of pollution policy in his "Economy and Environment/Morality and Meaning," a review of *The Uncertain Search for Environmental Quality*, by B. Ackerman, S. Rose-Ackerman, O. Henderson, and J. W. Sawyer, Jr., *Stanford Law Review* 29, no. 1 (November 1976): 183-204.

4. Section 6(f) of the act.

5. *Synthetic Organic Chemical Manufacturers Association v. Brennan*, 503 F. 2d 1160 (1974).

6. The chief exceptions have been court decisions striking down emergency temporary standards on the grounds that OSHA had not shown that a "grave danger" existed. All three of OSHA's first permanent standards were originally issued as emergency temporary standards (valid for six months) under Section 6(c) of the act.

7. *Industrial Union Department, AFL-CIO v. Hodgson*, 499 F. 2d 467 (1974).

8. U.S., Congress, Senate, Report no. 91-1282, 91st Cong., 2d Sess., p. 58.

9. *Industrial Union Department, AFL-CIO v. Hodgson*, pp. 477-478.

10. Interview with Donald Elisburg.

11. Interview with Dan Krivit.

12. Interview with John Stender.

13. Memorandum to Congressman William Steiger. The memo specifically complained that Schubert had not prevented Stender from issuing an emergency standard on pesticides (which was later thrown out by the courts) and had failed to get him to differentiate among the substances covered in the standard on the fourteen carcinogens.

14. Although formal authority rests with the assistant secretary, higher authorities do have tools for intervening. The solicitor's office, which reports to the secretary and undersecretary, is heavily involved in OSH legal issues because OSHA has no legal staff of its own. Under the accepted procedures on standards, the associate solicitor for OSH has had the informal authority to delay adoption of a new standard. Ultimately a secretary can usually get the president to fire an assistant secretary, but that step is a last resort.

15. Interviews with Daniel Boyd and John Stender.

16. Barry Kramer, "Health Hazards: Vinyl-Chloride Risks Were Known by Many before First Deaths," *Wall Street Journal*, October 5, 1974, p. 1.

17. For vinyl chloride, as for other permanent standards issued since 1974, a good history of regulation and a description of the major arguments and evidence can be found in the foreword to the standard itself published in the *Federal Register*. For vinyl chloride, see the *Federal Register*, October 4, 1974, pp. 35890 ff.

18. Bureau of National Affairs, *Reporter*, June 27, 1974, p. 86.

19. These figures are derived from exhibits V-10 and V-5 in the Snell final report, "Economic Impact Studies of the Effects of Proposed OSHA Standards for Vinyl Chloride," September 27, 1974, Contract No. L/A 74-167.

20. This and the following quotations are all taken from the October 4, 1974, *Federal Register*, pp. 35891–35892.

21. "Sharp Drop in Vinyl Chloride Exposure Is Ordered by Labor Agency for Workers," *Wall Street Journal*, October 5, 1974.

22. Interview with George Taylor.

23. Interview with Grover Wrenn.

24. Barry Kramer, "Goodrich Unit's PVC Facility in Quebec Has Had 9 Deaths Due to a Rare Cancer," *Wall Street Journal*, October 29, 1975.

25. James Singer, "New OSHA Head May Signal Change in Agency's Approach," *National Journal*, Dec. 27, 1975, p. 1733.

26. The findings of the study—"Vinyl Chloride Industrial Abstract Cast Study," prepared by the Center for Policy Alternatives, Massachusetts Institute of Technology (Cambridge, Mass., 1976) are reported in Mary Jane Bolle, "Cost-Benefit Studies for OSHA Standards: Use and Misuse," Congressional Research Service Paper 77-56E, August 22, 1977, pp. 26-29.

The conclusiveness of that study's findings are called into possible question by the 1975 statement of a Society for the Plastics Industry spokesman that the cost impact would not be noticeable until after April 1976, when use of respirators would no longer be allowed. See Bureau of National Affairs, *Reporter*, July 31, 1975, p. 295.

27. Bureau of National Affairs, *Reporter*, May 16, 1974, p. 1594.

28. Preface to Standard, *Federal Register*, Dec. 3, 1974, p. 41842.

29. Quoted in Carl Musacchio, "The Power Press Flap: Will It Reshape Standards Setting?" *Occupational Hazards*, October 1973, p. 110.

30. Transcript of hearing on power press standard, p. 107. The transcript is on file at OSHA's Technical Data Center, Washington, D.C.

31. *Federal Register*, Dec. 3, 1974, pp. 41842, 41843.

32. In the power press standard comment file, OSHA Technical Data Center, Washington, D.C.

33. *AFL-CIO* v. *Brennan* (no. 75-1105).

34. See U.S. Department of Health, Education, and Welfare, National Institute of Occupational Safety and Health, "Machine Guarding—Assessment of Need," Publication no. 75-173 (Washington, D.C., June 1975), pp. 190, 197.

35. For a discussion of OSHA's new safety standards and the economic studies that accompanied them, see John Mendeloff, "Costs and Consequences: A Political and Economic Analysis of the Occupational Safety and Health Act" (Ph.D. diss., University of California, Berkely, 1977), pp. 169-177.

36. For ten of the fourteen carcinogens, NIOSH had estimated that the population at risk for each was equal to or less than 1,000 workers. Only one—4,4 Methylene-bis (2-Chloroaniline)—involved more than a few thousand workers. Because NIOSH and OSHA proposed uniform work procedures (rather than exposure levels) for all of them, they were treated in one action. For information on the populations at risk, see the *President's Report on Occupational Safety and Health* (Washington, D.C.: Government Printing Office, 1973), pp. 152-161.

37. Ibid, p. 106.

38. Employers, for example, have fought hard against proposals to require that signs be posted warning workers of the cancer-causing potential of asbestos or vinyl chloride. According to Steven Kelman, employers in one lawsuit aimed at getting rid of warning signs openly expressed the fear that the signs would force them to pay higher wages. Unions have been concerned about the implication of OSHA's requirement that when medical exams find that a worker should be removed from a certain exposure, the company must remove him—without any guarantee that he will retain his wage rate.

39. The 1972 asbestos standard illustrates this practice. It states that even when engineer-

ing controls can't attain compliance, ". . . they shall nonetheless be used to reduce exposures to the lowest practicable level, and shall be supplemented by the use of work practice controls." *Code of Federal Regulations* 1910.1001(f)(2). Employers have denounced this requirement, which imposes both the costs of engineering controls and the inconvenience of personal protective equipment, OSHA's reply has been that respirators provide less certain protection, and hence improvements achieved by engineering controls, although insufficient by themselves, will reduce the harm resulting from those deficiencies.

40. Criteria documents for silica, sulfuric acid, benzene, and chloroform were also transmitted to OSHA by NIOSH during 1974. OSHA had not proposed standards for any of them by the end of 1976.

41. Arthur D. Little, Inc., "Economic Impact of Proposed Osha Standard for Asbestos," first report to the U.S. Department of Labor, April 28, 1972, p. 1.

42. Ibid., p. 2. Most of the economic studies conducted for OSHA, unlike this one, did not make any recommendations.

43. Selikoff's role is well reported by Paul Brodeur, *Expendable Americans* (New York: Viking, 1974).

44. Interview with Daniel Boyd.

45. Russell Settle, "The Welfare Economics of Occupational Safety and Health Standards" (Ph.D. diss., University of Wisconsin, 1974), chap. 4.

46. These seventy-two estimates derive from three assumptions about the number of asbestos-caused deaths, three assumptions about the trend of benefits and costs over time, two time periods of varying lengths, two discount rates and two measures of benefits. Ibid., table 15, pp. 158-161.

47. Ibid., p. 173. The discount rates used were 4 percent and 10 percent. The narrower concept includes only foregone gross earnings and the costs of medical treatment resources. These benefits comprise only about 20 percent of the value of the broader concept, in which the value of nonmarket time to workers and the value of the retirement years loom largest. Exactly how to value these is very problematic. Settle chooses to value a worker's nonwork hours at his after-tax wage rate and to assume that a worker would be earning that wage eighteen hours a day, every day of the year. Understandably, his valuation of the time of retirees is even more arbitrary.

48. The conference, which I attended, was sponsored by the U.S. Department of Labor and was entitled, "Evaluating the Effects of the Occupational Safety and Health Program." It was held in Annapolis, Maryland, March 18-19, 1975.

See Settle, "Welfare Economics," p. 93, for the assumption about effectiveness.

49. Ibid., p. 103-110.

50. Robert S. Smith, *The Occupational Safety and Health Act: Its Goals and Its Achievements* (Washington, D.C.: American Enterprise Institute, 1976), pp. 55-56.

51. See the second Bolt, Beranek, and Newman study, "Economic Impact Analysis of Proposed Noise Control Regulation," Report no. 3246, April 21, 1976, p. 3-1.

52. Executive Order 11821, *Federal Register*, November 27, 1974, p. 41501.

53. Interview with John Stender.

54. The December 1974 memo was written by a Labor Department official outside of OSHA and circulated among Stender and his top deputies. The cover letter written by one of the OSHA staff described the memo as "paralleling our discussion of last week."

55.The Labor Department's main battle with OMB didn't concern OSHA but rather the exemption from the IIS requirement of the interpretive rulings about prevailing wages that it makes under the Davis-Bacon Act. It won that fight.

56. Interview with Donald Elisburg.

57. Interview with ASPER official.

58. Interview with John Morrall. The IIS requirement did not include any mention of benefit-cost analysis, but CWPS argued that projects whose costs exceeded their benefits contributed unjustifiably to price increases.

59. In late 1977, President Carter announced his intention to replace inflationary impact statements with a requirement for "regulatory analysis," including a specification and review of alternative approaches to the problem addressed by the regulation. Labor unions had pressed to delete any requirement for economic analysis, but the proposed executive order would specifically require analyses of economic consequences. See the *Federal Register*, November 17, 1977, pp. 59740-59746.

60. Smith, *Health Act*, p. 85. For the central argument for this conceptual approach, see E. J. Mishan, "Evaluation of Life and Limb: A Theoretical Approach," *Journal of Political Economy* 79 (1971), pp. 687-705.

61. Smith, *Health Act*, p. 57.

62. See Harold Hochman and James Rodgers, "Pareto Optimal Redistribution," *American Economic Review*, September 1969.

63. See James Q. Wilson and Edward C. Banfield, "Public-Regardingness as a Value Premise in Voting Behavior," *American Political Science Review* 58 (1964): 876-887.

64. Interviews with David Bell and Grover Wrenn. The absence of clear decision rules does tend to enhance the power of the administrator. Wrenn observed that as an administrator he was glad Congress had not spelled out what must be done by OSHA in various circumstances, as it had with the Clean Air Act and EPA. Administrative discretion in the area of labor relations is usually quickly hammered away by the pounding of two strongly organized contenders. While Wrenn's mention of case law does reflect this pounding—each major standard has been appealed to the courts by one side or the other —the discretion remains largely untrammeled after five years. On economic issues, Wrenn predicts that discretion will continue to exist indefinitely. For a fine treatment of these issues, see James Q. Wilson, "The Dead Hand of Regulation," *The Public Interest*, no. 25 (Fall 1971), pp. 50-51.

65. Quoted in *Occupational Hazards*, October 1975, p. 49.

66. With a somewhat different focus, Zeckhauser has also emphasized the importance of the process through which safety decisions are made. See his "Procedures for Valuing Lives," *Public Policy* 23 (1975): 419-464.

This point bears on the argument that people don't perceive the extent of the costs of regulation and thus tolerate much more regulation than they would if they were better informed. (Irving Kristol had advanced this argument several times in his *Wall Street Journal* columns.) To the extent that people value a process in which costs are explicitly not considered, the argument is clearly off base.

More realistically, however, there are few, if any, goods for which the costs are irrelevant under all circumstances. There is some point at which any good—including the satisfaction derived from refusing to make trade-offs—becomes too costly to indulge. If a person were faced with the loss of all his friends or all his money as a result of that refusal, he would be likely to submit. For most people, however, the psychic benefits may far exceed whatever costs they actually incur (for example, as consumers) by a decision to ignore OSHA's costs, whether the decision is their own or society's.

67. Lewis Thomas, *The Lives of a Cell: Notes of a Biology Watcher* (New York: Viking, 1974), p. 103. On the other hand, Dr. Thomas coolly, if not icily, dismisses much of our medical spending as not cost-effective in improving health status.

68. G. Christian Hill, "Offshore Drilling Plan Stirs Heated Debate," *Wall Street Journal*, September 2, 1975, p. 1.

69. Of course many goods that no one considers priceless also cannot be marketed because of the difficulty of excluding nonpurchasers from sharing in their consumption or because of the purely technical problems of collecting payment.

70. On the FAA, see Stephen Rhoads, *Policy Analysis in the Federal Aviation Administration* (Lexington, Mass.: Lexington Books, 1974), pp. 70ff. For a report on the NHTSA study, see James W. Singer, "Product Safety Effort Challenged as Being Too Costly," *National Journal Reports*, May 3, 1975, p. 667.

71. See Keith E. Marvin and Andrew M. Rouse, "The Status of PPB in Federal Agencies: A Comparative Perspective," in Robert H. Haveman and Julius Margolis, eds., *Public Expenditures and Policy Analysis* (Chicago: Markham, 1970).

72. Quoted in William Lawrence, *Of Acceptable Risk: Science and the Determination of Safety* (Los Altos, California: William Kaufmann, 1976), p. 87.

73. Of course, several factors encourage standard setters to believe that workers are not able to protect themselves adequately. Workers are often ill informed, and their ability to change jobs is often restricted. These issues are not emphasized here because to varying degrees they are common to all of the regulatory issues discussed. For example, consumers' ignorance about auto safety design is one justification for auto safety standards.

74. For example, consider the mess a department secretary would get into if he tried to explain to a congressional committee why preventing a single death in an airplane crash would be more or less worthwhile than preventing a death in an automobile or bus accident.

75. I am endebted to Professor Lee Friedman for pointing out that OSHA requirements probably tend to increase the relative price of capital inputs. However, to the extent that OSHA creates a greater awareness of hazards among workers, the price of labor for risky jobs may rise as well.

76. James Q. Wilson has described the body of evidence supporting the proposition that "individuals and groups are politically more sensitive to sudden or significant decreases in their net benefits than they are to increases in net benefits. They are, in short, more threat-oriented than opportunity-oriented." ("Politics of Regulation," p. 139.)

77. Interview with Jack Sheehan.

78. Harold Levinson, "Pattern Bargaining: A Case Study of the Automobile Workers," *Quarterly Journal of Economics*, May 1960, p. 307.

79. "Would You Take $1,000,000 for Your Life?" Inverview with Louis Belicsky, *Job Safety and Health*, February 1975, p. 24.

80. For example, several sources report that a carcinogen program that NIOSH started was largely the result of one scientist's efforts. Because his attempts to create a more diligently protective spirit within NIOSH were appreciated, organized labor made its support for him clear to NIOSH leaders.

81. Some scientists and health professionals have been drawn to the OSH issue because

of their political commitment to environmental issues. They hope that their support for labor's tough standards in the workplace can at least neutralize some of labor's opposition to strict air pollution standards and other environmental regulation. Barry Commoner is one eminent example. See, for example, his article, "Labor's Stake in the Environment/The Environment's Stake in Labor," in *Jobs and the Environment: Three Papers,* Institute of Industrial Relations, University of California, Berkely (1973).

82. U.S., Congress, House, Committee on Education and Labor, *Occupational Safety and Health Act of 1969: Hearings,* 91st Cong., 1st sess., 1969, p. 1017.

83. In interviews with the author.

84. Interview with Anson Keller.

85. See the discussion of uncertainty by Nina Cornell, Roger Noll, and Barry Weingast, "Safety Regulation," in *Setting National Priorities: The Next Ten Years,* ed. Henry Owen and Charles L. Schultze (Washington: Brookings Institution, 1976), pp. 468–470.

86. Hal Luft of the Stanford Medical School illustrates this point with a story about a medical conference at which a doctor described an experiment on the efficacy of intensive care units (ICUs) for patients with recent coronaries. After randomly assigning some patients to go home and others to stay in the ICUs, the doctor reported that the patients who had stayed in the ICUs had experienced a slightly lower mortality rate, although the difference had not been statistically significant. Many in the audience were quite upset and demanded that the experiment be terminated and that none of the patients be deprived of the ICU care. The lunch break intervened, but following it the chagrined doctor announced that he had inadvertently mixed up the figures: the people who had gone home had experienced the lower mortality rate. No one in the audience insisted that the experiment be terminated and all patients should be sent home.

An experience of mine illustrates a similar point. I carried out a study of fatalities involving forklift trucks, which indicated that a large number of people (three to four a year in California alone) were killed when they were thrown out of an overturning forklift and crushed by the *overhead protective structure.* That structure, standard equipment since the later 1960s and required by OSHA, is intended to prevent injuries to the driver from falling loads. In that task, it is undoubtedly successful. The question remains, however, of whether the net effect of the overhead structures is beneficial.

The response of the state safety engineers with whom I spoke was to favor a new regulation requiring forklift operators to wear seatbelts. That regulation would seem to be a difficult one to enforce since drivers are constantly jumping on and off their vehicles. Keeping the overhead guards (with or without seatbelts) may be the best policy, but what is striking is the reluctance of the safety engineers to consider that getting rid of a safety requirement might lead to greater safety. More research on the issue was opposed on the grounds that it might play into the hands of opponents of seatbelts.

87. The wisdom of this emphasis is questionable, but so is the emphasis in almost all of our health programs on the prevention of death as opposed to the diminution of suffering and disability. For the argument on this point, see Leon Kass, "The Pursuit of Health," *The Public Interest,* no. 40, (Summer 1975).

Notes to Chapter 5
1. U.S., Congress, House, Committee on Education and Labor, *Occupational Safety and Health: Hearings,* 90th Cong., 2d sess., 1968, p. 12.

2. U.S., Congress, House, Committee on Education and Labor, *Occupational Safety and Health Act of 1970 (Oversight and Proposed Amendments): Hearings,* 92d Cong., 2d sess., 1972, pp. 274, 278. The state official was Charles A. Hagberg from Wisconsin.

3. William Steiger, "OSHA: Four Years Later," *Labor Law Journal* 25, no. 12 (December 1974): 728.

4. For a brief discussion of OSHA's impact on occupational diseases, see John Mendeloff, "Costs and Consequences: A Political and Economic Analysis of the Occupational Safety and Health Act" (Ph.D. diss., University of California, Berkeley, 1977), pp. 343–349. Probably the only way that evaluations could be conducted would be to have random inspections of workplaces that were likely users of toxic substances and see whether the proportion in compliance decreased over time. Whether this use of scarce industrial hygiene resources would be worthwhile is uncertain.

Note that the overall disabling injury rates described in the text are actually injury *and* illness rates, so diseases are included in the evaluation. This may impart a small upward bias to the overall rate, because illnesses are probably reported better under the new system.
  This evaluation concentrates on the manufacturing sector. While other sectors, especially construction, receive some attention, manufacturing is emphasized because better data are available and because the rise in manufacturing injury rates during the 1960s provided one of the spurs for legislative action.

5. I obtained information about the frequency and size of penalties in Massachusetts and California by telephone interviews, and in writing from New Jersey, Iowa, Wisconsin, New York, Maine, and Michigan. Maine, Iowa, and Michigan reported that they had never levied any fines on employers before OSHA.

6. "DIR Management Analysis Report on the Development of a Better Work-Targeting (I.V.I.) System for Safety Engineers Inspecting Industrial Plants." California Department of Industrial Relations, Study B, directed by Connie Trewin, October 1972, p. 10. The conclusion of the New York State study is cited in Robert S. Smith, *The Occupational Safety and Health Act: Its Goals and Its Achievements* (Washington, D.C.: American Enterprise Institute, 1976), pp. 65–66.

7. A review of Wisconsin's experiences with levying penalty payments when a safety code violation causes an accident appears in Risk Management Council's *Monthly Report*, September 1975, published by the Wisconsin Department of Industry, Labor, and Human Relations.

The California data were examined by me when I worked for the California Department of Industrial Relations. State law requires the Division of Industrial Safety (DIS) to investigate all fatal workplace accidents except those resulting from assaults and highway accidents. In addition, employers are required to notify DIS of all accidents causing amputations, permanent disfigurements, or hospitalization over 24 hours (except for observation). DIS can choose whether to investigate these nonfatal accidents. Usually inspectors try to pick those most likely to involve violations. Over 1300 such investigations were conducted during calendar 1976, although only about 1000 AI reports were on file. The main reason for this discrepancy is that some inspectors filed only when they discovered violations. Because the accidents reported in the file are heavily biased to include cases in which violations played a role, the data cannot be used to give an overall estimate of the proportion of injuries in which violations contributed to the accident. For fatalities, however, such an estimate can be constructed but in order to do so certain assumptions must be made. Of the 645 deaths processed under WC in 1976, all but 246 were the result of four phenomena unrelated to standards (highway accidents, assaults, heat attacks, and plane crashes). Of the remaining 246 deaths, 145 are accounted for in the AI reports. The question becomes whether we can say anything about the relation to violations of the other 101 deaths. Most likely all or almost all of these deaths were either (1) not investigated (despite the statutory requirement) because DIS felt that violations were unlikely to be involved; or (2) investigated but no violations were found, and the inspector didn't bother to fill out the AI report. If all standards-related deaths were investigated, then 14 percent (92 out of 645) of all deaths involved violations (or hazards for which the DIS investigators wrote "special orders"). The figure for serious violations alone was 74, or 11 percent. A maximum estimate can be constructed by assuming that the proportion of cases with violations was the same for fatalities lacking reports as for the fatalities on file. Multiplying this proportion (50 percent) times 101 gives 50 deaths. Adding that to 92 gives 142, or 22 percent of all 645 deaths.

Note, however, that although the violations cited in the AI reports were "related to" the accident, they were not necessarily the cause—that is, although the violation may have made it more likely, the accident may have occurred even in its absence.

8. I say "in part" because another reason why some of these standards are cited so infrequently pertains to their vagueness. Inspectors are reluctant to cite them unless an accident has actually occured, lending substance to the claim that a hazard really did exist; Otherwise, inspectors would search for a more specific standard or not cite at all.

9. Smith, *Health Act*, pp. 63–64.

10. The findings of the Conference Board's survey are described by Nicholas Ashford, *Crisis in the Workplace: Occupational Disease and Injury* (Cambridge, Mass.: MIT Press, 1976), p. 318.

11. Wild uncertainties about costs plague any discussion of OSHA. I found that my own attempt to construct some estimates degenerated as I multiplied each guessed-at number (or range) by another. I do present a discussion of these estimates in "An Evaluation of the OSHA Program's Effect on Workplace Injury Rates: Evidence from California through 1974," prepared for the U.S. Department of Labor Office of the Assistant Secretary for Policy, Evaluation, and Research (July 1976); see appendix B.

12. One way to maintain the same basic view of firm behavior would be to admit that safety information, like all information, cannot be obtained without some cost. The employer of ten workers may have decided that he didn't have the time to read safety manuals and that his plant wasn't large enough to warrant a visit from his workers' compensation insurer's safety inspector. Neither was he willing to pay the minimum fee charged by private safety consultants. When OSHA appears on the scene, he reads about it in his trade journal and sends for the book of standards. Confronted by hundreds of pages of tightly printed jargon, he decides that maybe he'd better play it safe and call in a safety consultant. The consultant explains which OSHA standards he is out of compliance with, and together they figure out the cost of compliance. The employer doesn't really know how many injuries would be prevented by each expenditure, but he does know what his injury experience has been. Consequently, he decides that compliance with some of the standards would not be worthwhile for him. On the other hand, he discovers from the consultant that some hazards can be corrected more cheaply than he had realized, and he proceeds to abate them. For this employer, the threat of OSHA penalties spurred an investment in information. OSHA in this instance generated a higher level of safety not by adding to the costs of noncompliance (penalties) but rather by reducing the perceived costs of compliance.

Although I am sure this scenario has been acted out in real life, it should not be given undue importance. Employers do, after all, have considerable incentive to seek out information that will help them increase profits. And as this example shows, if the new measures they learn about won't increase profits, they won't adopt them.

13. See Mendeloff, "Costs and Consequences," pp. 257-259, for the data on which this statement is based. Most inspections of establishments with over 500 workers are not general schedule inspections and do not cover the entire workplace. However, many if not most complaint inspections and accident investigations include at least a partial tour.

14. Coverage figures for 1974 appear in the *President's Report on Occupational Safety and Health* (Washington, D.C.: Government Printing Office, 1974), p. 22. More recent figures can be found in the monthly BNA *Occupational Safety and Health Reporter.*

These figures are based upon the inspectors' responses to the instruction, "Enter the number of employees affected by the OSHA inspection. . . . If a partial inspection is made, enter an estimate of the number of employees primarily affected by the inspection, e.g., if only one shop or part of a plant is inspected, enter the number of employees employed in that shop or part of the plant on all shifts." U.S. Department of Labor, Occupational Safety and Health Administration, *OSHA Management Information System Field Reporting Manual,* (Washington, D.C., May 1975), p. III-7. Of course, inspectors may tend to exaggerate.

15. *President's Report, 1974,* table 5, p. 23.

16. For example, one standard pertaining to falls in construction—"guardrails, handrails, and covers" (1926.500)—was cited as a serious violation over 700 times in 1974, constituting 15 percent of all serious violations cited by OSHA in that year. See *President's Report, 1974,* table 12, p. 25.

17. In "Safety and Health Provisions Before and After OSHA," Winston Tillery reports that a BLS survey of 503 contracts—the version of the contract in force before January 1971 and its successor, in force after January 1972—showed that the general changes in safety clauses were small. The provisions that changed the most were those requiring the employer (from 204 contracts before OSHA to 259 contracts after OSHA) or the employee (197 to 246) to comply with the state and federal laws and standards. *Monthly Labor Review,* September 1975, pp. 40–43.

18. By fiscal 1977, complaint inspections had soared to about 40 percent of non–follow-up inspections performed by federal OSHA. Part of the reason for this growth was the decision—triggered by OSHA's failure to check out an informal complaint about what turned out to be a major hazard (kepone)—to inspect in response to "informal" complaints (for example, from nonemployees or anonymous ones) as well as "formal" ones.

19. Jerome B. Gordon, Allan Akman, and Michael Brooks, *Industrial Safety Statistics: A Re-Examination* (New York: Praeger, 1971), table 8.10., p. 150.

20. The importance of this type of reaction to a safer environment is stressed by Sam Peltzman in *Regulation of Automobile Safety* (Washington, D.C.: American Enterprise Institute, 1975). I think the point is valid but that Peltzman overstates it. At any rate, it is less applicable to occupational safety than to auto safety.

Notes to Chapter 6
1. Aldona Di Pietro, "An Analysis of the OSHA Inspection Program in Manufacturing Industries 1972-73," U.S. Department of Labor, Office of the Assistant Secretary for Policy, Evaluation, and Research, Technical Analysis Paper (Washington, D.C., August 1976), mimeo.

2. Di Pietro points out that the failure to find any evidence that inspections caused injury rates to fall could have arisen because causality runs in the opposite direction as well—that is, workplaces with rising rates may be more likely to be inspected. She presents evidence that establishments with a high or rising rates were in fact more likely to be inspected in 1973. The finding on high-rate firms is probably, for the most part, an artifact of Di Pietro's use of two-digit SIC classifications; since OSHA inspects firms in high-rate four-digit industries, naturally it will tend to inspect the higher-rate workplaces within the more aggregated industry. The finding about rising rates is more pertinent and interesting. DiPietro does not ask how inspectors can find out where rates are rising, but the likely answer is through previous inspections. An inspector is probably more likely to

schedule a follow-up inspection or another general inspection when he sees (from reviewing the injury log, which he is required to do during the inspection) that the rate is rising. Accident investigations also contribute in a small way to inspecting workplaces with rising rates. Although none of these factors is very large, in combination they may obscure an inspection effect of a few percentage points, which is the likely magnitude of OSHA's impact. A recent reanalysis of this data has found an inspection effect.

3. Robert S. Smith, "The Estimated Impact on Injuries of OSHA's Target Industry Program," paper presented at the Department of Labor Conference on Evaluating OSHA (Annapolis, Md., March 18–19, 1975).

4. The reasoning behind this assertion begins with the fact that the high-rate industries tend to be those with particularly unsafe environments or work practices. Since in the absence of major technological changes these are intrinsic to the production process, the hazards are unlikely to be eliminated by compliance with standards. The finding that variations in injury rates among industries cannot be attributed to differences in the extent of industry compliance with standards reinforces the point. See Robert S. Smith, *The Occupational Safety and Health Act: Its Goals and Its Achievements* (Washington, D.C.: American Enterprise Institute, 1976), p. 65.

A review of injury rate trends by accident type for the target industries in California suggests that the CIB injury rate declined slightly for two of the three industries. However, when one looks at specific industries, it is not apparent that *aggregate* judgments about which accident types are most standards-related necessarily apply. See Mendeloff, "An Evaluation of the OSHA Program's Effect on Workplace Injury Rates: Evidence from California through 1974," prepared for the U.S. Department of Labor, Office of the Assistant Secretary for Policy, Evaluation, and Research (July 1976), appendix G.

5. In the TIP (Target Industry Program) industries, the 5 percent of ICDV injuries would decline 10 percent [−.5%] while the remaining 95 percent of all injuries would increase by 5 percent [+4.75%] for a net increase of 4.25 percent. In the non-TIP industries, the 10 percent of ICDV injuries would decline by 5 percent [−.5%] while the remaining 90 percent would increase by 5 percent [+4.5%] for a net increase of 4.0 percent.

6. The California study is cited in chapter 5, note 6. For 72 of the 91 injuries judged controllable, I felt that there was enough information to reconstruct the accident type— falls, CIBs, and so on. From those 72 cases, I calculated the percentage of controllable injuries in each accident type. For example, 23.6 percent of the 72 were CIB injuries. Since, according to the study, only 18 percent of all injuries were controllable, these controllable CIB injuries composed 4.3 percent of all injuries (.18 times 23.6 percent). For all disabling injuries reported in California in 1970, CIBs comprised 7.4 percent. Dividing 4.3 by 7.4 percent therefore gives the percentage of all CIB injuries, which were controllable—58 percent. The same procedure was followed for the other accident types.

7. These sources are cited in chapter 5, note 7. The California study was conducted by the author.

8. One difficulty with this focus on categories of injuries is that it may be subject to the "ecological" fallacy. For example, if 60 percent of all the injuries in an accident type category are standards-related, reductions of up to 40 percent could come entirely from injuries unrelated to standards, and the inference that the reductions resulted from compliance could be unwarranted.

9. For the most complete discussion of the determinants of occupational accident rates, see Walter Oi, "Economic and Empirical Aspects of Industrial Safety," prepared for the U.S. Department of Labor, February 28, 1974.

10. See R. H. Van Zelst, "The Effect of Age and Experience upon Accident Rate," *Journal of Applied Psychology* 38, no. 5 (1954).

The new-hire rate is the annual rate for the number of workers *newly* hired (that is, excluding workers recalled from layoffs) each month as a percentage of the total number of employees during the month. The average new-hire rate for the postwar period has been about 3.0. A plant with this rate and an average employment of 100 would hire an average of 3 people a month or 36 people a year.

11. The shortening job tenure of workers over the past ten years (within each age cohort) is documented in "Job Tenure of Workers, 1973," Special Labor Force Report no. 172 (Washington, D.C.: Bureau of Labor Statistics, 1975).

12. Professor Lee Friedman of University of California, Berkeley, pointed out to me that the injuries caused by the increase in inexperienced and young workers would not necessarily be suffered by those workers.

13. Van Zelst, "Effect of Age," pp. 316–317. Robert E. B. Lucas has shown that jobs held by younger male workers are more hazardous than those held by older male workers. See "The Distribution of Job Characteristics," *Review of Economics and Statistics* 56 (November 1974). The finding that young males have higher injury rates holds for the lost workday injury rates analyzed in this chapter.

14. See, for example, Jerome B. Gordon, Allan Akman, and Michael Brooks, *Industrial Safety Statistics: A Re-examination* (New York: Praeger, 1971).

15. Readers unfamiliar with regression analysis may benefit from the following simple example. Suppose that we have four years of data about injury rates and the new-hire rate, which we will pretend is the sole important influence on the size of the injury rate. The new-hire rates are 2.0, 2.5, 3.0 and 2.5, and the corresponding injury rates are 50 per 1000, 52 per 1000, 56 per 1000, and 53 per 1000. Then, on average, the effect of a 0.5 increase in the new-hire rate is to increase the injury rate by 3 per 1000. A multiple regression analysis carries out the same sort of operation on several variables simultaneously, estimating the average independent effect of each on the injury rate.

16. A Chow test was used to test the null hypothesis that the parameters for the 1950s (1948–59) and for the 1960s (1959–70) were the same. This null hypothesis could not be rejected. Both the unlagged NH and the earning coefficients were highly significant in both periods, but the lagged NH and age coefficients were insignificant in both with different signs. See the appendix for a discussion of how the age variable was constructed and how the new-hire variable was extended back to 1947.

17. There are several potential sources of bias. One is the malpractice insurance problem which ballooned in the mid-1970s, allegedly leading some doctors to practice a more "defensive medicine," one result of which may be that some injured workers who would once have been told to report back to work now are told to take time off from work. A second explanation could be a small change in the wording of the main question used to determine whether the injuries reported by employees involved lost workdays. (This issue is discussed in Mendeloff, "Evaluation," appendix D.) A third possibility is that higher benefit levels (or, after April 1974, shorter waiting periods) encouraged some workers—who wouldn't otherwise have taken off a day—to take days off work in order to get the higher benefits they qualified for after three days. Adding a WC benefits variable to the regression model did not indicate that higher benefits (either in constant dollars or as a percentage of the average weekly wage) increased the reported California injury rate; however, this result could possibly be attributable to an offsetting factor—higher benefits leading to higher premiums and greater injury prevention efforts. Alone, none of these developments is likely to create a worrisome bias, but together they do pose the possibility that recent rates are somewhat inflated.

18. For further discussion of data from other states, see Mendeloff, "Evaluation," appendix I. The same regression model was tested on the overall compensable injury rate for

Wisconsin manufacturing and gave results similar to the California finding. See ibid., "Costs and Consequences: A Political and Economic Analysis of the Occupational Safety and Health Act" (Ph.D. diss., University of California, Berkeley, 1977), appendix C.

19. The F statistics for these comparisons (with the larger sample running through 1974) were highly significant for all of the CIB regression variants, significant for the "strains" regression, but not significant for the other accident type rates or for the overall California rate (except for the variant that omitted a trend variable). The F statistics are reported in the list of regressions in the appendix. For the procedure used to calculate the F statistic in these circumstances (where the added number of observations is less than the number of parameters), see J. Johnston, *Econometric Methods*, 2d ed. (New York: McGraw Hill, 1972), p. 207.

20. Higher WC benefits or premiums provide injury prevention incentives only to the extent that experience rating translates reduced injury losses into reduced premiums. Since experience rating increases with firm size, we might be tempted to test the effect of WC changes by examining injury experience for different size classes of firms. Unfortunately, so many factors are bound up with firm size that tests of any one proposition are likely to be thwarted. For example, larger firms are also (1) more likely to have complied prior to OSHA; (2) more likely to have unions and safety directors who will utilize OSHA; and (3) more likely to be inspected (to the extent that their individual establishments are also large).

The relation of WC benefits/premiums and reported injury rates may be complex (see note 17). Perhaps higher benefits induce increased workers' claims of back injuries, which might explain why the net effect of high WC benefits/premiums might be zero. Perhaps WC benefit/premium increases really do lead to added safety efforts and reduced injuries for the CIB and other hard-to-fake types of injuries. However, we would still need to explain why, for example, the CIB rate was lower than predicted while the (hard-to-fake) struck by and striking against rate was not. In any event, if would be interesting to rerun the regression described in note 17 for each accident type rate.

21. According to a McGraw-Hill inventory of metalworking equipment, the percentage of metalworking machines that were numerically controlled grew (in northern California and northern Nevada) from 0.58 percent in 1968 to 1.03 percent in 1973; in southern California (and southern Nevada and Arizona), the figures were 0.71 percent and 1.30 percent. See "The Eleventh American Machinist Inventory of Metalworking Equipment 1973," *American Machinist*, October 29, 1973, table 13, p. 164.

22. Ibid. The 15 percent figure was estimated from the data in table 9, p. 160.

23. Graphs for these three and the other accident type fatalities appear in Mendeloff, "Costs and Consequences," pp. 323-328.

24. The assumptions and calculations underlying these estimates are presented in ibid., chap. 7, appendix A.

25. See Florida Department of Commerce, "Analysis of Work Injuries Covered by Workmen's Compensation, 1972," table 6, pp. 36-37. Note that Florida includes all cases with one or more full lost workdays, the same measure of disabling injury used in California.

26. A discussion of costs imposed by OSHA appears in Mendeloff, "Evaluation," appendix B. The "hardest" data pertain to capital expenditures on both safety and health beginning in 1972. The key questions are: (1) how much of this spending has been for safety? (2) how much of that sum would not have been spent in the absence of OSHA? (3) how should the capital spending be depreciated to arrive at a cost figure for the years through 1975? Then we need estimates of noncapital safety expenditures attributable to OSHA.

27. One of the tests I carried out, did address this question. The change in the manufacturing lost-workday rate (as reported in the BLS survey) was the dependent variable in a
regression with variables for the probability of inspection and the average penalty per
inspection. The key control variable was the change in the state new-hire rate. At the
time, data were available for only about 25 states for 1972–73 and 1973–74 regressions.
The new-hire rate coefficient was significant and comparable in size to its coefficient in
the time series described here, but neither policy variable was significant. Attempts to
control for the industrial composition of each state's manufacturing sector could aid this
test, but a basic problem remains the use of the overall injury rate, which tends to obscure any effects that may exist. (See Mendeloff, "Evaluation," appendix H.)

Notes to Chapter 7.

1. Smith recommended that "the standard-setting approach to occupational safety
should be repealed and replaced by a program which sets moderate fines on each injury,
to be paid by the victim's employer." Robert S. Smith, *The Occupational Safety and
Health Act: Its Goals and Achievements* (Washington, D.C.: American Enterprise Institute. 1976), p. 84, Cornell, Noll, and Weingast suggest that ". . . OSHA could be relieved
of all responsibility of trying to prevent industrial accidents and left free to concentrate
on the more complex problems of health hazards. Instead of setting standards as a means
of reducing industrial accidents, either an injury tax or a strengthening of Workmen's
Compensation would be at least as effective, and very likely cheaper." Nina Cornell,
Roger Noll, and Barry Weingast, "Safety Regulation," in *Setting National Priorities: The
Next Ten Years*, ed. Henry Owen and Charles L. Schultze (Washington, D.C.: Brookings
Institution, 1976), p. 503.

2. The political obstacles to an injury tax would not vanish if it were proposed as a
supplement to safety standards, rather than as a substitute. Union leaders might favor
this addition to standards, but it is unlikely that they would overcome their ideological
aversion enough to become active adherents. Business leaders would fiercely oppose
this tandem. Even if they preferred a tax to standards, having both would be the worst
alternative of all to them. With labor tepid and business apoplectic, the injury tax supplement stands little more of a chance than the injury tax alone.

By far the most vexing administrative problem would be how to deal with tax evasion—
that is, with the underreporting of injuries. The nature of the underreporting problem
would depend upon the procedures used to monitor injury performance. A tax could
be computed from reports filed directly by each firm with the federal government, or it
could work through a surcharge on the compensable losses reported to WC insurers—a
tax that would be remitted to the U.S. Treasury. The first method would pose great
difficulties: employers would have no reason to report injuries except the fear of sanctions, but the free-floating quality of the reporting system would undermine efforts to
detect underreporting. Use of the WC institutions would partially avoid both of these
problems; however, it would either require a major extension of federal authority in the
WC area or be limited to the states that already have good data systems.

These same issues arise in any proposal to use employers' reports of injuries, although
some of the proposals with this characteristic are politically feasible (see discussion of
the THIRE alternative). One advantage of simulating a tax by redesigning the enforcement program is that enforcers could limit it to states that have the required data without raising cries of unfairness. In contrast, the federal government could hardly adopt a
tax program for some states and not for others.

3. Even that conceptual judgment is tentative and subject to empirical verification, because deterrence, for example, depends on the perceptions of employers and not necessarily on the actual expected costs of noncompliance.

4. Congress has voted several times to exempt small firms from inspections, only to have

the provisions vetoed for unrelated reasons. In 1976 and 1977 Congress expressed its antipathy to what members saw as overenforcement of picayune regulations and adopted a one-year ban (under most circumstances) on first-instance penalties for nonserious violations. Court decisions have challenged OSHA's right to demand entry to workplaces without a search warrant.

5. In the House, the Rules Committee can issue a "closed rule," prohibiting floor amendments to a committee's bill, but no such procedure exists in the Senate. Consequently all legislative changes in the act have come through the appropriations process, where decisions are binding only for the fiscal year.

6. In theory, employers will comply voluntarily when the net private benefits of compliance are positive. When penalties are introduced, employers are likely to come into compliance next with those standards for which compliance is relatively worthwhile (that is, for which the private net benefits are negative but relatively small). The additional compliance achieved by further increases in the expected costs of noncompliance will impose still larger private losses. It is plausible that even though employers may not bear the full cost of injuries, the relative rankings of compliance actions would be the same for the social calculus as for the private one.

7. For the major work on emphasizing performance standards, see "OSHA Safety Regulation: Report of the Presidential Task Force," in *Ford Administration Papers on Regulatory Reform*, ed. Paul W. MacAvoy (Washington, D.C.: American Enterprise Institute, 1977).

8. Before 1976, about 10 percent of inspections were based on complaints and about 70 percent were general schedule. Since late 1976 about 30 percent have been based on complaints and only about 40 percent have been general schedule. Much of the increase in complaint inspections occurred because OSHA had been embarrassed by its failure to respond to an informal complaint at what turned out to be a horror show of a workplace—the kepone plant in Hopewell, Va. To avoid future charges of dereliction, OSHA decided to respond to informal complaints (from nonemployees and anonymous sources) as well as formal ones.

9. Rates for injuries caused by detectable violations currently do not exist, except in a very crude form. In order to construct them, a large-scale program of investigating perhaps a hundred randomly chosen accidents in each industry would be required.

Another modest change that OSHA could adopt would be to consider the public costs of inspections more explicitly and precisely. How should the "fixed costs" of inspections (like travel time) affect inspection priorities? Walter Oi has helped focus attention on this issue; see his article, "On the Economics of Industrial Safety," *Law and Contemporary Problems* 38(Summer-Autumn 1974). Also see the "TICVID" proposal in John Mendeloff, "Costs and Consequences: A Political and Economic Analysis of the Federal Occupational Safety and Health Program" (Ph.D. diss., University of California, Berkeley, 1977), pp. 465–468.

10. See chap. 5, note 7.

11. Section 8(c)(2) of the OSH Act states that "the Secretary . . . shall . . . prescribe regulations requiring employers to maintain accurate records of, and to make periodic reports on, work-related deaths, injuries, and illnesses other than minor injuries requiring only first aid."

12. All references to California accident investigation data are from an unpublished study by the author for the California Department of Industrial Relations. The Wisconsin figures are from the State Department of Industry, Labor, and Human Relations, Risk Management Council, *Monthly Report* (Madison, September 1975).

13. The reasoning here can be illustrated most simply by assuming a twentyfold increase

in AIs in California—up to the level of Wisconsin in 1969. The percentage of AIs finding violations would fall by about half (from 39 percent to 21 percent); thus, the increase in AIs finding injury-causing violations would be about tenfold.

14. According to a 1960 survey, about one-half of the states required physicians to report all medical treatment cases directly to a government agency. All but seven or eight states required some sort of physician's report. See International Association of Accident Boards and Commissions, *Guide to Work Injury Reporting: United States and Canada: 1960* (Washington, D.C.) table 6, p. 7.

15. It is also possible to say something about what type of injuries will be affected and how the size of the effects will vary. AIs focus employers' attention on the probability that violations will cause injuries and that the injuries will be investigated, not just on the probability that a violation will be detected. In general, substitution of AIs for scheduled inspections will decrease the effectiveness of the safety program with respect to detectable violations. Exceptions can occur when an establishment has an extremely small probability of being inspected (that is, because it has only a few employees) or when a violation has an extremely large probability of causing an injury. In those cases the probability that an injury would occur and be investigated could exceed the probability of detection during a routine investigation. For all injuries caused by nondetectable violations, the accident investigation expansion will be more effective.

16. A Supreme Court decision on whether OSHA needs to get a search warrant when an employer tries to block an inspection will probably be forthcoming in 1978.

17. A strong consultation program is a natural complement to THIRE. Small employers should be encouraged to seek assistance in reducing their rates, but employers should not be able to use consultations as a way to become exempt from inspections.

18. See, for example, Rollin H. Simonds, "OSHA Compliance: 'Safety is good business,'" *Personnel*, July–August 1973, pp. 30–38. Simonds discusses a study by Shafai-Sahrai which controlled for age and marital status as well as for industry. See also J. B. Cronin, "Cause and Effect: Investigations into Causes of Industrial Accidents in the United Kingdom," *International Labour Review*, 103(February 1971). Of course, workers' compensation experience ratings show that some firms within a manual classification consistently outperform or do worse than the norm.

19. An assumption that could support this contention is that an establishment can have a high relative injury rate because the management has been sloppy about safety, overlooking some cheap opportunities to prevent injuries. (Of course, from a broader perspective, the managers may have a comparative advantage in some other field, and their neglect of safety could be socially beneficial. But here we are concerned about finding ways to prevent more injuries.)

20. If we reward or punish establishments on the basis of their relative injury rankings, this restriction is highly desirable for two reasons. First, because injury-rate differences within an industry are more compressed than differences among establishments in all industries, it becomes politically easier to use a larger penalty for each "excess" injury and thus to provide stronger incentives for injury prevention. (To illustrate this point, suppose that all firms have 100 workers and that the average number of injuries is 20, with a range from 1 to 40. Suppose that in any given industry, the range spans only 10 injuries. For any given tax per injury, some firms in the comprehensive ranking would have to pay very high taxes because of their major divergence from the average. For that same tax rate, no firm in the industry ranking would have to pay as much.) Second, firms can improve their ranking (for example, move from one decile to another) within their industry more cheaply than they can improve it relative to all industries; consequently, a given financial incentive will generate greater preventive activity when proper categories are used.

21. Even though, at the margin, firms with poor safety performance may be able to prevent injuries more cheaply, an exclusive emphasis on them would undoubtedly soon forego cheaper prevention opportunities at better-performing firms. However, since the latter probably already have good safety programs; the special emphasis may be necessary for poor performers to induce them to make lumpy investments (like hiring a safety director).

22. California data indicate, for example, that 13.6 percent of inspectors' time was spent inspecting, and 7.6 percent was spent in employer conferences. These comprised about 37 percent of all nontravel, inspection-related time. Since that time averaged about fifteen hours per inspection (excluding construction), the average time spent with workers would be roughly three hours and with management representatives roughly five hours. See California Department of Finance, "A Review of the Implementation of the California Occupational Safety and Health Act (Cal-OSHA)," Report no. PR-125 (Sacramento, February 1976), table 7, p. 33, and table 8, p. 35.

23. Section 17(j) of the OSH Act.

24. The available data, which bear only on the number of violations, do not support the drop-off hypothesis. Each year the cumulative number of reinspected establishments grows, but the average number of violations per inspection has also been growing. The percentage of establishments found in compliance has been roughly constant. Of course, it is not known whether this aggregate finding applies specifically to the reinspected establishments.

No reliable data on average compliance costs are available. A few years ago the National Association of Manufacturers published a survey of its members, showing how much they thought compliance with OSHA standards would cost them. Their estimates ran about $35,000 for firms with less than 100 workers and about $75,000 for firms with 100 to 500 workers. It is very plausible that these figures are overestimates. See Nicholas Ashford, *Crisis in the Workplace: Occupational Disease and Injury* (Cambridge, Mass.: MIT Press, 1976), p. 318, for the survey findings.

25. For both political and analytical reasons, enforcement strategists should consider carefully the impact of their program on different size classes of establishments. For example, large establishments tend to have rates lower than the industry average and thus would be exempted (except for complaints and AIs) from a policy targeting workplaces with above-average rates; however, the inclusion of a full adjustment for the number of employees, as in table 7.1, means that large establishments that do have above-average rates will be very heavily inspected. Also, note that because most large establishments have relatively low injury rates, targeting based on divergence from the industry average (that is, the number of injuries in the industry divided by the number of workers) will place most establishments *above* the average.

26. Once the psychological costs of inspections are admitted into the discussion, the notion of precise implicit tax rates becomes mushy. Even without the psychological dimension, the "tax" would vary among firms depending on the costs of compliance at each one. But what really counts is not the actual implicit tax rate but the employers' perceptions of the tax rate. To calculate the implicit marginal tax rate, employers would need to know the expected costs of an inspection as well as how changes in the frequency of inspection would be affected by changes in the firm's injury rate. Enforcers can control the kind of information employers get about this second element. It is conceivable that injury prevention would be increased if employers were only told, "The worse you are, the more you'll see us," rather than given a formula like the one in table 7-1. For a recent discussion of the importance of how a program is perceived, see Walter Nicholson and Sonia Wright, "Participants' Understanding of the Treatment in Policy Experimentation," *Evaluation Quarterly* 1, no. 2 (May 1977).

27. A discussion of possible tools for reducing underreporting appears in Mendeloff, "Costs and Consequences," pp. 506–512.

28. U.S. Department of Commerce, *County Business Patterns, California* (1971), tables 1B and 1C.

29. My review of all of the 1976 California accident investigation reports that found violations indicated that the flagrantly detectable violations tended to occur at smaller establishments.

30. Because the number of inspections among poorer-performing establishments will increase, the cost-effectiveness of the detection treatment alone may decrease if the added inspections require compliance with increasingly less worthwhile standards. However, this tendency is likely to be outweighed by the much more efficient prevention measures spurred by the taxlike component.

31. The state of Washington has taken some of the most thoughtful steps on inspection policy. It uses a procedure that combines some of the features of THIRE and AI–Wall-to-Wall. Priorities are reset each month on the basis of (mainly standards-related) injuries during the previous month and the experience rating of the firm (as determined by WC losses over three years). Thus a firm whose overall injury performance had been superior would be free from scheduled inspections unless it experienced more than one (standards-related) compensable injury during the preceding month. (Steven Levette of the Washington Department of Labor and Industries provided this information.)

32. The federal government should support the development of a data base that can show the relative performance of each establishment for each type of injury, even if it is never used for enforcement. Such a data base could spur great advances in accident research. Good and bad performance for each type of accident could be easily identified; research teams could visit workplaces and try to determine why the differences exist and what methods appear to prevent the injuries. OSHA or state consultants in states with such a data base could use it in a similar way, identifying firms with special problems or offering assistance to solve them.

Notes to Chapter 8
1. Critics of weak coal mine safety enforcement long lamented the responsible agency's placement within the Interior Department, which is also responsible for fostering the development of coal resources. In a department with conflicting responsibilities, all agencies except the dominant one would probably do better outside of the department, yet the bureaucratic clash may provide a useful method for forcing the consideration of trade-offs.

The Transportation Department's attempt to introduce some uniformity into the safety assessment work of its various branches offers one example of the second idea.

2. For a discussion of professional hegemony within agencies, see Harold Seidman, *Politics, Position and Power: The Dynamics of Federal Organization* (New York: Oxford University Press, 1970), pp. 142–150.

3. Lifesaving is worth more in some situations than in others because it is worth more either to the people at risk or to others who care about them.

4. In promulgating the coke oven emissions standard in November 1976, OSHA did observe that estimates of annual compliance costs ranged from $130 million to $1.28 billion and took the position that ". . . costs are likely to fall in the $200 million range, rather than the $1 billion range." As for the effects, OSHA described the estimates that had been given but stated that "we do not believe that we can forecast accurately the amounts of annual reductions in mortality and morbidity." Indeed, "OSHA does not be-

lieve it is appropriate to quantify even a range of benefits of the final rule." The promulgation document is reprinted in Bureau of National Affairs, *Occupational Safety and Health Reporter*, October 28, 1976. The quotations appear on pp. 645–647.

If we did combine the high estimate of reduced annual worker mortality (240 lives) with the low estimate of annual costs ($130 million), the cost per life saved would be just over $500,000. Alternatively, if we combine the low estimate of reduced mortality (8 lives) with the high estimate of costs ($1.28 billion), the cost per life saved runs to about $150 million. (Morbidity would have to be considered as well.)

5. For example, OSHA tried to set up a new system specifically to get information about power press injuries, but the reports submitted were fragmentary and not necessarily representative of all power press injuries. Instead, OSHA could have chosen to send a team to investigate a random sample of punch press injuries that were already reported under the workers' compensation program in California.

6. In late 1977, President Carter did propose to replace the inflationary impact statement program with "regulatory analyses" that would require agencies to examine alternative methods of dealing with the problem at hand and the economic consequences of each. See the *Federal Register*, November 18, 1977, pp. 59740–59746.

Notes to Chapter 9
1. Arthur M. Okun, *Equality and Efficiency: The Big Tradeoff* (Washington, D.C.: Brookings Institution, 1975), p. 21.

2. Unfortunately, the real social discomfort often arises from being reminded that people can be so desperate. In cases where the only way a person can get a job is to be willing to take desperate risks, a social ban on risk taking at work will merely direct the desperation into other channels.

3. Note again that health standards are largely exempt from this criticism. Most serious types of occupational disease (as opposed to dermatitis) *are* caused by violations of standards.

4. David R. Mayhew, *Congress: The Electoral Connection* (New Haven: Yale University Press, 1974).

5. Interview with Gary Sellers, October 1975.

6. Paternalism is not used here in a pejorative sense. To reinforce their own entreaties, parents may support a legislative requirement that motorcyclists wear helmets. Is it always wrong for parents (or citizens generally) to express caring by restricting the right of other people to engage in hazardous activities?

7. Interview with Grover Wrenn, October 1975.

8. Like other students of OSHA, I believe its largest role should be in the health area; however, I also tend to be relatively sanguine about the potential of OSHA's safety program. OSHA has had some effect on the injury rate, and it can probably have more effect at a lower average cost if it adopts some of the inspection approaches outlined in this chapter. In addition, the strong case that can be made for federal support of occupational health research can be extended, at least in principle, to safety as well.

9. THIRE encounters many of the same data problems that the injury tax proposal does, but it can solve them more easily because it is a flexible administrative program. Thus, in a state with good WC data, OSHA (or the state agencies themselves in the twenty-three states that operate thier own OSHA-approved programs) could establish THIRE; in states without good data, it would not. The injury tax, however, which would require legislation, could hardly be levied in one state but not in another.

The principles underlying the THIRE strategy—simulation of a tax—may be applicable to other policy areas, for example, fixed-source water pollution or air pollution. The prerequisites are an ability to measure whether (and by how much) firms are exceeding the standard for emissions and an ability to impose costs in an incremental fashion for violations.

Notes to Appendix

1. Smith's model is developed in "Intertemporal Changes in Work Injury Rates," in Industrial Relations Research Association, *Proceedings of the 25th Annual Meeting,* 1972. Walter Oi has tested Smith's model on U.S. data for 1956–1970 for six two-digit manufacturing industries. He found that nine of the twenty-four coefficients had unexpected signs and that only one was significant at the .05 level with the predicted sign. Using a variant of my first-difference model (with the accessions rate, males 18–24, hourly earnings, and the percentage of nonproduction workers), I got slightly better results for those years. Three signs were unexpected, while five were significant. See John Mendeloff, "An Evaluation of the OSHA Program's Effect on Workplace Injury Rates," prepared for the U.S. Department of Labor (Washington, D.C., 1976), appendix G, and Walter Oi, "Economic and Empirical Aspects of Industrial Safety," prepared for the U.S. Department of Labor (Washington, D.C., February 1974).

2. The formula for calculating the t statistic for the difference between predicted and reported values is given in Jan Kmenta, *Elements of Econometrics* (New York: Macmillan, 1971,) p. 375.

3. The two-step procedure is described in ibid., pp. 287–288.

4. In the CTIR regressions in the following list, for equations 3 and 4 the reported values were higher than the predicted for each year. For equation 5, the predicted were higher for 1973, 1974, and 1975.

Selected Bibliography

Arthur D. Little, Inc. "Economic Impact of Proposed OSHA Standard for Asbestos." First report. Contract with U.S. Department of Labor, OSHA. April 28, 1972. Mimeo. Cambridge, Mass.

Ashford, Nicholas. *Crisis in the Workplace: Occupational Disease and Injury.* Cambridge, Mass.: MIT Press, 1976.

Ashford, Nicholas. "An Evaluation of the Occupational Health Mandate of the Occupational Safety and Health Act." U.S. Department of Labor Conference on Evaluating the Effects of the Occupational Safety and Health Program, Annapolis, Maryland, March 18-19, 1975. Mimeo.

Bauer, Raymond A.; De Sola Pool, Ithiel; and Dexter, Lewis Anthony. *American Business and Public Policy.* 2d ed. Chicago: Aldine, 1972.

Behavioral/Safety Center, Westinghouse Electric Corporation. "An Evaluation of Policy Related Research on Effectiveness of Alternative Methods to Reduce Occupational Illness and Accidents." Contract with National Science Foundation, July 1974.

Bendix Corporation. *Machine Guarding—Assessment of Need.* Contract with National Institute of Occupational Safety and Health. NIOSH Publication no. 75-173. June 1975. Washington, D.C.: Government Printing Office.

Blau, Peter M. *The Dynamics of Bureaucracy.* 2d ed. Chicago: University of Chicago Press, 1962.

Bolt, Beranek, and Newman, Inc. "Economic Impact Analysis of Proposed Noise Control Regulation," Report no. 3246. Contract with OSHA, U.S. Department of Labor, April 21, 1976. Mimeo.

Bolt, Beranek, and Newman, Inc. "Impact of Noise Control at the Workplace." Report no. 2761. 3 vols. Contract with OSHA, U.S. Department of Labor, January 1, 1974. Mimeo.

Brodeur, Paul. *Expendable Americans.* New York: Viking Press, 1974.

Buchanan, James M., and Tullock, Gordon. "Polluters' Profits and Political Response: Direct Controls versus Taxes." *American Economic Review,* March 1975, pp. 139-147.

Bureau of National Affairs. *The Job Safety and Health Act of 1970.* Washington, D.C., 1971.

Bureau of National Affairs. *Occupational Safety and Health Reporter.* All issues.

Burton, David J. "Estimated Costs of Compliance Related to the Proposed Coke-Oven Emission Standard." Contract with OSHA, U.S. Department of Labor, July 20, 1975. Mimeo.

Burton, John F., Jr.; Benham, Lee K.; Vaugh, M. Williams; and Flanagan, Robert J., eds. *Readings in Labor Market Analysis.* New York: Holt Rinehart & Winston, 1971.

Burton, John F., Jr. and Berkowitz, Monroe. "Objectives Other Than Income Maintenance for Workmen's Compensation." *Journal of Risk and Insurance* 38, no. 3 (September 1971).

Calabresi, Guido. *The Cost of Accidents: A Legal and Economic Analysis.* New Haven: Yale University Press, 1970.

California. State Department of Finance. *A Review of the Implementation of the California Occupational Safety and Health Act (Cal-OSHA).* Sacramento: State Printing Office, 1976.

California. State Department of Industrial Relations. "DIR Management Analysis Report on the Development of a Better Work-Targeting (I.V.I.) System for Safety Engineers Inspecting Industrial Plants—Study B." October 1972.

Chelius, James R. "The Control of Industrial Accidents: Economic Theory and Empirical Evidence." *Law and Contemporary Problems* 38 (Summer-Autumn 1974): 700-729.

Chelius, James R. "An Empirical Analysis of Safety Regulation." In *Supplemental Studies for the National Commission on State Workmen's Compensation Laws*, ed. Monroe Berkowitz, vol. 3. Washington, D.C.: Government Printing Office, 1973.

Chelius, James R. "Expectations for OSHA's Performance: The Lessons of Theory and Empirical Evidence." U.S. Department of Labor Conference on Evaluating the Effects of the Occupational Safety and Health Program, Annapolis, Maryland, March 18–19, 1975.

Commoner, Barry. "Labor's Stake in the Environment/The Environment's Stake in Labor." In "Jobs and the Environment: Three Papers," from a conference on Jobs and the Environment—Whose Jobs, Whose Environment? sponsored by the Institute of Industrial Relations, University of California, Berkeley, San Francisco, November 28, 1972.

Cornell, Nina; Noll, Roger; Weingast, Barry. "Safety Regulation." In *Setting National Priorities: The Coming Decade*, Ed. Henry Owen and Charles L. Schultze. Washington, D.C.: Brookings Institution, 1976.

Cronin, J. B. "Cause and Effect: Investigations into Aspects of Industrial Accidents in the United Kingdom." *International Labour Review* 103 (February 1971).

Cummins, J. David, and Olson, Douglas. "An Analysis of the Black Lung Compensation Program." *Journal of Risk and Insurance* 41 (December 1974).

Dahl, Robert A., and Lindblom, Charles E. *Politics, Economics and Welfare.* New York: Harper and Row, 1953.

Davies, J. Clarence III. *The Politics of Pollution.* New York: Western Publishing Company, 1970.

Davis, Otto A. and Kamien, Morton I. "Externalities, Information and Alternative Collective Action." In *Public Expenditures and Policy Analysis*, ed. Robert H. Haveman and Julius Margolis. Chicago: Markham, 1970.

DiPietro, Aldona. "Data Needs for the Evaluation of OSHA's Net Impact." Office of Evaluation, U.S. Department of Labor, August 19, 1975. Mimeo. Washington, D.C.

Discher, David P.; Kleinman, Goldy D.; and Foster, F. James. *Pilot Study for Development of an Occupational Disease Surveillance Method.* Contract with National Institute of Occupational Safety and Health. Publication no. 75-162. May 1975. Washington D.C.: Government Printing Office.

Doeringer, Peter B., and Piore, Michael. *Internal Labor Markets and Manpower Analysis.* Lexington, Mass.: D. C. Heath, 1971.

Edelman, Murray. *The Symbolic Uses of Politics.* Urbana, Ill.: Unversity of Illinois Press, 1967.

Fenno, Richard F., Jr. *Congressmen in Committees.* Boston: Little, Brown, 1973.

Foster D. Snell, Inc. "Economic Impact Studies of the Effects of Proposed OSHA Studies for Vinyl Chloride." Contract with OSHA, U.S. Department of Labor, September 27, 1974. Mimeo.

Foulkes, Fred. "Learning to Live with OSHA." *Harvard Business Review*, November-December 1973.

Freeman, A. Myrick, and Haveman, Robert H. "Clean Rhetoric, Dirty Water." *The Public Interest* 28 (Summer 1972).

Fromm, Gary. "Aviation Safety." *Law and Contemporary Problems* 33 (Summer 1968): 590–618.

Fromm, Gary. "Comment on Schelling." In *Problems in Public Expenditure Analysis*, ed. Samuel B. Chase. Washington, D.C.: Brookings Institution, 1968.

Gordon, Jerome B.; Akman, Alan; and Brooks, Michael. *Industrial Safety Statistics: A Re-examination*. New York: Praeger, 1971.

Greenstone, J. David. *Labor in American Politics*. New York: Random House, 1970.

Grosse, Robert. "Problems of Resource Allocation in Health." In *Public Expenditures and Policy Analysis*, ed. Robert H. Haveman and Julius Margolis. Chicago: Markham, 1970.

Herlick, Sanford. *The California Workers' Compensation Handbook*. San Bernardino, CWCH Publishing Company, 1975.

ICF, Inc. "Preliminary Analysis of Total Costs of OSHA's Current Occupational Disease Abatement Strategy." Contract with OSHA, U.S. Department of Labor, October 1976. Mimeo. Washington, D.C.

Kalis, D. C. "Update on the Cost of OSHA Compliance." *Occupational Hazards*, August 1974, pp. 42–44.

Kneese, Allen V., and Schultze, Charles L. *Pollution, Prices, and Public Policy*. Washington D.C.: Brookings Institution, 1975.

Kramer, Barry. "Health Hazards: Vinyl-Chloride Risks Were Known by Many Before First Deaths." *Wall Street Journal*, October 5, 1974.

Lane, Robert. *The Regulation of Businessman: Social Conditions of Government Economic Control*. Hamden, Conn.: Archon Books, 1944.

Lave, Lester B. "Safety in Transportation: The Role of Government." *Law and Contemporary Problems* 33 (Summer 1968); 512–535.

Levinson, Harold. "Pattern Bargaining: A Case Study of the Automobile Workers." *Quarterly Journal of Economics*, May 1960.

Lowrance, William W. *Of Acceptable Risk: Science and the Determination of Safety*. Los Altos, Calif.: William Kaufmann, Inc., 1976.

McCarry, Charles. *Citizen Nader*. New York: New American Library, 1972.

Marvin, Keith E., and Rouse, Andrew M. "The Status of PPB in Federal Agencies: A Comparative Perspective." In *Public Expenditures and Policy Analysis*, ed. Robert H. Haveman and Julius Margolis. Chicago: Markham, 1970.

Massachusetts Institute of Technology, Center for Policy Alternatives, "The Impact of Governmental Restrictions on the Production and Use of Chemicals." Contract with U.S. Council on Environmental Quality and U.S. Environmental Protection Agency. February 15, 1975.

Mayhew, David R. *Congress: The Electoral Connection*. New Haven: Yale University Press, 1974.

Mendeloff, John. "An Evaluation of the OSHA Program's Effect on Workplace Injury Rates: Evidence from California through 1974." Prepared under contract with the Office of the Assistant Secretary for Policy, Evaluation, and Research, U.S. Department of Labor, July 1976.

Mendeloff, John. "Costs and Consequences: A Political and Economic Analysis of the Federal Occupational Safety and Health Program." Ph.D. dissertation, University of California, Berkeley, 1977.

Miller, Richard S. "The Occupational Safety and Health Act of 1970 and the Law of Torts." *Law and Contemporary Problems* 38 (Summer–Autumn 1974); 612–640.

Mishan, E. J. *Economics for Social Decisions: Elements of Cost-Benefit Analysis.* New York: Praeger, 1973.

Mishan, E. J. "Evaluation of Life and Limb: A Theoretical Approach." *Journal of Political Economy* 79 (1971): 687–705.

Moran, Robert. "Occupational Safety and Health Standards as Federal Law: The Hazards of Haste." *William and Mary Law Review* 15: 777–797.

Nader, Ralph. "Brown Lung: The Cotton-Mill Killer." *The Nation*, March 15, 1971, pp. 335–337.

National Safety Council. "The Feasibility of Performing Cost/Benefit Analyses of Industrial Safety Programs at the Establishment Level." Contract with OSHA, U.S. Department of Labor, 1972.

New York. State Department of Labor. "Age and Sex Differences in Work Injury Rates." Special Labor News Memorandum no. 125, September 1, 1969.

Noll, Roger G. *Reforming Regulation.* Washington, D.C.: Brookings Institution, 1971.

Oi, Walter Y. "Economic and Empirical Aspects of Industrial Safety." Prepared for the U.S. Department of Labor, February 28, 1974. Xerox. Rochester, N.Y.

Oi, Walter Y. "The Economics of Product Safety." *Bell Journal of Economics and Management Science*, Spring 1973, pp. 3–28.

Oi, Walter Y. "An Essay on Workmen's Compensation and Industrial Safety." In *Supplemental Studies for the NCSWCL*, vol. 1, ed. Monroe Berkowitz. Washington, D.C.: Government Printing Office, 1973.

Oi, Walter Y. "On the Economics of Industrial Safety." *Law and Contemporary Problems* 38 (Summer–Autumn 1974): 669–699.

Oi, Walter Y. "On Evaluating the Effectiveness of the OSHA Inspection Program." U.S. Department of Labor Conference on Evaluating the Effects of the Occupational Safety and Health Program, Annapolis, Maryland, March 18–19, 1975.

Okun, Arthur M. *Equality and Efficiency: The Big Tradeoff.* Washington, D.C.: Brookings Institution, 1975.

Olson, Mancur, Jr. *The Logic of Collective Action.* New York: Schocken, 1968.

Page, Joseph. "Toward Meaningful Protection and Worker Health and Safety." Review of *Expendable Americans* by Paul Brodeur and *Muscle and Blood* by Rachael Scott. *Stanford Law Review* 27 (May 1975), pp. 1345–1360.

Page, Joseph, and O'Brien, Mary-Win. *Bitter Wages.* New York: Grossman, 1973.

Peltzman, Sam. *Regulation of Automobile Safety.* Washington, D.C.: American Enterprise Institute, 1975.

Price, David. *Who Makes the Laws?* Cambridge, Mass.: Schenkman, 1972.

Rees, Albert. *The Economics of Work and Pay.* New York: Harper and Row, 1973.

Rhoads, Steven. *Policy Analysis in the Federal Aviation Administration.* Lexington, Mass.: Lexington Books, 1974.

Rose-Ackerman, Susan. "Effluent Taxes: A Critique." *Canadian Journal of Economics* 6, no. 4, pp. 512–528.

Russell, Louise B. "Pricing Industrial Accidents." *Supplemental Studies for the NCSWCL,* ed. Monroe Berkowitz, vol. 3. Washington, D.C.: Government Printing Office, 1973.

Sands, Paul. "How Effective is Safety Legislation?" *Journal of Law and Economics* 11 (April 1968): 165–174.

Schelling, Thomas C. "The LIfe You Save May Be Your Own." In *Problems in Public Expenditure Analysis,* ed. Samuel B. Chase. Washington, D.C.: Brookings Institution, 1968.

Schultze, Charles L. *The Politics and Economics of Public Spending.* Washington, D.C.: Brookings Institution, 1968.

Seidman, Harold. *Politics, Position, and Power: The Dynamics of Federal Organization.* New York: Oxford University Press, 1970.

Seline, John R. "Toward the Development of an Economic Impact Model for OSHA Standards." U.S. Department of Labor Conference on Evaluating the Effects of the Occupational Safety and Health Program," Annapolis, Maryland, March 18–19, 1975.

Settle, Russell Franklin. "The Welfare Economics of Occupational Safety and Health Standards," Ph.D. dissertation, Unversity of Wisconsin, 1974.

Simonds, Rollin H. "OSHA Compliance: 'Safety is good business.' " *Personnel,* July–August 1973, pp. 30–38.

Simonds, Rollin H. and Grimaldi, John V. *Safety Management: Accident Cost and Control.* Homewood, Ill.: Richard D. Irwin, 1963.

Singer, James W. "Labor Report/New OSHA Head May Signal Change in Agency's Approach." *National Journal,* December 27, 1975, pp. 1725–1734.

Singer, James W. "New OSHA Task Force—Political Payoff or False Alarm?" *National Journal,* July 10, 1976, pp. 973–975.

Singer, James W. "Product Safety Effort Challenged as Being Too Costly." *National Journal Reports,* May 3, 1975, pp. 658–668.

Smith, Robert S. "An Analysis of Work Injuries in Manufacturing Industry." In *Supplemental Studies for the NCSWCL,* ed. Monroe Berkowitz, vol. 3. Washington, D.C.: Government Printing Office, 1973.

Smith, Robert S. "Compensating Wage Differentials and Hazardous Work." Office of Evaluation, Technical Analysis Paper no. 5, U.S. Department of Labor, 1973. Mimeo. Washington, D.C.

Smith, Robert S. "Evaluating the Impact of OSHA on Occupational Safety and Health." Office of the Assistant Secretary for Policy, Evaluation, and Research, U.S. Department of Labor, April 1975.

Smith, Robert S. "The Feasibility of an 'Injury Tax' Approach to Occupational Safety." *Law and Contemporary Problems* 38 (Summer–Autumn 1974): 730–744.

Smith, Robert S. "Intertemporal Changes in Work Injury Rates." In *Proceedings of the Industrial Relations Research Association,* 1973.

Smith, Robert S. *The Occupational Safety and Health Act: Its Goals and Its Achievements.* Washington, D.C.: American Enterprise Institute, 1976.

Somers, Herman, and Somers, Ann. *Workmen's Compensation.* New York: John Wiley, 1954.

Spengler, Joseph S. "The Economics of Safety." *Law and Contemporary Problems* 33 (Summer 1968); 619-638.

Steiger, William A. "OSHA: Four Years Later." *Labor Law Journal* 25:12 (December 1974): 723-728.

Stender, John H. "Enforcing the Occupational Safety and Health Act of 1970: The Federal Government as a Catalyst." *Law and Contemporary Problems* 38 (Summer-Autumn 1974): 641-650.

Stigler, George. "The Optimum Enforcement of Laws." *Journal of Political Economy* 78, no. 1 (May-June 1970): 526-536.

Strauss, George, and Sayles, Leonard R. *Personnel: The Human Problems of Management.* 2d ed. Englewood Cliffs, N.J.: Prentice-Hall, 1967.

Surry, Jean. *An Annotated Bibliography for Industrial Accident Research and Related Fields.* Labour Safety Council, Ontario Department of Labour. Toronto, April 1969.

Surry, Jean. *Industrial Accident Research: A Human Engineering Appraisal.* Labour Safety Council, Ontario Department of Labor. Toronto, 1971.

Teplow, Leo. "Comprehensive Safety and Health Measures in the Workplace." Mimeo. 1975.

Thaler, Richard, and Rosen, Sherwin. "Estimating the Value of Saving a Life: Evidence from the Labor Market." Rochester, N.Y.: University of Rochester, Department of Economics, Mimeo. 1974.

Tillery, Winston. "Safety and Health Provisions Before and After OSHA." *Monthly Labor Review,* September 1975, pp. 40-43.

U.S. Congress. House. Committee on Education and Labor. *Occupational Safety and Health Act of 1968: Hearings.* 90th Cong., 2d sess., 1968.

U.S. Congress. House. Committee on Education and Labor. *Occupational Safety and Health Act of 1969: Hearings.* 91st Cong., 1st sess., 1969.

U.S. Congress. House. Committee on Education and Labor. *Occupational Safety and Health Act of 1970 (Oversight and Proposed Amendments): Hearings.* 92d Cong., 2d sess., 1973.

U.S. Congress. House. Committee on Education and Labor. *Occupational Safety and Health Act of 1970 (Oversight and Proposed Amendments): Hearings.* 93d Cong., 2d sess., 1975.

U.S. Congress. Senate. Committee on Labor and Public Welfare. *Legislative History of the Occupational Safety and Health Act of 1970.* 92d Cong., 1st sess., 1971.

U.S. Congress. Senate. Committee on Labor and Public Welfare. *Occupational Safety and Health Act of 1968: Hearings.* 90th Cong., 2d sess., 1968.

U.S. Congress. Senate. Committee on Labor and Public Welfare. *Occupational Safety and Health Act of 1970: Hearings.* 91st Cong., 1st and 2d sess., 1970.

U.S. Congress. Senate. Committee on Labor and Public Welfare. *Occupational Safety and Health Review, 1974: Hearings.* 93d Cong., 2d sess., 1975.

U.S. Department of Labor. Occupational Safety and Health Administration. *Compliance Operations Manual.* Washington, D.C.: Government Printing Office, 1972.

U.S. National Commission on State Workmen's Compensation Laws. *Compendium on Workmen's Compensation*, ed. Marcus Rosenblum. Washington, D.C.: Government Printing Office, 1973.

U.S. National Commission on State Workmen's Compensation Laws. *The Report of the NCSWCL.* Washington, D.C.: Government Printing Office, 1973.

U.S. National Commission on State Workmen's Compensation Laws. *Supplemental Studies for the NCSWCL*, ed. Monroe Berkowitz. 3 vols. Washington, D.C.: Government Printing Office, 1973.

U.S. Office of the President. *President's Report on Occupational Safety and Health.* Washington, D.C.: Government Printing Office, 1972; 1973; 1975; 1976.

Van Zelst, R. H. "The Effect of Age and Experience Upon Accident Rate." *Journal of Applied Psychology* 38, no. 5 (1954).

Vroman, Wayne. "The Incidence of Compensation Insurance Premium Payments." In *Supplemental Studies for the NCSWCL*, ed. Monroe Berkowitz, vol. 2. Washington, D.C.: Government Printing Office, 1973.

Wallick, Franklin. *The American Worker: An Endangered Species.* New York: Ballantine, 1972.

Weidenbaum, Murray L. *Government-Mandated Price Increases.* Washington, D.C.: American Enterprise Institute, 1975.

Wildavsky, Aaron. "Economy and Environment/Rationality and Ritual." Review of *The Uncertain Search for Environmental Quality*, by B. Ackerman, S. Rose-Ackerman, D. Henderson, and J. W. Sawyer, Jr. *Stanford Law Review* 29, no. 1 (November 1976): 183–204.

Wilson, James Q. "The Dead Hand of Regulation." *The Public Interest* 25 (Fall 1971): 39–58.

Wilson, James Q. "The Politics of Regulation." In *Social Responsibility and the Business Predicament*, ed. James W. McKie. Washington, D.C.: Brookings Institution, 1974.

Wisconsin. State Department of Industry, Labor, and Human Relations. "Inspection Effectiveness Study." Contract with OSHA, U.S. Department of Labor, September 30, 1971. Madison, Wisconsin.

Woodward Associates. "Study to Determine the Engineering and Economic Feasibility of Retrofitting ROPS on Pre–July 1, 1969, Construction Equipment." Contract with OSHA, U.S. Department of Labor, July 15, 1974.

Zeckhauser, Richard. "Procedures for Valuing Lives." *Public Policy* 23 (1975): 419–464.

Zeckhauser, Richard, and Nichols, Albert. "The Occupational Safety and Health Administration: An Overview Prepared for the Senate Committee on Government Operations." Mimeo. Washington, D.C., n.d.

Index

Abatement policy, 45, 185n
  on engineering controls, 45
  of granting of extensions, 163
Abel, I. W., 18
Accident investigation program, 127-130.
    See also Inspections
  cost-effectiveness of, 130-131, 132
  vs. scheduled inspections, 200n
Accidents. *See also* Injuries
  injury rate for, 114
  preventable, 95
  underreporting of, 124
  work injuries categorized by, 97
Administrators, and injury rate estimates,
    118
Adoption feasibility
  of accident investigation program, 131,
    132
  of OSHA safety program, 123
  of THIRE, 141
AFL-CIO, Standing Committee on OSH,
    54
Age, and injury rate, 101, 104
Agencies, regulatory, 5. *See also* State
    agencies
Allocation process, in THIRE program,
    136
American Conference of Governmental
    Industrial Hygienists, 58
American National Standards Institute
    (ANSI), 24, 36, 37
  power press committee of, 56, 57
American Petroleum Institute, 78
Amputation, reporting of, 128, 129
Appeals, 2, 19. *See also* Courts; Review
    Commission, Occupational Safety
    and Health
Appropriations Conference Committee, of
    House and Senate, 4
Arbitration, 90
Arthur D. Little, Inc., 53, 61-63
Asbestos, 42
  Arthur D. Little study on, 61-63
  hazard of, 179n, 182n
  and informed workers, 187n
  Settle's benefit-cost study of, 63-64,
    70
  standard for, 59, 61, 64
  TWA for, 63
Asbestosis
  incidence of, 61, 62
  prevention of, 63
Ayres, William, 17

B-11 Committee, ANSI, 57

Barnako, Frank, 38, 39
Bauer, Raymond A., 15
Bell, David, 69, 189n
Beneficiaries
  economics of, 67
  of OSHA's programs, 34-35
Benefit-cost analysis, 63. *See also*
    Cost-benefit analysis
Benefits
  distribution of, 31-34
  of OSHA standards, 145
Berman, Richard, 57
Beryllium, disease caused by, 14
B. F. Goodrich Company, 44, 52
Bias, on injury studies, 196n
Bill
  Curtis, 50
  Daniels, 19, 38, 49, 183n
  Domenick, 50
  S2823, 22
  Steiger, 19, 38
Bingham, Eula, 41
Black Lung Compensation Program,
    12-13, 17-18, 180n
Bolt study, on noise, 65
Boyd, Daniel, 47-48, 51, 54-55
Boyle, Tony, 18
Bronchogenic cancer, incidence of, 61,
    62
Bureau of Labor Statistics (BLS), survey
    of injury rates, 102, 162
Burton, Phillip, 18
Business. *See also* Employers; Management
  and consensus standards, 38
  criticism of OSHA, 151
  and safety incentives, 88
Byssinosis, 9, 12

California
  AI program in, 129
  reporting requirements in, 128, 192n
  safety program of, 105-115
California study, 86, 195n
CAL-OSHA, 106, 128
Cancer
  bronchogenic, 61, 62
  mesothelioma, 61, 62
  and vinyl chloride standards, 52
Carbon monoxide, standard setting
    for, 61
Catastrophes, reporting of, 128
"Caught in or between" (CIB) category
    of accident, 95. *See also* CIB injuries
Chamber of Commerce, U.S., and national
    consensus standards, 37

Chiles, Lawton, 22
Chow test, 196n
CIB injuries, 98, 111–112
  cost of, 118
  and fatalities, 116
Coal industry
  disaster in, 154
  and Farmington, West Virginia, blast, 17
  safety enforcement in, 202n
Coal Mine Safety Act, 12, 18
Coalworkers, pneumonconiosis of, 9. See also Workers
Coke oven emissions standards, 76, 202n
Collective action, 178n
Collective bargaining, and OSH program, 16
Commerce, Department of, 146
"Compensable losses," 11–12
Compensation
  "hazard pay," 10
  for risk of death, 9
Complaint inspections, 199n
Compliance
  and enforcement program, 93
  noncompliance, 83, 85, 119
  per-worker cost of, 183n
  voluntary, 199n
  weak incentives for, 88
Compliance Operations Manual (COM), 43–44
Conference Board survey, 88
Congress, U.S., and standard setting, 50–79. See also House of Representatives; Senate, U.S.
"Consensus" standards, 1, 37, 38, 39, 82
  adoption of, 157–158
  assessment of, 39
  beneficiaries of OSHA in, 166
  impact of OSHA on, 34
  injury rate in, 117
  relevance of OSHA standards in, 89
Consumer Product Safety Commission (CPSC), 5
Corn, Morton, 41, 55–56
Cost-benefit analysis
  of detectable violations, 90
  of noise, 185n
  of safety, 6
  for vinyl chloride exposure, 187n
Costs
  of accident investigation, 130
  distribution of, 31–34
  vs. health effects, 47
  for mechanical press modifications, 57

of OSH Act implementation, 21, 145
  uncertainties about, 193n
Cotton workers, byssinosis of, 9. See also Workers
Council of Economic Advisers (CEA), 4
Council on Wage-Price Stability (CWPS), 65, 66
Courts
  and mechanical press standards, 58
  and standard setting, 48–50
Criteria documents (CDs), 59
Curtis bill, 50

Daniels, Domenick, 19
Daniels Bill, 19, 38, 49, 183n
Decisions, life and death, 68–71. See also Lifesaving
Demography, and injury rates, 101, 104, 134
Deterrence, 87–93
Dexter, Lewis Anthony, 15
Domenick bill, 50
Dow Chemical Corporation, 52
Dusts, 10

Earnings, and injury rate, 103, 104
Econometrics, of injury rate, 171
Economics. See also Cost-benefit analysis
  of lifesaving, 69
  of standard setting, 49, 67–71
Economists, and OSH program, 155
Education and Labor Committee, House, 17, 18–19, 30
Effectiveness, of OSHA, 94–120, 164–166
Eizenstat, Stuart, 4
Electrical accidents, 114, 116
Elisburg, Don, 66
Employers. See also Business; Management
  and incentives for safety, 23
  and OSHA inspections, 137
  underreporting of, 138
  and WC premiums, 11
Enforcement, 1, 201n
  criticism of, 36
  effects of, 83
  engineering controls vs. personal protection in, 43–46
  safety vs. health in, 41–43
Engineering controls, 188n
  for health standards, 43–44
  vs. personal protective equipment, 43–46, 162–164
Environmental Protection Agency (EPA), 5
  and noise standards, 52
  vinyl chloride position of, 55

Epidemics, occupational disease, 118, 153
Experience, and injury rates, 100
Expertise, support of, 62
Exposure levels, 43, 59. *See also* Standards
Extensions, granting of, 163
Eye injuries, 95, 114, 116

Fairness
  of accident investigation program, 131,
    132
  of OSHA's safety program, 123
  of THIRE, 140–141
Fatalities
  reporting of, 128
  and violations, 87
Feasibility. *See also* Implementation
    feasibility
  of engineering compliance, 76
  policy on, 43
Federal action, arguments for, 151–154.
    See also Government
Federal Aviation Administration (FAA),
    159
  benefit-cost studies of, 71
  constituency of, 74
  safety regulations of, 72
Federal Trade Commission, 5
Fenno, Richard F. Jr., 30
Firestone Company, 53
Firms. *See also* Business
  safety practices of, 91
  underreporting of, 138
Flood Control Act, 147
Florida, WC data from, 111, 117
Ford, Gerald R., 65
Forklift accidents, 191n
Fraser, Douglas, 57
Friedman, Lee, 190n
Fumes, 10

General Electric Company, 14
Gordon, Jerome B., 92
Government intervention of, 6–20, 24–35.
    See also State agencies
Grievances, 90
Guenther, George, 38, 51, 158

"Hazard pay," 10
Hazards
  defining, 152
  health vs. safety, 41–43
  recognition of, 13
  workers' awareness of, 90
Health
  vs. safety, 13–15, 161–162

  standards for, 58–67
  value of, 78
Health enforcement program, of OSHA,
    42
Health standards, problems with, 27
Heat stress, 61
Highway safety. *See* National Highway
    Traffic Safety Administration
    (NHTSA)
Hodgson, James, 38
House of Representatives
  Appropriations Conference Committee,
    4
  Education and Labor Committee of, 17,
    18–19, 30
  subcommittee hearings, 17
Hygienists, and number of inspections, 42

Implementation feasibility. *See also*
    Feasibility
  of accident investigation program, 131,
    132
  of OSHA's safety program, 124
  of THIRE, 141
Incentives
  for injury prevention, 121
  to reduce hazards, 99
  safety, 11
  and THIRE alternative, 136–138
  worker, 10
Income distribution, 34–35
Industry
  and initial standards, 37
  vinyl chloride standards in, 55–56
Industry groups, and injury tax, 28
Inflationary impact statements (IIS's),
    65, 147, 189n
Injuries
  eye, 95, 114, 116
  ICDV category of, 86, 94, 95
  ICVs, 86, 115
  OSHA's effect on, 86, 94, 165–166
  preventable, 95
  rate determination for, 98–102
  social costs of, 117–118
  underreporting of, 124
Injury data, research with, 143–144
Injury rates, 183n
  and accident types, 114
  in California, 106
  determination of, 116
  econometrics of, 171–176
  effect of inspections on, 194n–195n
  effect of OSHA on, 105
  effect of tax on, 182n

Injury rates (continued)
  fall in, 143
  major components of, 113
  prediction of, 115
  regression analysis of, 111
  trends in, 195n
  and WC benefits/premiums, 197n
Injury tax, 26–28, 182n
  imitation of, 132
  politics of, 28–31
  potential of, 121–122
  problems of, 198n
  union reaction to, 155
Inspections
  characteristics of, 193n
  complaint, 199n
  and ICDV injuries, 87
  need for professionalism in, 41
  performance-based, 126
  policy on, 201n, 202n
  random, 139
  routine, 3
  and safety-vs.-health issue, 41–42
  scheduled, 127
  studies on effect of, 94–95
  and THIRE alternative, 133
  wall-to-wall, 129, 132
Intervention, government, 6–20
  method of, 24–35
  and social costs, 13
Iowa, WC data from, 111
IUD v. Hodgson, 49, 50, 58, 65

Javits, Jacob, 17, 19, 49, 181n
Job evaluation plans, 10
Johnson, Lyndon B., 17

Keller, Anson, 80
Kneese, Allen, 25, 29
Krivit, Daniel, 19, 21, 51

Labor, Department of
  and abatement policy, 46
  citations of, 184n
  and method of intervention, 24
  safety agencies in, 146
  and standard setting, 49, 51
  standards of, 36
  unions as clients of, 73–74
Labor, and OSHA standards, 75–81. See
  also Workers
Labor unions, and OSHA, 3. See also
  Unions
Lance, Bert, 4

Legislative process, for standards enforcement, 154–157
Legislators. See also Congress; Politics
  and incentives for safety, 26
  and injury rate estimates, 118
  and politics of safety, 29–30
"License to maim," 31
Lifesaving
  attitudes towards, 69
  economics of, 73
  FAA value for, 74
  value of, 78, 179n
Lobbyists, 23
Longshoremen, injury rates among, 99

McCormack, John, 18
Management. See also Employers
  and job classification, 11
  and OSHA standards, 75–81
Manufacturing
  beneficiaries of OSHA in, 166
  impact of OSHA on, 34
  injury rates in, 102
  relevance of OSHA standards in, 89
Market, private, and safety technologies, 7
Mayhew, David, 30, 31
Mead, Walter, 70
Meany, George, 17
Mechanical punch presses
  and CIB accidents, 113
  standards for, 56–58
Medical exams, 32, 153
Mesothelioma, incidence of, 61, 62
"Minimax regret," rule of, 80
Mintz, Benjamin, 46, 47
Monitoring equipment, 14
Motor vehicle accidents, 95
Multiple regression analysis, for injury rate
  determination, 98, 111

Nader, Ralph, 18, 74, 154, 156, 160, 178n
Nader study, of OSHA, 39
Nagle, Robert, 18, 21, 37, 40
National Fire Protection Association
  (NFPA), 24
National Highway Traffic Safety Adminis-
  tration (NHTSA), 5, 159
  benefit-cost studies of, 71
  criticism of, 74
National Institute for Occupational Safety
  and Health (NIOSH), 1, 149, 159
  criteria documents of, 59
  and vinyl chloride exposure, 52, 54, 55
National Machine Tool Builders
  Association, 58

Nebraska, WC data from, 111
New-hire rate, 100
  defined, 196n
  and injury rate, 103, 104, 198n
New York State study, of workers'
  injuries, 86
New York Times, 4
NHTSA. *See* National Highway Traffic
  Safety Administration (NHTSA)
NIOSH. *See* National Institute for
  Occupational Safety and Health
  (NIOSH)
Nixon administration, 17, 37
"No hands in dies" provision, 56, 57, 58
Noise, 10
  Bolt study on, 65
  effect of OSHA on violations, 45–46
  standard setting for, 51–52, 61
Noncompliance, 83, 85, 119. *See also*
  Compliance

Obey, David, 69, 78
O'Brien, Mary-Win, 40
Occupational Safety and Health Act
  amendments to, 50
  impact of, 1
  implementation of, 157–164
  legislative history of, 82
  penalties of, 85, 136
  political history of, 15–24
  procedural rights of, 123
Occupational Safety and Health Administration (OSHA)
  accident investigation program of,
    127–130
  cost effectiveness of, 121
  costs imposed by, 197n
  criticism of, 3
  deterrent force of, 88
  effectiveness of, 94–120, 164–166
  effect on safety practices, 91
  enforcement policy of, 178n
  impact of, 164–167
  increased safety through, 85–87
  mechanical press standards of, 58
  operations of, 2–3
  policy alternatives for, 124–127,
    167–170
  public cost-effectiveness of, 122
  public hearing on power press standards,
    56–57
  and safety alternatives, 142
  social cost-effectiveness of, 123, 166
  standard setting of, 68
  unions as clients of, 73–74

Occupational Safety and Health Review
  Commission (OSHRC), 2, 19, 44, 46
Office of Management and Budget (OMB),
  65
Office of Standards Development (OSD),
  48, 147
O'Hara, James, 17
Ohio, WC data from, 111
Oil, Chemical, and Atomic Workers, 15
Oil spills, economics of, 70
OSHA. *See* Occupational Safety and
  Health Administration (OSHA)

Page, Joseph, 40
Paternalism, 68, 152
  of government, 14, 68, 203n
  and risk sharing, 73
Penalties, OSH Act, 85, 136
Performance, standards for, 126. *See also*
  Standards
Pesticides, standard on, 186n
Petrochemical industry, beneficiaries of
  OSHA in, 166
Plants, nonunion, and OSHA, 33
Politics
  of injury tax, 28–31
  and OSHA, 184n
  of regulation, 73–75
  of safety standards, 28–31
  of THIRE, 169
Polyvinyl chloride (PVC), 53. *See also*
  Vinyl chloride
Pool, Ithiel de Sola, 15
Power press injuries, 203n
Preventive measures, and social costs, 7
Procedures
  debates over, 22
  standard setting, 48–52
Profitability, and safety programs, 92
Program-planning budgeting system
  (PPBS), 71
Protection, costs of, 3
Protective equipment, 153, 188n
  vs. engineering controls, 163–164
  for meeting standards, 45
Public
  and OSHA, 34
  and regulatory policy, 5
"Public-regardingness," 152

Reform
  of OSHA's safety program, 124–127
  in standard setting, 145–150
Regression analysis, 111, 196n

Regulation
  costs of, 189n
  and OSHA policy, 4-5
  politics of, 73-75
Reporting
  requirements for, 128
  underreporting, 138-139, 143
Republican party, 154
  and OSHA, 51
  and OSH Act, 20, 22
Reuther, Walter, 18
Review Commission, Occupational Safety
    and Health, 2, 19, 44, 46
Risk of death, compensation for, 9
Risk premiums, and job classification, 11
Roll-over protective devices (ROPS), 93
Rosen, Sherwin, 34

Safety
  cost-benefit analysis of, 6
  vs. health, 13
  increased, 87-93
  inspection strategies in, 162
Safety directors, and OSHA inspections,
    137
Safety engineers, 92, 112
Safety performance, ranking, 134-135
Safety program
  OSHA's, 121-144
  state, 105
Safety standards, politics of, 28-31
Samuels, Sheldon, 47
Sate plan, 178n
Sayles, Leonard R., 10
Schaffer, C. Boyd, 47
Schubert, Richard, 51
Schultz, George, 12, 22-23
Schultze, Charles L., 4, 25, 29
Scientists, and protection of workers, 78
Selikoff, Irving, 62, 63
Sellers, Gary, 18, 158
Senate, U.S.
  Appropriations Conference Committee,
    4
  Labor and Public Welfare Committee,
    19, 22, 50, 124
  Labor Committee of, 37
Settle, Russell, 63-64
Shearing presses, and CIB accidents, 113
Sheehan, Jack, 16, 18, 76
Smith, Adam, 9
Smith, Robert, 6, 11, 24, 64, 67, 88
Social costs. See also Costs
  of disabling injuries, 117

and government intervention, 13
and preventive measures, 7
Social Security system, 12
Society for the Plastics Industry, 53
Standards
  benefit-cost studies of, 148
  coke oven, 76
  consensus, 1, 37, 38, 39, 82, 157-158
  development of, 1
  economics of, 67-71, 182n
  and environmental issues, 191n
  health vs. safety, 81
  initially adopted, 36-41
  NIOSH revisions of, 61
  occupational health, 58-67
  OSHA-enforced, 36
  politics of, 28-31
  relevance of, 85-87
  setting of, 48-52, 145-150, 158-161
  specification vs. performance, 126
  TWA, 53, 55
  uncertainty about, 79
  union leaders position on, 77
  Walsh-Healey, 184n
Starr, Chauncey, 73
State agencies
  criticism of, 153
  and safety alternatives, 142
State data, and OSHA's impact, 105-115
State programs, 24
Steel industry, 11
Steelworkers, 16, 76
Steiger, William, 19, 23, 31, 37, 51, 82
Steiger Bill, 19, 38
Stender, John, 47, 51, 52, 55, 57, 65
Strains category, of injury, 113
Strauss, George, 10
Surgeon general, vinyl chloride position
    of, 55
Sylvania Corporation, 14

Target industry program, OSHA's, 94
Targeting Inspections of High Injury Rate
    Establishments (THIRE), 133-142
  assessing, 140-142
  cost-effectiveness of, 140
  and incentives, 136
  operations of, 133-136
  political appeal of, 169
  potential weakness of, 137
  problems of, 203n-204n
  and small establishments, 139
  susceptibility to underreporting, 138,
    143

Taxes. *See also* Injury tax
accident investigation as, 130
effluent, 181n
Tax system, of intervention, 26–28. *See
also* Intervention
Taylor, George, 54, 57
Technological change
and hazards, 99
and injury rates, 134
Teplow, Leo, 38
Textile industry, and reporting of
byssinosis, 12
Textile Workers Union, 31
Thaler, Richard, 34
THIRE. *See* Targeting Inspection of High
Injury Rate Establishments (THIRE)
"Threshold limit values," (TLVs), 58
Time-weighted average (TWA), 53, 63
Tort liability, 25
Toxic substances category, of injury, 95
Transportation, Department of (DOT), 71
Trends, in injury rate, 102

Ultraviolet radiation, standard setting for,
61
Underreporting, 138–139, 143. *See also*
Reporting
Unemployment, and OSHA, 32–34
Union leaders
and asbestos standard, 63
and change, 180n
and injury tax, 28–29
and job classification, 11
and OSHA's standard setting, 80
on risks, 77
Unions
criticism of OSHA, 151
and incentives for safety, 23
influence with OSHA, 160
and injury tax, 155
and OSH program, 15, 17
and THIRE alternative, 133
United Auto Workers, 32, 57
United Mine Workers (UMW), 18
United Rubber Workers (URW), 15, 77
United Steelworkers Union (USW), 16

Victims, identifying, 72–73
Vinyl chloride
history of regulation of, 186n
and informed workers, 187n
standard setting for, 52–56
Vinyl chloride monomer (VCM), 53
Violations. *See also* Noncompliance
and Daniels Bill, 19

and fatalities, 87
penalties for, 3
and safety-vs.-health issue, 41–42

Walsh-Healey Contracts Act, 24, 36, 37,
43, 185n
Williams, Harrison, 19, 124
Williams-Steiger Act, 82
Wilson, James O., 190n
Wirtz, Willard, 37, 82
Wisconsin
reporting requirements in, 128
WC data from, 111
Wisconsin study, of accident investiga-
tions, 98
Workers
and impact of OSHA, 32
informed, 9–10, 13, 14, 156, 183n
and types of accidents, 96–97
Workers' compensation (WC) programs,
11, 181n
Wrenn, Grover, 54–55, 69, 189n

Z-16 definition, for injury reporting
system, 102